W9-CCV-970

The Invisible Computer

Books by Donald A. Norman

Textbooks

Memory and Attention: An Introduction to Human Information Processing. (First edition, 1969; second edition, 1976.)

Human Information Processing. (With Peter Lindsay. First edition, 1972; second edition, 1977.)

Scientific Monographs

Models of Human Memory. (Edited, 1970.)

Explorations in Cognition. (With David E. Rumelhart and the LNR Research Group, 1975.)

Perspectives on Cognitive Science. (Edited, 1981.)

User Centered System Design: New Perspectives on Human-Computer Interaction. (Edited with Steve Draper, 1986.)

General Interest

Learning and Memory, 1982.

The Psychology of Everyday Things, 1988.

The Design of Everyday Things, 1990. (Paperback version of *The Psychology of Everyday Things.*)

Turn Signals Are the Facial Expressions of Automobiles, 1992.

Things That Make Us Smart, 1993.

CD-ROM

First Person: Donald A. Norman. Defending Human Attributes in the Age of the Machine, 1994.)

The Invisible Computer

Why Good Products Can Fail,
the Personal Computer Is So Complex,
and Information Appliances Are the Solution

Donald A. Norman

The MIT Press
Cambridge, Massachusetts
London, England

©1998 Donald A. Norman

This book was set in Stone Sans and Stone Serif by Wellington Graphics.

Printed and bound in the United States of America.

Library of Congress Cataloging-in-Publication Data

Norman, Donald A.
    The invisible computer : why good products can fail, the personal computer is so complex, and information appliances are the solution
    Donald A. Norman.
       p. cm.
    Includes bibliographical references and index.
    ISBN 0-262-14065-9 (alk. paper)
    1. High technology industries—Marketing   2. Human-computer interaction.
    3. Human-centered design. I. Title.
QA76.5.N665   1998
004.16—dc21   98-18841
                                                                              CIP

Contents

Preface

Thomas Edison was a great inventor but a poor businessman. Consider the phonograph. Edison invented it, he had better technology than his competitors, and he did a sensible, logical analysis of the business. Nonetheless, he built a technology-centered phonograph that failed to take into account his customer's needs. In the end, his several companies proved irrelevant and bankrupt.

Sound familiar? Today's PC business has a number of parallels. Look at ease of use. The early phonograph was too complicated for office use. "Persevere," early users were told, "it only takes two weeks to master." It took a hundred years for the phonograph to evolve to the state it has reached today. It has been modified so thoroughly that all of the underlying technologies differ and even the term *phonograph* is seldom used, being replaced by *tape deck, cassette recorder,* and *CD player.* By analogy, the computer industry is in the era of 78 rpm shellac phonograph records—it still has a long way to go.

A major goal of this book is to hasten the day when the technology of the computer fades away out of sight, and the new technology that replaces it is as readily accepted and easy to use as a cassette tape recorder or CD player. The problem is that whether it be phonograph or computer, the technology is the easy part to change. The difficult aspects are social, organizational, and cultural.

Today's technology is intrusive and overbearing. It leaves us with no moments of silence, with less time to ourselves, with a sense of diminished control over our lives. But all this can change. Now we are trapped in a world created by technologists for technologists. We have even been told that "being digital" is a virtue. But it isn't: People are analog, not digital; biological, not mechanical. It is time for a human-centered technology, a humane technology.

The personal computer is perhaps the most frustrating technology ever. The computer should be thought of as infrastructure. It should be quiet, invisible, unobtrusive, but it is too visible, too demanding. It controls our destiny. Its complexities and frustrations are largely due to the attempt to cram far too many functions into a single box that sits on the desktop. The business model of the computer industry is structured in such a way that it must produce new products every six to twelve months, products that are faster, more powerful, and with more features than the current ones. The result is that the entire industry is trapped by its own success, trapped into a cycle of ever-increasing complexity from which it cannot escape.

It doesn't have to be this way, but the current paradigm is so thoroughly established that the only way to change is to start over again. In this book I show how to make a new start, how to start with simple devices—information appliances—then slowly establish this new paradigm as the natural successor to today's complexity. The proper way, I argue, is through the user-centered, human-centered, humane technology of appliances where the technology of the computer disappears behind the scenes into task-specific devices that maintain all the power without the difficulties.

This change requires a new attitude. For manufacturers, it requires a new approach to the development of products, hiring people with human-centered skills in addition to those with technology-centered ones, changing the product process, perhaps restructuring the company.

The original title of this book was *Taming Technology,* for that is the goal. Then the title changed to *Information Appliances,* for that is the method. Now it is *The Invisible Computer,* because that is the end result, hiding the computer, hiding the technology so that it disappears from sight, disappears from consciousness, letting us concentrate upon our activities, upon learning, doing our jobs, and enjoying ourselves. The goal is to move from the current situation of complexity and frustration to one where technology serves human needs invisibly, unobtrusively: the human-centered, customer-centered way.

The Life Cycle of Technology

The purpose of this book is to take a realistic look at the world of technology, the better to understand why good products can fail and inferior products succeed. I take a close look at the reasons the personal computer came to be so complex and how that complexity is so intertwined with its heritage that only a complete rethinking of the fundamental ideas can change it. I believe that there is indeed a solution, the development of information appliances. Information appliances hold great hope and promise, but the path toward adoption is treacherous, a minefield full of fierce competitors. The existing technology, the personal computer, exerts a deadly gravity well that prevents the unwary from escaping its pull.

All technologies have a life cycle, and as they progress from birth, through troubled adolescence, and on to maturity, their characteristics change. During this life cycle, the customer segment varies, starting with the early adopters, those technology enthusiasts who nurture the fledgling early products and help them gain power and acceptability. In the early days of a technology, the engineers rule. Each successive new product boasts of improved technology: faster, more powerful, better this, better that. Technology rules the day, guided by feature-driven marketing.

When technologies mature, the story changes dramatically. Now the technology can be taken for granted. The customers change and they want different things. Convenience and user experience dominate over technological superiority. These new customers are late adopters, people who wait for the technologies to mature, to prove themselves and to provide value for their money, value without hassle. Late adopters are the vast majority; they far outnumber the early adopters, those who are seduced by technology.

The mature phase of a product has to be driven by customer needs. Now it requires a human-centered development cycle. As a result, the company must change: It must learn to make products for its new customers, to let the technology be subservient. This is a difficult transition for a technology-driven industry to understand, a difficult change to make. Yet this is where the personal computer industry stands today. The customers want change, yet the industry has faltered, unwilling and unable to alter its ways.

The high-technology industry is driven by engineers, by technology itself. It has flourished through a period of phenomenal growth accompanied by high profits. As a result, the industry has succumbed to a technology fever, to the disease of featuritis, to pushing new technologies at the customer faster than even the most compliant customer can absorb. Normal consumers who make up the bulk of the market consist of people who just want to get on with life, people who think technology should be invisible, hidden behind the scenes, providing its benefits without pain, anguish, and stress. These people are not understood by the wizards of high technology. These people are left out. I consider myself one of these people.

If information technology is to serve the average consumer, the technology companies need to change their ways. They have to stop being so driven by features and start examining what consumers actually do. They have to be market driven, task driven, driven by the real activities of those who use their devices. Alas, this requires a dramatic change in the mindset of the technologists, a change so drastic that many companies may not be able to make the transition. The very skills that made them so successful in the early stages of the technology are just the opposite of what is needed in the consumer phases.

A basic goal of this book is to help companies make the transition from being technology centered to being human centered. I explain why today's technology is inappropriate for the average consumer. I explain the way that market factors have an impact on sales. I explain why today's PC is fundamentally flawed. And I show the procedures that must be followed to go on to the next generation of information technology that breaks away from today's technology-centered world to one that truly can fulfill the needs of consumers.

The Book

The journey starts in chapter 1 with the story of Thomas Edison and the phonograph. Although Edison's phonograph boasted superior technology, Edison did not understand his customers and, as a result, his several phonograph companies all failed. Technology alone does not a market make; being first and being best are not the most relevant variables in the world of high technology.

Chapter 2 discusses the changes that take place in a product as it passes from youth, through adolescence, and then to maturity, the stage where it must become human centered. In chapter 3 I propose a new form of information technology: the information appliance. Here, technology becomes invisible and the emphasis is on the human activity the appliance is meant to serve.

Chapter 4 considers the personal computer, examining why the PC is so complex; chapter 5 explains why there is no simple magical cure. In chapter 6 I examine the nature of infrastructures and the difference between two different kinds of economic goods: substitutable and non-substitutable (infrastructure) goods, the first leading to a sharing of markets, the second to domination.

If we are to move to human-centered development, we must understand people better; this is the topic of chapter 7. The first lesson is that there is a serious mismatch between the properties of machines and of people. Our modern technology is digital: People are analog, and the difference is profound.

The Achilles' heel of the modern PC is its difficulty. If information appliances are to succeed they must avoid the trap of technological difficulty. I advocate a human-centered design approach that puts human needs first, technology second. This is the message of chapters 8, 9, and 10.

But all is not lost. Chapter 11 explains the conditions under which disruptive technologies can take over from older, established means, changing the infrastructure where necessary. Chapter 12, the concluding chapter, points out that information appliances are just such a disruptive technology. We can move to a world of information appliances.

The ideal system so buries the technology that the user is not even aware of its presence. The goal is to let people get on with their activities, with the technology enhancing their productivity, their power, and their enjoyment, ever the more so because it is invisible, out of sight, out of mind. People should learn the task, not the technology. They should be able to take the tool to the task, not as today, where we must take the task to the tool. And these tools should follow three axioms of design: *simplicity, versatility,* and *pleasurability.*

Acknowledgments

This book has been made possible by many people, more than I can enumerate here. I give particular thanks to Joel Birnbaum and Bill Sharpe of Hewlett-Packard. Indeed, Joel hired me to help deliver on the dream of information appliances. Tim McCollum and Haig Baronikian provided commentary and discussions on key topics. Sandy Dijkstra and Rita Holm of the Sandra Dijkstra Literary Agency have, as usual, been invaluable. Bob Prior of the MIT Press helped restructure and refine the early draft into a much superior book. The whole team at the MIT Press has been helpful, especially Michael Sims, who tidied up the writing and set me straight on the history of the phonograph. As always, Julie helped ensure it was readable, deleting sentences, paragraphs, and pages, restructuring and rearranging (she even tried to delete this sentence). As for Bran Ferren of Walt Disney, who keeps asking whether I'm still having fun: Yes, Bran, yes. I have been, I am, and I forever intend to.

CARUSO GLUCK McCORMACK

Everybody naturally wants to hear the best music

If you had your choice of attending two concerts—the greatest artists in all the world appearing at one, some little-known artists at the other—which would you choose? You would quickly decide to hear the renowned artists who are famous for their superb interpretations. And this is exactly the reason why the Victrola is the instrument for your home. The world's greatest artists make records for the Victor exclusively:

Caruso, Alda, Braslau, Calvé, Culp, de Gogorza, De Luca, Destinn, Elman, Farrar, Gadski, Galli-Curci, Garrison, Gluck, Hempel, Homer, Journet, Kreisler, Martinelli, McCormack, Melba, Paderewski, Powell, Ruffo, Schumann-Heink, Scotti, Sembrich, Tetrazzini, Whitehill, Williams, Witherspoon, Zimbalist.

There are Victors and Victrolas in great variety of styles from $10 to $400, and there are Victor dealers everywhere who will gladly demonstrate them and play your favorite music for you. Ask to hear the Saenger Voice Culture Records.

Victor Talking Machine Co., Camden, N. J., U. S. A.
Berliner Gramophone Co., Montreal, Canadian Distributors

New Victor Records demonstrated at all dealers on the 1st of each month

Victor Supremacy

"Victrola" is the Registered Trade-mark of the Victor Talking Machine Company designating the products of this Company only.

Warning: The use of the word **Victrola** upon or in the promotion or sale of any other Talking Machine or Phonograph products is misleading and illegal.

Important Notice. Victor Records and Victor Machines are scientifically coordinated and synchronized by our special processes of manufacture, and their use, one with the other, is absolutely essential to a perfect Victor reproduction.

To insure Victor quality, always look for the famous trade-mark, "His Master's Voice." It is on all genuine products of the Victor Talking Machine Company.

"HIS MASTER'S VOICE"
REG. U.S. PAT. OFF.

Victrola XVII, $265
Victrola XVII, electric, $325
Mahogany or oak

1

Drop Everything You're Doing

"Drop everything you're doing," my CEO said to me. "I have a really important job for you to do."

This was my rude introduction to the world of high technology. I had just left the hallowed halls of bickering academia to join the harried frenzy of industry. Everything was different, yet, to some extent, everything was the same. In academics there is much emphasis on cleverness and creativity. It doesn't matter how successful you were in the past. What counts is: What did you accomplish this year? What did you publish? What do colleagues and opponents think of your work? It is more important to be clever than to be correct, better to be profound than practical. In the pecking order of the university, those who are the most abstract and irrelevant are at the top, those most practical and useful are at the bottom.

The world of high-technology business doesn't work the way you think it does. Technical, business, and social factors affect the way new technologies are deployed. Once ideas are let out of the laboratory, common sense disappears, especially in the rush to show that one company's products are superior to another's very similar ones.

In industry, there is much emphasis on action, on shipping products. Profit margins and sales figures rule the day. It doesn't matter how successful you were in the past: How much have your market share, sales, and profits increased this year, this quarter, this month? Market success

Figure 1.1
Victor Talking Machine Company advertisement, *National Geographic*, December 1917.

is everything, much more prized than the nature of the product. It is better to be first than best. Everything is always in a rush: to get to market, to beat your competitor, to get the product out in time for the holiday season, or the school season. In the research university there is much thought, little action. In industry, there is much action, little time for thought.

The request of the Chief Executive Officer of my company, I would soon discover, was not unusual.

"But you told me to drop everything last week," I replied, "I've barely gotten started on that job."

"That's OK," said my CEO, "this one is more important. Drop everything you're doing, and by the way, you have a 9 AM meeting tomorrow on the east coast. You can sleep on the plane. My assistant has already arranged for the tickets."

The abrupt and secret nature of this particular task was not at all unusual. The high-technology industry rushes to do this, to do that. The race is to the swift and the clever, not to the best. The continual rush makes it impossible to step back and reflect, to take a broader view. To the product manager, thinking about the future means to think six months ahead, maybe twelve. To the researcher, thinking about the future means to think ten years ahead, maybe five. The gap between these styles is almost unbridgeable. Don't believe everything you read. In fact, don't believe anything. How much impact do science and research actually have on products? Less than you might think, less than you might hope.

We live in interesting times. We are indeed in the midst of a major revolution, one brought about by the converging interests and technologies of communication, computation, and entertainment. Technological revolutions have several interesting properties. First, we tend to overestimate the immediate impact and underestimate the long-term impact. Second, we tend to place the emphasis on the technologies themselves, when it is really the social impact and cultural change that will be most dramatic. And, finally, we think revolutions are fast, with changes occurring in months or, at worst, a few years.

In reality, technological revolutions are fast only from a historical point of view. Look at the revolution triggered by Gutenberg's development of the movable-type printing press. Its impact was rapid—within 100 years it was felt all across Europe. To the historian, 100 years is a short time; for someone living at the time, it is an eternity—more than most lifetimes. All new technologies take a long time to affect the lives of ordinary people. The telephone was invented in 1875, but it didn't have a major impact until the 1900s. The airplane was conceived in the late 1800s and flown successfully in 1903, but it didn't become commercially available for passengers for 30 years and, even then, it was a risky, foolhardy means of transportation. The fax machine was invented in the mid 1800s and even today has not yet made much of an impact in the home.

Today we often hear that the pace of change has speeded up, that changes happen in "internet time," in months or weeks, not decades or years. False. The internet had its start in the 1960s as a government-sponsored research network for universities and company research laboratories. Thirty years later, at the end of the 1990s, it still is not present in the majority of homes in the United States, and its adoption in other countries is even lower. The digital computer is fifty years old, the personal computer more than twenty, yet fewer than half the homes in the United States have computers and the number is far lower in other countries. These rates of adoption might be faster than the airplane and the telephone, but not by as much as you might have been led to believe. Technological revolutions are rapid when measured by the time span of civilization, but slow when measured by the time span of an individual's life.

Nonetheless, we now really are in a period of rapid change, of rapid convergence of technologies. One hundred years from now, our descendants will wonder about the primitive life we led, where we had to contend with diverse communication facilities: government mail systems for personal delivery of letters handwritten or typed on paper; private companies for more rapid delivery of time-sensitive material and small packages; a separate system—fax—for the delivery of pictures of material; electronic mail for typed material; yet another system—the telephone and its associated answering machine and voice mail technology—for voice messages; and no video mail. It doesn't take much thought to recognize that all these are similar systems and that society would be better served with one solution that merged the delivery of personal and business mail, voice messages, images—whether static or moving—and graphics. It also doesn't take much time for those trying to merge these technologies to throw up their hands in frustration at the myriad hurdles society places in their path.

Where Edison Went Wrong

Today's high-technology business is in a muddle. It has arrived at its current state by its heavy emphasis on technology, quite often technology for technology's sake. The modern computer is the culmination of this process and, as I explain more fully in this book, it has led to an overly complex, fundamentally difficult machine—but one that increasingly has come to dominate our lives. Today we cannot do business or conduct much of our daily activity without the use of modern information technology, both the computer infrastructure and the associated communication technology. But the computer does not really meet our needs. It suffers from the rush, the haste, and, for that matter, the arrogance of the technology industry. This is an industry that puts the device first, the customer second. The real needs of consumers are ignored.

Today, at the start of the twenty-first century we find the industry dominated by personalities, by major magnates whose personal presence controls the development of technology. The same was true at the start of the twentieth century: Edison, Bell, Marconi, and Westinghouse all played major roles in the development of the early days of the information industry, and all were colorful, powerful, and very public figures. Let us begin with those early years, when the first information technologies were introduced to the marketplace: the telegraph, the telephone, the phonograph and, later, the radio. For my purposes, the story of Thomas Alva Edison is the most relevant; he played a major role in many of those early information industries, from communication (the telegraph and telephone), to entertainment (the phonograph and movie projector), to the underlying infrastructure (the incandescent light, electric power distribution, and electric dynamos and motors).

Thomas Alva Edison was a great technologist—one of the best—but not a great businessman. Not only was he an inventor, but he started one of the first industrial research laboratories, hiring some excellent technicians and scientists. Moreover, he realized that no invention could succeed by itself; it needed an entire infrastructure to work. With this in mind, he put together all the other components of the total system. He had all that logic indicates should be necessary: He was first with the technology, the technology was usually superior to that of his competitors, and he understood that success required the construction of appropriate infrastructure. What he did not have was a solid sense for marketing. He often did not sufficiently understand his customers.

Edison had many strengths, but he also had several major weaknesses. It is for those deficiencies that I am telling this story, for the deficiencies are common ones, still with us. This book is really about the high-technology industry, and especially the personal-computer industry, and how they should change. Edison's story is a great place to start. In many ways, Edison invented the high-technology industry. His work combined the information processing and communication industries. He played a major role in the development of the entertainment industry by inventing the phonograph and the motion picture camera and projector. And like the business tycoons of today, he had a cantankerous, colorful personality, suing and spying upon his competitors, courting the press, hyping his inventions often even before they were invented, and leading a lively, eccentric, and very public life. The feuds, suits, and rivalries among technologists at the turn of the nineteenth century far exceeds the similar excesses of today.

Consider the phonograph. Edison was first, he had superior and more versatile technology, and he did a brilliant, logical analysis of the business. But the logical approach is the wrong way to go about understanding the needs of customers. You have to talk to them, watch them;

this is the only way to understand their interests, their motives, their needs. Edison thought he knew better and, as a result, he built a technology-centered phonograph that failed to take into account his customer's needs. I'll return to this story later, but for now, note that at the end, his several phonograph companies were unsuccessful.

Sound familiar? It's like today's personal computer business, and there are even more parallels. Do you think the computer is difficult and the phonograph simple? The phonograph was judged to be too complicated for office use; it took about two weeks to master, but only if you were willing to persevere. It took years to get the phonograph to the state it is in today, changed so thoroughly that all of the underlying technologies differ and even the term *phonograph* is no longer used. By this analogy, the computer industry still has a long way to go and, if we are fortunate, the end result will be quite unlike today. The problem is that whether phonograph or computer, the technology is the relatively easy part to change. The difficult parts are social, organizational and cultural.

Today's technology imposes itself on us, making demands on our time and diminishing our control over our lives. Of all the technologies, perhaps the most disruptive for individuals is the personal computer. The computer is really an infrastructure, even though today we treat it as the end object. Infrastructures should be invisible: and that is exactly what this book recommends: A user-centered, human-centered humane technology where today's personal computer has disappeared into invisibility.

This change will not be easy. It requires a disruptive technology. For manufacturers, it requires a new approach to design, a human-centered design. This means hiring new kinds of people, changing the design process, perhaps restructuring the company.

Why not? Remember, there are far more people in the world who do not use computers than there are who do: That is the marketplace, that is where the opportunities lie. Companies shouldn't always talk to their customers: they should talk to those who are not (yet) customers. Among other things, this was Edison's main fault. He thought he knew better than his customers; he didn't provide them with what they wanted, he provided them with what he predetermined was best for them. This was a bad idea then, it's a bad idea now.

Why Being First and Best Isn't Good Enough

Success does not always go to those who are first to market, nor to those with the best product. Alas, the history of technology is filled with failures of those who were first. Quick, what was the name of the first manufacturer of automobiles in the United States? Duryea was the first.[1] Most people today have never even heard the name.

The history of the phonograph is illustrative.[2] Edison invented the phonograph in 1877, and by 1878 the Edison Speaking Phonograph Company was marketing the first machines. It even made a profit for the first few years. At first, the technology was crude—the recordings were made on tinfoil, the machine was delicate. Edison and his competition engaged in a series of technological improvements, substituting wax for tinfoil, discs for cylinders, electric motors for hand- or spring-propelled drives, and so on. People weren't quite sure what the machine would be used for, and so, at first, it was used primarily for public demonstrations (with paid admission). Edison thought they could lead to a paperless office in which dictated letters could be recorded and the cylinders mailed to the recipients, without the need for transcription. He also tried putting a small phonograph into a doll and selling it as a talking toy. Owners of the early machines held parties where guests could record songs and games and enjoy listening to them being played back. Prerecorded speeches and songs became popular, and this eventually became the primary usage.

The practical phonograph did not arrive until the late 1880s, by which time Chichester Bell and Charles Tainter had developed a competitive company, the American Graphophone Company, that recorded on wax-coated cardboard cylinders rather than tinfoil. In the early 1890s Emile Berliner became the first to produce prerecorded stamped disc records commercially with his machine, the gramophone.

Edison's phonograph had a number of superior features to the competition.[3] But having the best technology is no route to success either. Edison had the best technology. Sony's Beta technology for video cassette recording is widely considered to have been superior to the VHS format for video cassette recorders and tape championed by a conglomerate led by JVC and Matsushita, but Beta lost. The Macintosh operating system clearly had advantages over the DOS operating system for personal computers, but it lost, first to DOS, and then to Microsoft Windows, a system that took ten years to catch up to the Macintosh, but that now dominates the world of computers. Edison's recordings were superior, but he used technology that was incompatible with that of his competitors. His competitors provided a product that fit the customer's needs better than did Edison's phonograph, and as a result, the superiority didn't matter: the competition won.

Being first helps, but it is not enough. Being best helps, but it is not enough. What was Edison's mistake? He used a technology-centered approach. His logical analysis of the technologies did not take into consideration the consumer's viewpoint.

When Edison invented the phonograph, he studied both the cylinder and the disc, the form of the medium in use today in CDs and DVDs. He recognized the superiority of the cylinder as a recording medium. He knew that as the cylinder revolves, each part passes under the stylus at the same speed. With discs, the outside edge moves past the stylus more rapidly than the parts near the center, and so the sound at the center deteriorates. Because the stylus in Edison's phonograph was propelled across the record by a feed screw, record wear was decreased in comparison with the disc, where the groove itself propelled the needle. Edison's machine could also be used to make home recordings. The cylinder's

Figure 1.2
The competing infrastructures of the phonograph. *(top)* The Edison Home Phonograph of 1901, which played wax cylinders. *(bottom)* The Victor Talking Machine Company's Monarch Junior of 1902, which played discs. (From the collection of Michael Sims.)

semipermanent jeweled stylus was more convenient than the discs' steel needles, which had to be changed after every record side.

But the discs offered many advantages over the cylinders. They were less fragile than the wax cylinders. Their hard shellac surface allowed greater playback volume, if a more raucous, scratchy sound, than the soft wax cylinders. They took up far less space, and were easier to store, package, and ship. They could accommodate longer playing time simply by increasing their diameter, and they had a second side that could provide more music without increasing storage space, for less money. Most important, they were far easier to mass produce.

The real use of the phonograph record, discovered after much trial and error by a variety of manufacturers, was to provide prerecorded music. Emile Berliner moved quickly to exploit this and his company rapidly picked up a dominant market share. His gramophone became the Victrola, manufactured by the Victor Talking Machine Company, later RCA Victor. Berliner and his successors rapidly established recording studios across the world and engaged the world's most famous musicians in the effort.

Edison's failure to recognize the real value of the phonograph is understandable: New technologies often end up being used very differently than anyone—especially their inventors—predict. The real error lay in letting his competitors get ahead of him and in failing to recognize the practical advantages of the disc over the cylinder in terms of ease of use, storage, and shipping, to say nothing of mass production. Instead, Edison scoffed at the raucous, scratchy sound of the disc machines compared to the superior sound of the cylinders.

Eventually Edison did realize the importance of compatibility and convenience. The problem was that by the time he switched over to discs in 1913 he was no longer the market leader. Worse, he failed to understand the real desires of his customers; once again, he let logic triumph over marketing wisdom.

Even after he began manufacturing discs, Edison continued to use the vertical recording method, called "hill and dale," in which the sound wave was represented by the vertical motion of the needle and a corresponding depth of the groove. The needle vibrated up and down as the record rotated. The competition used lateral recording, which meant the needle vibrated side-to-side as the record rotated. Once again, the differences are mostly technical, but the real point is that the world wanted a single system. Early phonographs could only play back one system, either vertical or lateral, so whichever system customers bought, they couldn't play back the recordings of the other. In chapter 6 I discuss the problems of nonsubstitutable, infrastructure goods, when the infrastructure of one company differs from that of another. Basically, if you have the dominant infrastructure, you win. If you choose the wrong one, you lose, and you lose big. Because the Victor Talking Machine Company had the dominant infrastructure, Edison lost.

Which method of recording was actually better? Edison, of course, thought hill and dale superior, and in numerous "tone tests" he sought to prove that an audience could not distinguish the sounds produced by his phonograph from those of a live singer.[4] Once again, it didn't matter. The sound quality of Victor's lateral recordings was "good enough."

Another serious mistake that Edison made was in the choice of recording artists. Edison decided that big-name, expensive artists were not much different from the lesser-known professionals. In this, he is probably correct. Take the ten best piano players, or opera singers, or orchestras in the world, and the difference between those ranked at the top and those at the bottom is not likely to be noticeable by the average listener. But the top two or three musicians are a lot better known, whereas few people can recite the name of the tenth best performing artist or group. Edison thought he could save considerable money at no sacrifice to quality by recording those lesser-known artists. He was right; he saved a lot of money. The problem was, the public wanted to hear the big names, not the unknown ones. It had been cleverly educated in this by Victor. As a Victor advertisement put it (see figure 1.1, page xiv):

If you had your choice of attending two concerts—the greatest artists in all the world appearing at one, some little-known artists at the other—which would you choose? You would quickly decide to hear the renowned artists who are famous for their superb interpretations. And this is exactly the reason why the Victrola is the instrument for your home. The world's greatest artists make records for the Victor exclusively.[5]

Edison pitted his taste and his technology-centered logical analysis on the belief that the differences among musicians were not important: He lost. He thought his customers only cared about the music; he didn't even list the performers' names on his disc records for several years. He failed to understand that people want to hear the big names. It doesn't matter if others are just as good. It doesn't even matter if they are better—it is the name that matters.

This would have been less important had it not been for Edison's choice of an operating system that was incompatible with the machines most people owned, hill and dale recording rather than lateral. If Edison had used the same standard way of recording the sounds as his competition, then it wouldn't have mattered that the big names were on Victor records. People would have been able to buy Edison phonographs and play Victor records. But with a specialized, incompatible infrastructure, if customers wanted the name musicians, they had to buy both the records and the phonographs from Victor. To put it in today's terms: There were two competing, incompatible operating systems. Eventually some companies did make instruments that could play both kinds of records, but by then, it was too late.

The Victor Talking Machine Company cemented its lead over Edison when it introduced the Victrola in 1907; this machine, with its amplifying horn concealed within the cabinet, became so popular that the word *victrola* became the generic term for any record player for the next five decades. Again, understanding the desires of the customer, who was growing tired of the intrusive, ever-larger horn, let a company maintain its dominance in the market.

Note the moral of this story, for it will apply over and over again in the high-technology marketplace. Know your customer. Being first, being best, and even being right do not matter; what matters is what the customers think. Edison was first, and he did have the best sound quality; but because he failed to fulfill his customer's desires, he fell behind in sales. He lost out by pushing the cylinder even though the customers preferred the more convenient disc. Edison pushed the phonograph as a recording medium when customers were more interested in listening to prerecorded music. When Edison finally did switch to discs, he wouldn't use famous—and expensive—musicians, but instead hired excellent but lesser-known musicians. As a result, he was never able to capture market share from his competition, especially from the Victor Talking Machine Company. And finally, he used a different technology than that of his leading competitors: at first cylinders instead of discs, and then vertical instead of lateral recording. Edison had studied all the methods; he thought his choices were superior. Maybe they were.

This is the important lesson about infrastructure technologies. It doesn't matter whether or not your technology is superior; it only matters that what is being offered is good enough for the purpose. Moreover, if you lead the marketplace in sales, it is permissible to use a nonstandard infrastructure. After all, if you have the majority of customers, then what you do becomes the standard. Your competitors have little choice but to follow. If you are not the leader, then having a nonstandard infrastructure is a bad idea. Ultimately, it leads to extinction.

But It's a Horrible Product

"But it's a horrible product," I complained. "It's not the sort of thing our company is famous for. We are known for ease of use, but look at this thing. Look at the remote control—38 buttons! I thought we were famous for simple, easy-to-use products. Nobody will be able to use this device!"

The time was almost midnight. It was the first few weeks of my new job, and already I was fighting with the vice president in charge of the new consumer products division. Wisely, however, he chose the site and time of the battle: his living room, from 10 PM to whenever we finished. And he provided the wine, a fine, rich northern Italian red. By now, we were in the second hour of discussions, on the second bottle of wine.

"Yes, yes," he said, "everything you complain about is absolutely true. But it doesn't matter. You see, nobody is going to buy the product."

"What!" I exclaimed, "If nobody is going to buy it, why are we in such a rush to produce it, such a rush that you won't let us take the time to fix the problems and do it right?"

"Ah," he replied, "it's a business strategy. See, by getting this product to market now, we announce to the world that we are not just a computer company, that we make things for the living room, for the home entertainment center. It's really too expensive for most people, and besides, most people have no use for it. But we will have established a foothold in the marketplace. Market share is everything. Speed is essential. Whether or not it works doesn't really matter. By being first, we will dominate. Then, we have time to make lots of products, and to make them right. And to make sure we make them right, I will put you in charge, OK?"

This was yet another introduction to the world of business. Being right wasn't always the point—being first was much more important. And what a disarming way to win me over; ply me with good wine, agree with every criticism, and put me in charge. I left a bit after midnight, complaining that I was tired and had an 8 AM meeting. "Actually, I have a 7 AM meeting myself," he said, "but I still have a few hours work to do. Midnight in California is a perfect time to make phone calls; it's 9 AM in Europe and 5 PM in Japan—perfect for both countries." That's life in the world of high technology. The pace is unrelenting. Action is prized. There is little time for thought.

The product shipped. It was a failure. Sales were miserable. And no, I was never actually put in charge. I did try to fix the complexity with an alternative, superior design, but we had only one month to get the new design into production, and two weeks of that were taken away from us because the factory in Portugal was going on vacation. Time, or rather the lack of it, I was starting to learn, is one of the greatest barriers to quality.

Would it have mattered if I had managed to fix the problems I knew about? Probably not. Was the executive correct? Probably. The product failed mainly because there was no real need for it. It didn't fall into any well-understood product category. It was targeted for the family room or living room, to sit on top of the television set, but consumers didn't yet have any experience with this kind of device, so they didn't know what they would use it for. It wasn't meant as a computer peripheral, but this is how it was reviewed and judged. As a result, reviewers didn't find it compelling; for a peripheral, it was too expensive and too slow. For these people, the attractive industrial design was irrelevant. Ease of use—or its absence—was equally irrelevant.

This product really was ahead of its time. So the fact that it was hard to use didn't matter. Yes, at least one product review commented upon the lack of usability, but that isn't what killed the product. Was the vice president right to say that market share and being first mattered more than doing it right? Yes, he was. The problem, I now realize, is that this was a new product category, a disruptive technology, but it was being aimed at the mass market, for the everyday user to put in the living room on top of the TV set. As I point out in chapters 2 and 11, disruptive technologies require special handling. The early adopters will be technologically sophisticated. For them, industrial design and ease of use is irrelevant. They would be perfectly happy with a horrible product as long as it delivered some capability they felt they needed. This one didn't deliver, at least not yet, not in its first manifestation. It might have succeeded in the long run, but it only got one chance.

What kind of a world is this, anyway, where horrible products don't matter? Welcome to the world of the technology enthusiasts, of the early adopters, of the fan clubs, and of the belief that technology comes first. But also welcome to the real world, where products do not exist in a vacuum, where for a product to be accepted by the public it has to fit into some recognizable niche, to provide value the customers understand. The right product can fail if introduced at the wrong time. The telephone took decades to be understood and accepted. The radio was first dismissed as a toy. The fax machine was invented more than a hundred years before it became an essential tool of industry. So, too, with the automobile. So, too, with almost every new technology.

When a new product category is invented and manufactured, it does not fit naturally into people's lives. In order to survive, it has to be introduced gradually. It has to be able to demonstrate its unique benefits that outweigh the trials and tribulations of all early technologies. Product categories, as a result, have a special life cycle in which they at first offer novel capabilities at the price of complexity, limited functions, and high cost. Over a period measured in decades or longer, they transition into everyday objects that offer what have become essential capabilities with simplicity, appropriate functionality, and low cost. They start out being technology dominated, of interest only to those few adventurous souls who are willing to pay the costs in order to get the benefits. They end up as everyday consumer items of value to everyone.

This is the story of the automobile, of the telephone, of the phonograph. It will be the story of the personal computer, although right now the computer is still in its early days, still complex and expensive. The computer has yet to make the transition to being an everyday object, with simplicity and low cost. Personal computers are not yet consumer items of value to everyone. To make the transition requires a very different view of the world than is held by the technology enthusiasts. It requires a consumer-centered view. Edison, for one, was resistant to such a view, and his companies failed.

Once upon a time, when the computer industry was young, the miracle was that you could make a small, personal device that could actually accomplish something useful. Youngsters in garages could put together products that soon became thriving businesses. Technology was king; those who mastered it could do no wrong. Those who could innovate became the stars—rich, influential stars. The push was to develop better and better technology, fancier and fancier tricks. Hurrah for this invention, hurrah for that. The fire was fueled by capitalism: Invest in the correct small company and you could increase your investment manyfold. Everyone fought for a piece of the action, and the action was hot new technology. Never mind that people couldn't use it. Never mind that the products kept getting more and more complex, more and more difficult to build, to maintain, to understand, and to use. Never mind. People kept buying—in part because they too were trapped by the technology mania, in part because they were forced to.

The notion that the marketplace decides only applies if there are real choices to be made. In the early days of a technology, it is often a choice between purchasing unwieldy, expensive technology that is difficult to use and maintain and doing without. To the technology enthusiasts, the technology, whatever its failures, offers advantages that they simply can't live without. In the relentless pace of business, there is always the nagging fear that the new technology offers a superior competitive advantage, and if you didn't keep up, your competitor might get an edge.

Technological Change Is Simple; Social, Cultural, and Organizational Change Is Hard

When will electronic mail replace much of the paper mail now hand-delivered by the international postal system? Not for a long time, because to make the change requires agreement with unions, satisfying concerns about worker's rights and national pride, and overcoming the sheer inertia of culture. Some countries legislate against anything that might interfere with the transport of mail. Electronic mail is not necessarily welcomed.

Want to make it easier to send a fax to the home? You must cope with the existing international standards for telephones, originally intended to carry only a few signals: a dial tone, busy signal, ringing signal, and voice to the connecting parties. Today it would be useful if a message could electronically indicate whether it is voice, computer modem, or fax, or whether it might go to a personal machine, or directly to a voice or fax mailbox. This can't be done, even though the technology that would be required is relatively simple. The problem is that the existing infrastructure is not compatible with such signals.

To the person using these technologies, the infrastructures are irrelevant. With a telephone answering machine, one leaves voice messages.

On a fax, one sends a copy of the image of the page. Email seems like fax in that one types a message and then commands the system to send the document visible on the screen, but what gets sent from one machine to another is very different from a fax; a fax will look like a degraded replication of the original, while email sends the computer code for the individual letters, and the receiving end recreates the text with its own choice of font. Fax looks like the original, email does not, even if it has the same words.

People trying to communicate wonder why they can't get voice messages over email. They can't understand why the letters so visible on the paper or on the screen from a fax can't be edited or operated upon in the same way as the similar appearing words from email.

In reality, these technologies use very different, barely compatible infrastructures. This historical accident makes it difficult to reconcile the differences. Voice mail is an analog representation of sound waves, encoded and stored according to the conventions of the telephone switching networks. Fax is also an analog signal, a picture of the letters and words, encoded in such a way as to pass through the telephone networks even though they were designed for voice, not data. The only way data can be sent over conventional telephone lines is to change the digital signals into audio tones that can pass through the network, then transform them back into data at the other end; hence all those tones and strange sounds created by fax machines and modems.

Email contains a digital representation of the letters, encoded in a binary encoding of the alphabet according to a scheme named by the acronym ASCII: American Standard Code for Information Interchange. ASCII is also a historical relic that doesn't work well in today's international society, where it cannot handle all the letters and diacritical marks of European languages, let alone the nonalphabetic characters of Asian languages. The first letter of the acronym ASCII indicates the problem: "A" for "American."

The impact of cultural influences is apparent in the different ways in which fax and email are used in business. Email and fax serve almost identical functions, yet they have come to be used rather differently. Email is the medium of informality; fax is more formal. Email tends to be typed quickly, by the person doing the correspondence. A fax tends to be prepared with the normal office procedures, with secretaries or administrative assistants neatly polishing the words and with care taken in grammar, spelling, and format. The differences reflect their historical origins.

Today's fax standards and machines resulted from a development process by large companies for business use. The technology of fax fits well within standard office routines, the same procedures used for letters, with responses written or dictated for a secretary to type. In both cases, a formal letter is produced. The only difference lies in the method of transmission and reception. Letters are put into envelopes and picked up and delivered by the mail service. Faxes are put into the office fax machine and the appropriate number dialed. The formality of a fax reflects the formality of the letter.

Email has evolved from the world of computer science, primarily in universities and government and industrial research laboratories. It was developed for quick notes between researchers, sometimes dealing with business, but more often with personal matters, such as restaurant suggestions or arranging meetings and social gatherings. Informality, ungrammatical writing, and misspellings were common. A well-formatted, properly constructed, formal message is considered out of place in email. In addition, the restriction to the limited character set of ASCII and the lack of formatting tools severely limits the style, leading to the use of special conventions, such as *asterisks* or UPPER CASE to indicate an *EMPHASIZED* word, and special symbols, such as ;-) to mean that the preceding remark was meant in jest (the symbols ;-) looking somewhat like a winking, smiling face if viewed sideways).

The difference between email and fax makes an important point: Once a technology becomes entrenched, it is very difficult to change. Thus, it would be valuable if email would allow formatting and the inclusion of pictures and diagrams right in the text, much as is possible in a book or letter. Similarly, it would be useful if faxes encoded the characters so that one could perform a computer search on the text, or copy and paste words and phrases from a fax into other documents. The problem is that these functions would require new standards and agreements among all the manufacturers and users of the relevant technologies to adopt equipment compatible with the standards. Such a task is almost impossible once technologies have become established. Too many organizations would have to change, too much expense in existing facilities would have to be expended. Hence, the social, cultural, and organizational aspects of a technology are more difficult to change than the technical ones.

Today we are at a critical juncture in the deployment of information technology. The world is dominated by the personal computer and its attendant communication and network structures. The personal computer has evolved historically to become the standard tool for doing things, despite its many flaws, despite its complexity, despite the fact that it is ill-suited for many of the tasks that it performs. As this chapter has shown, what is best is not necessarily what succeeds: The nontechnical aspects of a technology can dominate.

Once an infrastructure gets established, it is difficult to change. Even when it is clear that new methods would provide superior results, the old ways linger on, for they are so deeply embedded into the culture of a society, so deeply ingrained in the ways that people have learned to live, work, and play, that change can take place only very slowly, sometimes taking decades.

There is a better way, a world of information appliances. The task, then, is to look carefully at the alternatives. Examine information appliances. Examine just why the personal computer is so complex. We cannot forget the lessons of history: The best products do not always succeed. Social, cultural, and organizational factors can predominate over technological advances. Nonetheless, the world of technology today is far too complex; there has to be a better way. And there is.

Let us begin by examining the way market forces affect the life cycle of a product. At different points in its life cycle, a product appeals to very different market segments, who demand different attributes. As a result, the way that a product is developed, designed, and marketed has to change radically as a product moves from it early youth to maturity. The nature of these changes tell us what needs to be done to move from today's world of the personal computer to the power and simplicity of information appliances.

2

Growing Up: Moving from Technology-Centered to Human-Centered Products

Let me tell you about Gertrude. Gertrude disliked technology and, above all, computers. Nonetheless, in the early 1970s Gertrude went out and purchased one of the first personal computers, an Apple II, despite her lack of enthusiasm for technology, despite her skepticism. She became an early adopter because the new devices provided a service that could not be had in any other way. I learned an important lesson from Gertrude.

In the early days of the personal computer, I was one of the skeptics who failed to see the importance of this new and, to me, disruptive technology. I was a comfortable and long-term user of computers, starting with mainframes, such as the Remington-Rand Univac and minicomputers, such as Digital Equipment Corporation's PDP and VAX lines. This was long before the days of the graphical user interface: I was an expert user at Unix, arcane commands and all. When I saw the first Apple II, I considered it as a giant step backward. Information was stored on audio cassette tape. The display was a low-quality, low-resolution home television set. The keyboard was deficient. The machine was slow and woefully lacking in power compared to the minicomputers and mainframes. It all seemed so primitive—how could these new, limited systems be of any value?

Figure 2.1
(top) Miss Evelyn C. Lewis, the 1922 "Miss Washington," listens in with her radio set. She is tuning in by adjusting the condenser at the left. (Photograph courtesy of Corbis-Bettmann.) *(middle)* A Stromberg Carlson table-top radio, 1945. (Photograph courtesy of Corbis-Bettmann.) *(bottom)* A Sony Sports Walkman. (Courtesy of Sony Electronics Inc.)

Gertrude changed my mind. I was chair of the Department of Psychology at the University of California, San Diego, and Gertrude was the department's accountant. She refused to use computers. I tried hard to get her to use my laboratory VAX, but no, she was adamant. She pored over the huge printouts provided at regular intervals by the university financial department, reconciling the numbers with her manual adding machine. She was a whiz at her hand-operated calculator.

But one day she went out and bought an Apple II specifically so that she could use Visicalc, the first spreadsheet. This technology-hater fell in love with the spreadsheet, technology quirks be damned. The command set was complex and, even to me, a long-term computer user, intimidating. But Gertrude was determined; for her, the value was worth the pain. One of her duties was to do budget projections: Assuming we hired this many people or bought these pieces of equipment or supplies, what would be the impact on our budget? These were tedious to do by hand, especially as her clients, me and the grant-writing faculty, would often ask for revisions: "Suppose we increased this and got rid of that, what would it do to the budget?" For Gertrude and many others like her, it was worthwhile to buy a computer just for this one program, just for this one task, much to Apple Computer's surprise and delight.

In the early days of a technology, it doesn't matter if it is hard to use, expensive, or ungainly. It doesn't matter as long as the benefits are sufficiently great: if the task is important, valuable, and can't be done in any other way.

Technology Life Cycles and the Consumer

Technological products have a fascinating life cycle as they progress from birth through maturity. The same product that was attractive and desired in its youth can be irrelevant and ignored at maturity. Once through the unstable days of adolescence, everything changes. Customers view products in a new light, seeking very different things. The dimensions upon which the product is judged change. As a result, the way the product is conceived, developed, and marketed must also change.

The very talents of a company that made it successful in the early stages of a technology are exactly wrong for the latter phases.[1]

In the early days of a technology, some people will buy because of the functions it offers. These are called *early adopters,* people who buy because they are in love with technology and will buy almost any new item, or whose needs for the newly developed functions are so great that they are willing to put up with any other problems. Gertrude is a classic example.

New technology, functionality—that's what these early adopters purchase. Products are advertised and sold on the basis of their feature lists and technological claims. Marketing becomes the act of beating the competition's claims. Marketing teams go out and ask customers what new features they require, and then return to the company to implore the technologists to provide them in the next release of the product. Each company works hard to demonstrate that its products are technologically superior, that they have some new advantage that causes them to be faster, smaller, more powerful, or unique in whatever way seems appropriate to the audience. After a while, these claims take on a life of their own.

The result is technology-driven, feature-laden products. Each new release touts a new set of features. Advertisements proudly list them all, extolling their virtues. Seldom are the customer's real needs addressed, needs such as productivity, ease of use, getting the job done. Instead, the feature lists proclaim the technological feats, as if the mere purchase of enhanced technology thereby makes everything else OK. The notion that a product with fewer features might be more usable, more functional, and superior for the needs of the customer is considered blasphemous.

The situation is not helped by the product reviews in the press. Every field of technology spawns its own set of industry conferences and technical and popular journals. Financial analysts, whose job is to write about the minute differences among the companies, and the popular press, who write the reviews of new product releases, need some way of differentiating among the products they write about, so they take to inventing measurements. There seems to be some belief that their personal opinions are suspect. If they were simply to say "I liked this feature" or "I hated that feature," it would be regarded as personal opinion and carry little weight. As a result, they have created the myth that quantitative measurements are superior, for, after all, they are not subject to personal bias. All the reader has to do, goes the claim, is notice that the numbers measured for one product are better than those for another. Now the reviewer can say "When I held the scroll bar down in product X, it took 11 seconds to go from the start to the end of a document, but only 6 seconds with product Y." No matter that no user ever goes from the start of a document to the end in this way; here is a measurable, if irrelevant, difference between products.

Quantitative measurements are indeed valuable. They are at the heart of the scientific method, for they are precise and repeatable. But the choice of what is to be measured and what not is just as personal and just as biased as any other opinion. What is measured is deemed important, making what is not measured appear to be of little value. Reviewers measure what is easy to measure, regardless of whether these reflect any real utility for the users. Companies labor to improve on these highly quantifiable, highly marketable measures of performance, no matter that they are inapplicable to real life. Fortunes are won and lost, companies climb and collapse on the basis of such irrelevant measures and marketing claims.

I've just described the computer industry, although the general trends are common to the first few generations of products from many technology areas, from automobiles around the turn of the century to early televisions. This is where the computer industry is today; it still believes in technological frenzy. Megabyte, gigabyte, terabyte. Kilobaud, megahertz, gigahertz. New software releases gobble up speed and capacity, demanding more and more and more. But does the consumer understand what all these mean? Is the consumer well served? Strange you should ask.

When a technology matures, the story changes. You could even claim that a mature company is no longer a "technology" company—it's a products or a service company. After all, in everyday speech, we use the word *technology* to refer to things that are new, where the technology dominates over usability and usefulness. We call the digital computer "technology." We call the internet "technology." But what about a pencil or paper? How about a gas stove or a safety pin? In actuality, all are technologies, all follow advanced scientific and engineering practice in their design and manufacture. But pencils, paper, stoves, and pins are so commonplace that we take them for granted. We assume the technological features are reliable and robust, and so, on the whole, we ignore them.

Once technologies mature, we take their basic performance for granted. We assume it works just fine for our purposes. As a result, we look for other properties: price, value, prestige, appearance, and convenience. We purchase by brand name as much as by actual product. Even large, costly items such as automobiles and television sets are purchased more by price, appearance, prestige value, and brand reputation than by technical distinctions.

Marketing tries hard to make one product different from another by touting minor technical differences, often by giving them fancy names: "Only PixelTech has black-matrix, diagonal pixel-plating," they will proudly proclaim, even if we, the everyday users, are unable to understand, let alone evaluate, the claim.

The computer industry is still in its rebellious adolescent stage. It is mature enough that its technology, functions, and reliability should be taken for granted, but it still has a good deal of immaturity. It keeps trying to grow bigger, faster, more powerful. The rest of us wish it would just quiet down and behave. Enough already. Grow up. Settle down and provide good, quiet, competent service without all the fuss and bother. Ah, but to make this change from youth to maturity is to cross the chasm between the technological excitement of youth and the staid utility of maturity. It is a difficult chasm to bridge.

A vast chasm separates the requirements of the people on the early side of a product life from those on the late side. The first, the early adopters, want technological superiority, and they will suffer any cost, whether initial purchase price or cost of maintenance and usage, for the benefits. The other, the conservative late adopters, want reliability and simplicity: Their creed is "turn it on, use it, and forget it."

Products have to be developed, marketed, and sold very differently for these two groups of people. Alas, the aging teenagers who rule the computer companies of the world are still stuck on the youthful side of the chasm and they seem unable to make it across. It is time for computers to grow up, to enter the mature world of consumer appliances. The appliance argument is all about the consumer's comfort zone—the mature side of the chasm. It is all about ease of use, dependability, attractive appearance, prestige, and brand. The consumer world is a very different world than the high-tech world of technology-addicted developers and reviewers.

There are many ways to judge a product, many dimensions. Different dimensions are important at different phases of a product's life cycle. Similarly, different customer segments become relevant. In the early days of a product, what matters is that it provides unique capabilities. This is where the early adopters come in, the people who will buy regardless of the complexity or other difficulties just to be on the cutting edge. Early adopters are important—they help establish a market. But they are not the typical buyer—they have more technical abilities, they will put up with more grief, and they are willing to spend more money.

As the market develops, competition arises, the technology matures, and quality improves. This is the adolescent stage of a product. At some point, the technology can be taken for granted; that is, everyone has roughly comparable technology, so other dimensions of the product take on added relevance: reliability, maintenance, cost. This is where the pragmatic wave of adopters comes in, people who wait until they see whether the new technology stabilizes, whether it can actually deliver on its promises.

Eventually, the product reaches adulthood. It is mature, stable, reliable. Now, new dimensions are important; cost, appearance, and convenience play more important roles, with the technology and its functionality and reliability taken for granted. Now we get the late adopters, conservative purchasers who wait until the product has reached consumerhood, the final state of maturity. Now, the product provides real value. The technology moves to the background. Convenience and reliability are more important than technological superiority. Appearance, prestige, and pride of ownership start to matter.

Consider the wristwatch. Do you buy the one that keeps the most accurate time? Not usually. You assume they all keep accurate time, at least accurate enough for everyday purposes. In fact, some of the cheapest watches keep better time than some of the most expensive; the cheap electronic watches have time controlled by a precise, quartz crystal whereas the expensive watches are mechanical and hand made. Do you buy the watch that is most rugged? Not usually. They all are very rugged, at least rugged enough. Moreover, a cheap watch is so inexpensive that if it breaks, it is easier and less expensive to buy a replacement than to fix it, and cheaper to buy several new watches rather than one expensive one.

Although a watch is actually a piece of precision machinery, accurate to around 10–20 parts per million (one to two seconds a day), watches have long ago passed through the stage of being technology centered to the current stage of being entirely market driven, human centered. Watches are high-technology marketed as jewelry, as fashion, as objects of emotion. And yes, some are sold as functional, useful timepieces. Watchmakers have learned to manufacture a wide variety of watches to fit the varied requirements of their customers. They divide up their markets very carefully and then work at getting customers to buy from more than one category.

Digital watches tend to be inexpensive but capable of advanced functions, so these cater to the cost conscious and the gadgeteer. It is no surprise, by the way, that these are the watches favored by the engineers in high-technology computer companies. Note that although digital watches could be made to be attractive, with jeweled cases and precious metals just like analog watches, they seldom are, because these watches appeal to the practical.

Other watches are sold for their beauty, for their fashion, for their prestige value. Some are fun, some cute, some folksy, some sleek and sophisticated. Almost all the expensive watches display the time with mechanical hands, not because this is better, but because this is what the market demands. The cheaper analog watches are actually digital inside, powered by batteries and controlled by quartz crystals and stepping motors, not that the average user knows or cares. These are sold as jewelry, and the consumer is encouraged to own multiple watches, wearing the one that fits the mood, the activity, or the outfit.

The most expensive and most prestigious watches are those that are completely mechanical, some still hand made. Watches can be made expensive in two ways: One is through the addition of jewels and expensive metals, the other through "complications," added mechanical functions that show several time zones, phases of the moon, or the passage of the stars. These are complex and difficult functions to accomplish in analog, mechanical watches, hence the high cost. The fact that the same functions could be done cheaply in a digital watch is quite irrelevant to this market; these people would never wear an inexpensive plastic watch.

One brand, Swatch, brings out multiple versions of its watches with different design themes, encouraging users to collect them. This scheme is so successful that some purchasers never wear their watch, for an unused, unopened box has more value on the collector's market. Finally there are luxury, prestige watches, where the prices range from $2,000 for a luxury watch to over $10,000 for the most prestigious ones. Prestige, yes, that is what it is all about. This highly technical industry sells jewelry, fashion, and prestige. One company, SMH, has 14 different brands, the better to target the various market segments (Swatch is one of them). One of SMH's subsidiaries, ETA, makes most of the watch movements in the world.

SMH's annual report makes it clear that they consider three major factors to be of prime importance in the sales of their watches: innovation, public relations, and emotion. The computer business certainly understands innovation and it thinks it understands public relations. But emotion? When a highly technological product such as a watch is sold on emotion, then you know the technology has matured, that it is a true consumer product. When the most expensive products are actually less accurate, with fewer functions than the least expensive, then you know you are no longer in a technology-driven market—you are in a consumer market. When the technology becomes good enough, then technology is no longer the variable that controls purchases. Emotional reaction, pride of ownership, and pleasurability can all become major selling points. The computer industry has a way to go.

Moving from a Technology-Centered Youth to a Consumer-Centered Maturity: A Graphical Depiction

In its early days, a technology cannot meet all the needs of its customers. Leading-edge adopters, the early adopters, need the technology, and they are willing to suffer inconvenience and high cost to get it. Meanwhile, they keep demanding better and better technology, higher and higher performance. With time, the technology matures, offering better performance, lower price, and higher reliability. These phases are shown in figure 2.2. Note that when the technology exceeds the basic needs of most of its customers, we are at the transition point shown in figure 2.2; now there is a major change in customer behavior.

When the technology reaches the point where it satisfies basic needs, then improvements in the technology lose their glamour. Now customers seek efficiency, reliability, low cost, and convenience. Moreover, new kinds of customers keep entering the market as the product matures. In the early phases were the early adopters, those who were willing to gamble on the new technology because they felt the benefits far exceeded the costs. More conservative customers held back, waiting for the technology to prove itself, to become reliable. This is the cycle of market adoption described by Geoffrey Moore in his book *Crossing the Chasm* (see figure 2.3).

For many years, those who study the way innovative ideas and products enter society have classified the people who are the targets of innovation into five categories: innovators, early adopters, early majority, late majority, and laggards.[2] Each plays a different role in the development of a technology, with the innovators and early adopters driving

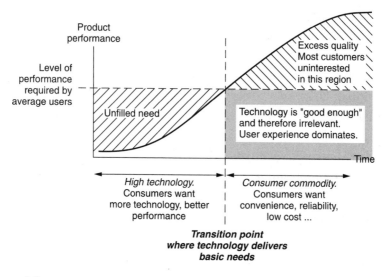

Figure 2.2
The needs-satisfaction curve of a technology. New technologies start out at the bottom left of the curve, delivering less than the customers require. As a result, customers demand better technology and more features, regardless of the cost or inconvenience. A transition occurs when the technology cannot satisfy the basic needs. (Modified from Christensen [1997].)

the technology and the early and late majority sitting on the sidelines, waiting until it is safe to jump in. Note, however, that in terms of the sheer size of the market, it is these latter customers who dominate—hence the term *majority*. These customers demand convenience, ease of use, reliability; they want solutions that simplify their lives, not technologies that complicate them. To Moore, there was a chasm between these two kinds of adopters. On each side of the chasm, a company must take a very different attitude toward its market, toward how it conceives of its product.

In truth, of course, this segmentation of the customer base is highly oversimplified. The world market consists of billions of people, with a wide variety of interests, skills, socioeconomic and educational levels, and concerns. Which products are necessities, which luxuries, depends upon the culture, the lifestyle, and a host of other variables. The needs

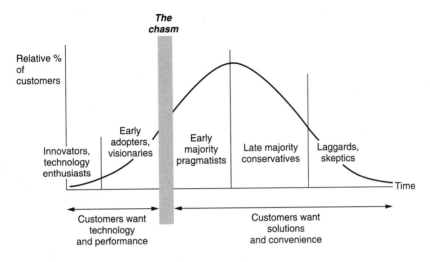

Figure 2.3
The change in customers as a technology matures. In the early days, the innovators and technology enthusiasts drive the market; they demand technology. In the later days, the pragmatists and conservatives dominate; they want solutions and convenience. Note that although the innovators and early adopters drive the technology markets, they are really only a small percentage of the market; the big market is with the pragmatists and the conservatives. (Modified from Moore [1995]).

vary, the threshold being low for some, high for others. Any individual plays multiple roles in society: parent or child, student or worker, employee or manager, serious adult or playful youth. Each role can have different levels of technological needs or lie at different parts of the adoption cycle. Note, too, that the time axes of the diagrams are measured in years or decades. The digital computer industry is just now crossing the chasm, although the computer has been with us for more than fifty years, the personal computer more than twenty. The internet started over thirty years ago. A technological product can take longer to mature than a person.

Oversimplifications are useful if they capture the essence of a phenomenon. The distinction between early and late adopters may be oversimplified, but I have found that it resonates with people all around the world. It captures well the changes in attitudes about a technology as it matures and becomes integrated with a society's culture.

Note how the analyses of figures 2.2 and 2.3 fit nicely with one another. What do late adopters want? Convenience, low cost, a good user experience. When is this possible? When the technology exceeds the transition point of figure 2.2. This corresponds to the location of the chasm in figure 2.3. As figure 2.4 illustrates, once technology reaches maturity, the entire nature of the product changes; it has to be designed, developed, and marketed differently.

Although early users are relatively few in number, they drive the technology. These are the customers who love a challenge, who want to be on the leading edge. The technology enthusiasts and visionaries see the promise offered by the new technology and are willing to take some risks, for, in their eyes, the benefits outweigh any difficulties they might face. This early group includes the product reviewers for the industry journals and the popular press. Product reviewers like to be viewed as visionaries; their job is to spot trends and extol their virtues. Moreover, product reviewers don't have to live with the products they recommend; they write their columns and go on to the next thing.

The vast majority of people are pragmatic and conservative. They are the late adopters who take a more realistic view of the world. They tend not to buy new technologies. Instead, they watch and learn from the experience of the early adopters. They wait until things have settled down, the prices have dropped, and the technology has stabilized. They wait until the product is truly capable of meeting their needs, wait for firm evidence that it brings economic value without disruption of their existing way of doing things. These buyers want convenience, reliability, and value. They do not want disruption.

The problem faced by the technology company is that the strategy for dealing with the customers in the early phase of a technology is contradictory to the strategy required in the mature phase. At first, the selling point is the technology and the list of features. At maturity, the selling points require that the attributes of the technology be minimized. The buyers now focus on solutions and convenience, on their experience with the product. They want to talk with experts in their problem

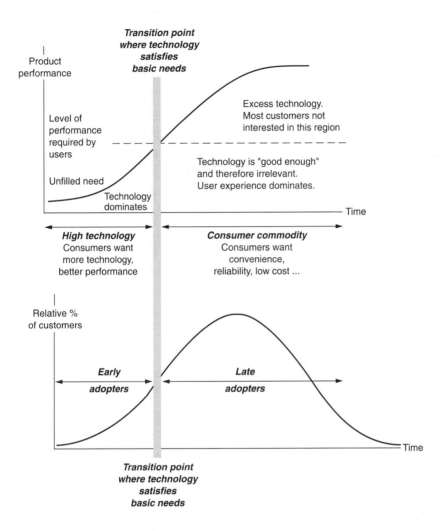

Figure 2.4

The change from technology-driven products to customer-driven, human-centered ones. As long as the technology's performance, reliability, and cost fall below customer needs, the marketplace is dominated by early adopters: those who need the technology and who will pay a high price to get it. But the vast majority of customers are late adopters. They hold off until the technology has proven itself, and then they insist upon convenience, good user experience, and value.

areas, not experts in technology. What impact will it have on their business, their life?

Now picture a company that has introduced a successful product, that has achieved great success with the early adopters. These are just a small part of the potential marketplace, and if the company wants to grow, it must change its entire approach in order to satisfy the needs of the late adopters. They have to transform themselves from a technology-driven company into a customer-driven or, in my terms, a human-centered one. But the companies who have become successful with the early technology often find that success makes their old skills obsolete. Much of what brought them success is exactly the wrong behavior now. They aren't ready to deal with the requirements of this new kind of market. They don't know how. Many don't even know they have to change; they fight the transition every inch of the way, introducing more elaborate technologies more laden with features to a marketplace that no longer cares.

Making the Transition to a Customer-Driven Company

In mature markets, technology is taken for granted. Convenience, price, and prestige are the driving forces. Among other things, convenience means ease of use, that the product can be purchased, turned on, and used, with no lengthy learning cycles, no need to call telephone support services, no need to consult complex manuals or to take classes. And no feeling of puzzlement, no loss of control. Prestige is measured in many ways, often by the brand reputation, often by the physical appearance: attractive, sophisticated design, texture, and color.

In the youth of a technology, a company can survive on pure engineering. The products are conceived and built by technologists. A small marketing and sales group takes care of advertisement and sales. Growth is fueled by technological enhancements. Customers and reviewers love it, crying out for more and more features, faster performance. At the same time, the market rises rapidly, profit margins are high. Technology reigns.

In its turbulent adolescence, as the technology matures, as the major needs of customers are able to be satisfied, the early pragmatic buyers enter the marketplace. These customers have greater demands: They want to be shown that the product is worth the investment. Moreover, they have a set of market requirements, not just technological ones. The technology company discovers it needs marketing. As a result, marketing organizations are formed to convince the customers of the product's worth. In turn, these marketing representatives come back to engineering asking for more and different kinds of features in the products. This may be the first time that the company has had representatives whose job is to talk to customers. It requires a change in perspective on the part of the engineers, the technical community. Mind you, we are still in the technology-driven phase of the market, transitioning to a feature-driven technology.

Marketing soon establishes itself as equal to engineering in influence and power. Before long, individuals from the marketing side of the company make their way up the executive ladder, in part because they understand the business side of the enterprise. Marketing starts to be represented on each technology team, usually resulting in tension between them and the engineering staff. Marketing representatives consult the company's customers and return with lists of necessary and desirable features. These lists drive successive releases of the products. Engineers often resent the influence of marketing. They feel that marketing people do not understand the technology and that their lists ask for outrageous things. In turn, marketing may feel that the engineers don't understand the needs of the customers, that they simply want to build neat gadgets, regardless of true market needs. The company is slowly maturing, but at a cost of internal tension.

But what happens when the product hits the mainstream, when even the conservative customers are starting to buy? Here is where the mass market is, here is where the most demanding customers are. And here is where the old style of doing business simply does not work anymore. The company must change the product, change the way things are done. The transformation is not easy. All the old skills are wrong for the new marketplace. The tensions between marketing and engineering were the early signs of trouble, but now that even greater changes are required, war can erupt.

As the marketplace matures, other pressures build. In the early days, there was little competition, and in any event, it was often difficult for a company to keep up with the demand. Profit margins were high. In the mature phases, there are multiple competitors, each of which is capable of satisfying the customer's technical requirements. Products can no longer differentiate themselves by features; other means are required. Now comes the importance of style, ease of use, reliability, convenience. Cost becomes a major factor in purchase decisions. With the advent of multiple competitors, often international, and with the advent of cost-sensitive buyers, profit margins drop rapidly. The financial market, which once thought of the company as the daring, pioneering leader, growing at a rapid pace and bringing in high returns, suddenly turns hostile; market share is dropping, and although sales may be rising, profits are often declining, sometimes out of existence. The financial community blames the company and lowers its predictions of future earnings; the stock prices crumble.

At the very time when a company needs to step back and take a new look at itself, when it needs to reorganize and restructure, the financial story puts severe pressures on its ability to do this. Time is the one thing it does not have. Suddenly, it has to meet market requirements, but the old guard wants to do it by adding yet more new technology, bringing out new products at an ever-faster rate, and fighting the falling revenues by cutting back on the size of the company. It is a tumultuous time. Geoffrey Moore called it a "tornado."[3]

Toward a Human-Centered Product Development

In the beginning stages of a technology, products are driven by the needs of technically sophisticated consumers. When technologies mature, however, everything changes. Now, the technology is no longer exalted; it has long since passed the stage of being "good enough" for most consumers. Moreover, the technology is commonplace enough that many competitors can produce roughly equivalent performance. As a result of the increased competition, prices drop. In the mature market, new classes of customers emerge: the mass market. These are the pragmatic, conservative customers who wait until the technology settles down, who wait until they can get value for their money with a minimum of fuss and bother. They want results. The new customers are less technically sophisticated than the old. The same product that satisfied the early adopters now creates confusion. They require assistance, hand-holding. Companies must build up elaborate service organizations to handle the customer needs. Yet this service is so expensive and the profit margins so low that a single call to the service desk can be costly enough to wipe out the entire profit from the item.

The computer industry has responded to these pressures by doing more of the same, only more forcefully. After all, their most successful strategies in the past were to increase the number of functions and features of each product. This is only natural human behavior. But it is the wrong behavior in these circumstances.

Changing times require changing behavior. The entire product development process must change. The strategy of the industry must change. No longer can sheer engineering suffice. Now, for the first time, not only must the company take marketing seriously, it must introduce yet a third partner to the development process: user experience. Moreover, the entire development process has to be turned around so that it starts with user needs and ends with engineering.

Why is everything so difficult to use? The real problem lies in product development, in the emphasis on the technology rather than on the user, the person for whom the device is intended. To improve products, companies need a development philosophy that targets the human user, not the technology. Companies need a human-centered development.

The Three Legs of Human-Centered Product Development: Technology, Marketing, and User Experience

Many skills are required to build successful products. Obviously, there must be an appropriate technology, one capable of delivering the required functions and performance at reasonable cost. For a product to sell, marketing experts must ensure that the product provides the features that customers require and that the product attributes are highlighted in advertisements, product literature, and product appearance. An enjoyable and effective user experience does not come about accidentally; it requires considerable focus and attention to the needs, abilities, and thought processes of the users. Finally, if the company is to remain profitable, the product must be built upon a solid economic foundation, providing the required attributes for a price that is acceptable to the consumers but that still yields a profit to the company.

Human-centered development requires three equal partners, three legs to the triad of product development: technology, marketing, and user experience. All three legs provide necessary and complementary

The business case

Figure 2.5
The three legs of product development in the mature, customer-centered phase of a product. When the technology matures, customers seek convenience, high-quality experience, low cost, and reliable technology. A successful product sits on the foundation of a solid business case with three supporting legs: technology, marketing, and user experience. Weaken the foundation or any of the legs and the product fails.

strengths. Weaken one leg and the product falls. The three legs stand upon the foundation of the business case and support the product itself. Weaken the foundation of sound business practices and the company may not succeed. And finally, the product must be appropriate for its position in the technology life cycle. An emphasis on technology is inappropriate for products in the consumer cycle of a technology.

Early in life, the stool does not have to be balanced. Early adopters care most about the technology, so this is the leg that must carry the weight. User experience and marketing simply have to be "good enough." As the product matures, marketing plays a more important role, tracking the technological needs of the customers and ensuring that the product is differentiated from the competition. User experience starts to increase in importance, but it does not drive the product requirements.

Things change dramatically during the mature phase of a product when it has crossed the chasm and is being marketed and sold to late adopters, those practical and conservative members of the market who seek convenience, a positive user experience, efficiency, reliability, and prestige. Here, a product fails if it is easy to use and understand but has deficient technology so that it is too slow and limited in ability. Here, a product fails if it has wonderful technology but is too difficult to use. And here a product fails if it has wonderful technology, accomplishes wonderful things, and is easy to use but is too expensive. All three legs must be in balance.

The Xerox Star is a case in point, a product that failed despite superb user experience; it had insufficient technology and marketing. This was the world's first commercially available computer with a graphical user interface. It was brilliantly designed, so much so that it set the standard for the entire second generation of the PC. It developed the high-level design principles that motivated the development of the Apple Lisa and Macintosh hardware and software and the Microsoft Windows operating system. In some ways it still surpasses current systems. The Xerox Star had ease-of-use features and a philosophy that has not been equaled since. Many of the developers of systems in the marketplace today would do well to study the Star.[4]

Despite all its virtues, the Xerox Star suffered a number of faults. It was ahead of its time[5]—it was a consumer product in an era of technology-driven ones; it was designed for late adopters before the market was ready. The sales force didn't know how to sell it. At first, they targeted the information technology professionals, technology addicts all. This customer segment failed to understand why ease of use should matter. Although the Star was intended for the late adopters, the end-users of a technology who care about convenience and use, it was premature for them; they weren't yet ready to adopt such new technology. And because the Star was a product category that was still early in the technology life cycle, the technology itself wasn't quite ready. The Star was slow, painfully slow. It had hardly any software, so it didn't really do much. Most important of all, it lacked a spreadsheet. And it was expensive. Brilliant design, but so what; it failed in the marketplace. The same, by the way, holds for the Apple Lisa: Brilliantly designed with features that have still not been equaled. And a failure in the marketplace.

The Apple II and the IBM PC illustrate another case in point: products that succeeded despite limited technology and poor user experience. They had great marketing, but more important, they handled tasks of sufficient value that their users were willing to tolerate the deficiencies. In many respects both the IBM PC and the Apple II were miserable machines. They were clumsy and, by today's standards, difficult to use. But they had a piece of software—the spreadsheet—that made it all worthwhile: Visicalc for the Apple II and Lotus 1-2-3 for the IBM PC. The spreadsheet didn't exist prior to its invention as Visicalc for the Apple II computer. It became possible to do accounting and budget projections in ways that simply could not be done before. A large number of people purchased the Apple II or the IBM PC solely so that they could use the spreadsheet. Gertrude was not alone.

These were machines for the early adopters, for those who were willing to overlook the deficiencies because of the great benefits. Superb functionality can conquer, can make for a viable business, but without full support for all three legs of the tripod, it will never stand as a business for the everyday consumer. There is a vast difference between the product that sells to the early adopters and the one that attracts a loyal following among the many. The sophisticated, easy to use, easy to understand Xerox Star and Apple Lisa were wrong for the early adopters. These people were quite happy with the clumsy, awkward Apple II and IBM PC. In turn, today, now that the market has reached maturity, ease of use and customer features are required; for today's customers, the philosophy that underlay the Lisa and Star is completely appropriate, whereas that of the Apple II and IBM PC is completely wrong. The entire design philosophy and development process changes once technologies mature. In a mature market, a human-centered development process is not only appropriate, it is required.

Human centered development requires three different skill sets, three legs of product development: technology, marketing, and user experience. Let me now review the properties of each.

Technology

For the high-technology, information-based products that are the focus of this book, it hardly seems necessary to justify the role of the technologist, for that role is well understood. It is technology that allows it all to happen, that drives the product by making possible new functions, better quality, and lower costs. As we saw from the story of the Xerox Star, the lack of sufficient technology can be a factor in a product's downfall. When the Star came out, the technology was still too expensive and limited. As a result, the machine was far too slow to be useful.

My students and I conducted some early studies of the Xerox Star at a company near my university that was one of the early large adopters of the Star. We found that despite the users' acceptance of the concepts and the principles of operation, the universal complaint was about the limited functions available and, above all, the slowness. The Star's help function, brilliantly conceived and excellently implemented from the user's point of view, was so slow as to be worthless. One user complained that after requesting help, you could leave and go get a cup of coffee, brewing a new pot if necessary, and after you leisurely returned to your desk, the help function might be ready. An exaggeration perhaps, but the story well illustrates the level of frustration.

One of the factors militating against the Apple Lisa was the high cost of the technology. The Lisa required a lot of memory for those days (an amount that today would be considered pitifully small), and this drove up the costs more than most people were willing to pay, especially as the early Lisa had very few applications of value to the user.

In the mature days of a technology, ease of use and convenience are key, but that is because the technology is taken for granted. The Xerox Star and the Apple Lisa came out in the early days of the industry. They didn't yet have the technology, neither the appropriate speed nor a sufficiently powerful set of applications. First things first: first technology and proper functions, then reliability and cost, then ease of use.

Even the Apple Macintosh was thought to be too expensive in price and too limited in capability. It, too, almost failed. It was saved by the development of yet another new technology, the laser printer and page description languages (Adobe Postscript, in this case), that made desktop publishing possible. The Macintosh had its "killer application," an ability to produce high-quality publications literally "on the desktop." Prior to the Macintosh and its associated laser printer, it took a highly skilled technical crew to produce quality publications.

Without proper technology, even the best of ideas fail. It is the technologists who determine what is and is not possible, how much time it will take, and what it will cost. All are critical determinants of product success. Without the technology there is nothing. With the technology? Well, there may still be nothing without the other two legs of marketing and user experience.

Marketing

The marketing organization fulfills many roles within a company, but the one of most concern during the development process is expertise in understanding the pulse of the customer. Marketing, of course, is not a single concept, it covers a wide range of activities, requiring a wide range of skills. But above all, it is the role of marketing to provide expert information on the customers themselves: who they are, what they buy, and how much they will pay.

In many cases, when customers first encounter a particular product at the store, they have no way of distinguishing among competing manufacturers except by what is visible in front of them, by what the sales literature and salespeople tell them, and by their perceptions of the product based on the reputation of the brand. One of the more important tasks of the marketing organization is to ensure that the product be presented in the best possible light; the visual appearance, the capabilities of the product, the reliability, and the brand reputation all play a critical role. Nothing should be left to chance, not the design, not the packaging, not the appearance, not even the training of the salespeople.

It is important to distinguish between users and customers; they are not necessarily the same. A good marketing organization understands and exploits these differences. Customers are those who purchase the products, users are those who use them. In many situations, products are bought by purchasing agents or managers, often choosing on the sole basis of initial cost. Wholesalers and channel distributors determine what retail stores will be given to sell, based on their particular beliefs of what people will buy. Contractors purchase kitchen appliances for the houses they are building, usually on the basis of price and perceived prestige, which may have little to do with the desires of the home purchasers. And even when the customer will be the actual user, the criteria that are used at the time of purchase often have little to do with those that matter when the product is actually in use.

Customers buy products for many reasons, not necessarily the ones the product developers care about or that companies would prefer. Exciting technology? Yawn. Great ease of use? Yawn. Great visual design? Well, this usually gets their attention, but not necessarily their purchase. They choose on the basis of features that may have little or nothing to do with how they will actually use the product. Moreover, the reasons for purchase vary with the nature of the industry and the type of purchaser.

One critical aspect of marketing is the positioning of the product in the marketplace.[6] Positioning is the act of establishing what the customer thinks about the company and the product. It determines how the customer perceives the products of the company. Customers buy on perceptions, not on reality; unless they have used the product themselves or have referred to friends or consumer testing organizations that have experience with the differences among the products, all they have is perception. That's one reason the concept of positioning is so important in marketing.

It's essential to position the company, the brand, and the product so that it has desirable connotations. Positioning determines the customer's perception of quality, prestige, value, reliability, and desirability. In high technology, there are many positioning options. Some computer manufacturers aim to position themselves as the quality leaders, enabling them to charge a slight premium in price. Some try to position themselves as broad industry leaders, providing much more than mere technology: "the document company," "the solutions company," "the information company," the "imaging company," all in the guise of establishing the perception that this is a company that you can trust for all of your needs. "Buy everything from us and you can be assured that it will all work together harmoniously." This argument relies on the customer's perception that a company is a single entity, and anything under its brand name comes from the same group of people.

The reality is that companies often consist of independent, warring divisions whose members do not cooperate with one another. Different divisions in the same company can be in active competition with one another. Sometimes companies have more harmonious relationships with their partners from other companies than with divisions of the same company. Many products are made by one company, but carry the label and brand of another. The internal parts of a product may be made by a different company than the one who made the exterior, and whose brand name appears on the faceplate. No matter what the real story is, the customer's perceptions are what determine the sale, and the customer's perceptions are determined by how the company has positioned itself.

Marketing plays an essential role in creating products that people will buy. Good marketing ensures that the product meets market expectations, that it is priced properly, and that it has features that appeal to users at the point of sale. The tools of the marketing organization are many, from market surveys, analyses of customer segments with attention to their purchasing power and habits, and the collection and analyses of actual retail sales from leading stores and distributors, to continual interaction with customers through visits, focus groups, questionnaires, and other sampling methods. Marketing is a critical leg in the tripod of product development.

Edison failed at marketing. Recall that his analysis of musicians indicated that there was little or no difference between the world's most famous musicians and those just below them. He may have been right. Edison also believed he had the superior technology. He may have been right. But he failed at understanding just why people buy specific products; he failed at marketing.

It is not enough to be first. It isn't enough to be best. It isn't even enough to be right. In the ideal situation a company should be all of those, but in addition, it is essential to understand why customers buy products, what they are looking for, and how their needs and perceptions drive sales. Having the best product means nothing if people won't buy it.

User Experience

The user experience group (UE) deals with all aspects of the user's interactions with the product: how it is perceived, learned, and used. It includes ease of use and, most important of all, the needs that the product fulfills.

Note the contrast with marketing and technology. Marketing is concerned with whether the customer—who is not always the same person who uses the device—will actually purchase the product. Marketing's primary emphasis is on those characteristics that affect the purchase of the item. UE's primary emphasis is on the usage phases of the product, from taking it home, unwrapping, assembling, and initial learning, through continued daily use to maintenance, service, and upgrading, where required. UE affects point of sale primarily through appearance, the graphical and industrial design, and the brand reputation for ease of use, convenience, and quality.

Ease of use has many benefits for a company. Not only are customers more likely to be satisfied with the product, but the need for service desks should decrease. In most high-technology companies, and especially in the computer industry, each manufacturer spends a huge amount of effort and money providing help services, large numbers of experts who sit at their telephones all day (and night), trying to aid the frustrated users who call with problems and complaints. Each call can be time consuming, a frustrating experience for caller and helper both. In the mature marketplace, where there is fierce competition, relatively low prices, and low profit margins, a single call from a customer can often cost the company enough to wipe out any profit from the sale of the item. Here is where one of the largest economic impacts of good product development can be measured.

Companies are concerned about the cost of their help-line services. They put much time and effort into improving the efficiency and usefulness of the telephone calls handled by the service. But this is treating the symptom, not the cause. Why not put the effort into revising the product so the calls would be unnecessary in the first place? That's the role of user experience: to develop products that fit the needs of their users, that satisfy their needs, both in terms of function and aesthetics, and to ensure that the products are easy to understand and to use. In addition, satisfied users become repeat purchasers, likely to recommend both the product and the company to friends and colleagues, enhancing the overall reputation.

User experience covers a wide range of attributes of the product. Some are technical, such as developing a conceptual model for the user that guides the developers in their design decisions and even the choice of technology, the better to ensure that the entire product development presents a cohesive, understandable face to the user. Some come from the experimental, social, and behavioral sciences, using field and observational methods to observe potential users to understand their real needs and to determine just what products might be of value. Experimental procedures and controlled observation can be used to test the initial product concept and prototypes to ensure that they are indeed usable and understandable, and that they deliver on their promise.

Some parts of user experience concentrate upon the aesthetics, ensuring that the perceptual properties are attractive and enticing: appearance, feel, sound, size, and weight. These require the skills of the graphical and industrial designers, whose contributions can transform products into "objects of desire."[7] Elegant, aesthetic, visually pleasing products not only sell better, they even appear to work better. Whether it be a fountain pen, a watch, or a computer, appearances matter.

Alas, a full-fledged UE group is rare in today's technology companies. Most companies have a few people scattered here and there who work on the user interface (variously called *human interface groups* or *human factors*). There are technical writers and industrial designers, perhaps a few graphical designers. But these people are seldom in one organization, seldom given much power. They are usually relegated to the junior, minor ranks, called upon at the tail end of product development to "make it easy to use," "make it pretty," "explain how to use it." This is not the way to deliver quality user experience. I return to this topic in chapter 9.

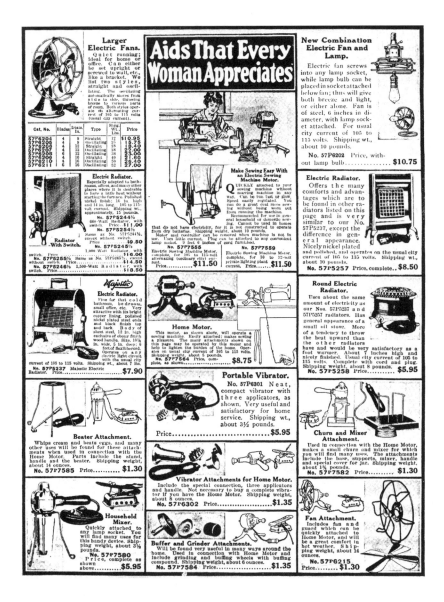

3

The Move to Information Appliances

One day in the late 1980s, while I was still a professor at the University of California, San Diego, I got a telephone call from Jef Raskin asking if I would visit his new company. Raskin had been a professor in the Visual Arts Department but had left the university and moved to Silicon Valley. I flew to San Jose and drove to Palo Alto. I hadn't seen Jef for years, so I entered his office and greeted him warmly. "Sign this," he said, pushing a legal document at me. It was a nondisclosure document. Ah yes, I had forgotten about the ways of Silicon Valley: first the legalities, then the friendship. Anything I learned during the course of the day could not be disclosed to anyone. I signed. The formality over, Jef relaxed and returned my greeting. The name of his company was Information Appliance and his device was intended to be the first of many. Although this was my first introduction to the concept of information appliances, Raskin had coined the term in 1978.[1]

A few years earlier, Jef had been at Apple Computer where he had started a project that he named "Macintosh." He intended to change the way the world thought about computing. Steve Jobs liked the idea so much that he took it over, displacing Raskin. Jobs made the Mac into a successful product that did indeed revolutionize the world of

Figure 3.1
An offering in the 1918 Sears Roebuck catalog. Before electric motors became invisibly embedded within home appliances, you would have to use your home electric motor. Note the variety of attachments ("applications") that could be used with the motor: churn and mixer, fan, buffer and grinder, beater, and sewing machine, among others.

personal computers, but in a manner that was quite different from Jef's dream.

Now Raskin had a chance to try again. The result was an innovative, fascinating writing appliance—not to be confused with word processors. The design got sold to Canon, who marketed it as the Canon Cat. You've probably never heard of it. It didn't get marketed very well, so it never was able to capture sufficient attention to receive a fair test in the marketplace. Of course, that is part of the message of this book: Good products can fail, inferior products can succeed.

Since then, the term *information appliances* crops up periodically. Recently it has appeared as the name for a variety of small devices, as if making something small were somehow related to making it an appliance. The term has been applied to small hand-held computers, to personal data assistants (PDAs), to the network computer (NC), and to a variety of internet browsers, especially those designed for use on the home television set or built into telephones. The name has become popular, even if the concept is not understood.

To me, the primary motivation behind the information appliance is clear: simplicity. Design the tool to fit the task so well that the tool becomes a part of the task, feeling like a natural extension of the work, a natural extension of the person. This is the essence of the information appliance. It implies specialization of function, thus allowing a customized look, shape, feel, and operation. The primary advantages of appliances come from their ability to provide a close fit with the real needs of their users, combined with the simplicity and elegance that arises from focus upon a single activity. At the same time, it is important not to lose some of the advantages of the personal computer, such as its ability to combine the output of any arbitrary application into another. To ensure that we keep this power, appliances will need to communicate freely and effortlessly with one another, allow us to use an appliance for one activity, then point it at a target appliance and push the "send" button: whoosh, the information is transmitted to the other. This facility requires a world-wide standard for information exchange so that devices can exchange information with one another, regardless of manufacturer. The goal is that the user will have to do nothing more than select the desired information and push the button labeled "send." The act of receiving should be done automatically.

Making a proper information appliance has two requirements: the tool must fit the task and there must be universal communication and sharing. Neither is easy.

The Information Appliance

appliance *n.*
A device or instrument designed to perform a specific function, especially an electrical device, such as a toaster, for household use. See synonyms at **tool.**
synonyms: *tool, instrument, implement, utensil*
American Heritage Dictionary, third edition (Electronic Version)

information appliance *n.*
An appliance specializing in information: knowledge, facts, graphics, images, video, or sound. An information appliance is designed to perform a specific activity, such as music, photography, or writing. A distinguishing feature of information appliances is the ability to share information among themselves.

The prime goal of the information appliance is to break through the complexity barrier of today's personal computers, the PCs. Computers are complex, difficult to learn, difficult to use, difficult to maintain. Moreover, as chapters 4, 5, and 8 illustrate, this complexity is fundamental to the beast; there is no way to overcome it. After all, whenever one device is asked to do the work of many, it must compromise on how well it can handle each individual task. Design a tool for a specific task, and its physical form, features, and structure can be a perfect fit to that task. Try to make a device that does two unrelated tasks, and the specialization that made it so ideal for the first gets in the way of the second. Moreover, once a single device can do two things, lo and behold, a third must be added: some way to inform the device which task

is to be performed, and which is to be interrupted, or resumed. In computers, this is one of the functions of the operating system.

Computers are the extreme case of devices that do multiple tasks. With the PC, with minor exceptions, all tasks must be performed on the same keyboard, display screen, and pointing device, no matter how well or poorly suited these are for the task at hand. Moreover, the operating system that allows the switching among tasks is more complex than any of the tasks it serves. Finally, the business model of the PC industry does not lend itself to simplicity, for a continual evolution in product complexity is considered essential for the continued ability of manufacturers to stay in business. From the consumer's point of view, the entire story is backward.

The evolution of electric motors provides a useful analogy. A motor, by itself, is not very useful to the average person. Motors are enablers, they are infrastructure. Couple a motor to the appropriate components and the result can be of great value. In the early days, electric motors, were large and expensive. A single motor was coupled to multiple belts and pulleys, the better to service a variety of specific tasks. In 1918, Sears Roebuck sold a "home electric motor," along with attachments such as a fan, an egg beater, a sewing machine, and a vacuum cleaner: one motor complemented by a variety of attachments (see figure 3.1, page 50).

Today, the modern house has dozens of motors, but they are invisible, hidden inside such things as clocks, fans, coffee grinders, food mixers, and blenders. Motors make all of these possible, but note how the word *motor* doesn't appear in the names of these appliances. The motors are embedded within these specialized tools and appliances so that the user sees a task-specific tool, not the technology of motors. Embedded motors are commonplace, but because they are invisible, the average

Figure 3.2
Information appliances. *(top)* A digital camera, which allows for immediate viewing of the image, which is often of more value and interest than a print. *(bottom)* A business calculator carried in the pocket and able to produce whatever answers are required, on the spot. Both can share their information with other devices. (Photographs courtesy of Hewlett-Packard Company.)

person doesn't have to know anything about their operation or the details of their technology, or even have to know they are there.

The same story can be applied to computers. A computer, by itself, is not very useful. Computers are enablers, they are infrastructure. When a computer is coupled to the appropriate components, its value is greater. Add specific computer programs, applications such as word processors, spreadsheets, and email, couple them to peripheral devices such as storage units, printers, and telephone modems, and the value increases. This is the traditional model of computing, and the result is like those early electric motors with a large number of accessories. The job does indeed get done, but at a cost of complexity and inconvenience. The tool itself dominates the activity.

When computers are embedded within information appliances, they can perform their valuable functions without the user necessarily being aware that they are there. Consider watches, microwave ovens, bread makers, coffee makers, dishwashing machines, clothes washers and dryers, all controlled by computers, but without advertising the fact, without requiring their users to know anything about their existence, let alone about their operating systems or memory capacity. In the car, these embedded computers control the fuel injection, ignition timing, antilock braking, and other systems such as security, safety, sound, and displays. In some cars they transform the fuel gauge into the more useful display that tells how far the car can be driven on the remaining fuel. They are hidden inside the most recent telephones and television sets. Computers make all of these devices possible, but note how the word *computer* doesn't appear in the names of the devices; it remains behind the scenes, invisible. Embedded computer systems are becoming commonplace, but because they are invisible, people may not realize they are there.

Although computer technology has been with us for over fifty years, it is still maturing. The microprocessor chip has been around for far less time. A few years ago, embedded computers and task-specific information appliances were not yet practical. However, the microprocessor, memory, and communication technologies are all reaching a sufficient stage of maturity that information appliances are possible with adequate performance, high reliability, and reasonable cost. As a result, it is now possible to change the focus of product development to that appropriate for a mature technology, from a focus on technical achievement to an emphasis on satisfying user needs.

In the appliance model of computing, every different application has its own device especially tailored for the task that is to be done. Each device is specialized for the task it performs, so learning how to use it is indistinguishable from learning the task—which is how it should be. Each device works independently of the others. Switching tasks means switching devices. Resuming a task is as simple as moving back to the appropriate device.

Examples of Information Appliances

The best way to understand information appliances is to experience them. Information appliances have actually been with us for some time in the guise of musical instruments, measurement devices, and calculators. Devices such as electric guitars, digital voltmeters, electrocardiograph monitors, and school calculators are all appliances, as are fax machines and telephones, both fixed and cellular. Moreover, some of these are capable of communicating with one another, thereby dramatically enhancing their capabilities. Professional test instruments commonly can send their readings to one another through a standardized instrument bus so that a set of devices takes on arbitrary power and utility.

Perhaps the best example of an effective, well-accepted family of information appliances is that of electric musical instruments, such as electric guitars, keyboards, drum machines, and synthesizers, along with the wide variety of sound generation and processing algorithms that supplement the musical devices. The musical appliance is really made possible by the emergence of a widely accepted international standard for sharing information among all appliances: Musical Instrument Data Interchange (MIDI). Because of MIDI any company can invent a new musical appliance that can then freely interact with all others. A keyboard can connect to a synthesizer, rhythm machines, control pedals, and other instruments, creating orchestras that unleash the power of digital recording and synthesis. New instruments can be invented, such as a voice device that allows singing to be converted to MIDI sequences that are then fully mixed with the other devices. I have even seen conducting wands that allow a person to conduct an orchestra, with the synthesizer creating the sounds of a symphony to the rhythm, tempo, and modulation of the waved wand. MIDI made the musical appliance possible. It allows musicians to put together a large variety of instruments and sound-shaping devices, the better to create new compositions. Even amateurs can partake in the fun. Some MIDI devices provide automatic accompaniment to the player, generating the second part of a duet or, in the case of rhythm machines, generating an entire percussion or bass accompaniment. This function also allows performers to accompany themselves or to perform all the different parts of a composition, then easily combine them. Because MIDI provides a complete record of the notes being played, intelligent tutorial devices have been constructed to teach musical skills.

Musical instruments are the prototype information appliance, but the aspirations go far beyond music. A calculator is another example of an information appliance, but it lacks the power of a standardized way of sharing its information with other devices, thus considerably weakening its power and the range of activities in which it might participate. The audio entertainment center could be considered a form of information appliance, receiving video and audio information and transforming it into the form best suited for enjoyment.

But think of direction-giving appliances, of guides to restaurants that couple into the direction-giving device, of devices that guide one through a national park, a museum, an amusement park or a department store. Sign up for an activity, then remain free to wander until the appliance says your turn has come. Find all the other people in your party. Receive information about the items in front of you.

Digital cameras are another excellent example of an information appliance, complete with communication protocol, often through wires, but more and more through wireless infrared connection; take a picture, aim the camera at a printer, send the picture to the printer through the infrared port and make a print immediately—as many as you wish. Cameras are part of a system of appliances that include portable viewers (so everyone can share the picture only seconds after they have been taken), storage devices, printers, and sending devices so that the pictures can be sent by email or posted on internet sites around the world. You can even send a picture from one camera to another, allowing people to share their photographs in yet another way.

These early appliances set the stage. They could be greatly enhanced were they all to share a common communication protocol, so all could speak to one another, letting creative users discover imaginative new combinations of devices and function.

A major technological change that characterizes the start of the twenty-first century is the merger of the infrastructures of communication and computers. This merger has major implications for many different domains, including education, business, and entertainment. The communication function is essential, and a major component of this technological change is the social interaction that is now made possible. Employees can keep in touch with their offices even as they travel, parents can keep in touch with each other and with their children. Teen-agers communicate with each other day and night, regardless of where they happen to be. Travelers can request assistance when stuck in some remote location, and people can report accidents or disabled motorists, sometimes even as the event is taking place. Information is more available to all of us, no matter where we are, whenever we need it.

Medical sensors are under development that can do analytical tests with minimal cost and effort. Microelectronic mechanical systems (MEMS) technology is already starting to appear in products. MEMS devices are truly tiny, even microscopic. They are made in the same way—and at the same scale—as microprocessors. Tiny stalks can be moved by electrostatic forces to make waves of silicon cilia that move blood cells across its surface, or that vibrate minuscule reflective surfaces—mirrors—to create bright projected images on large screens (the Texas Instruments Digital Light Processing projector uses this method).

Imagine tiny cameras, tiny radio, light, and infrared transmitters, tiny, yet powerful, computer chips. Efficient, colorful displays, both small (for embedding in your eyeglasses) and large, so groups can view them. Smart sensors that locate your position anywhere on earth, so you need never remain lost for long. Sensors that diagnose your ailments. Sensors that enhance privacy and sensors that diminish it. Sensors for probing and prying. Sensors capable of detecting nails, wires, and pipes hidden behind walls, lost objects below the ground, lost car keys, even lost people. Sensors on wild animals so that biologists can track them, wherever in the world their migration takes them. Someday we will be able to tag all our possessions with inexpensive sensors that will let us know where each is to be found.

New technologies will eliminate the need for house, office, and car keys, as well as money. We will have a plethora of memory aids, writing aids, learning aids, educational aids, entertainment aids. Aids to help us communicate with one another. Aids for navigation. The possibilities for future appliances are rich and amazing. In the appendix to this book, I provide fuller descriptions of some present and future information appliances.

Tradeoffs

Life is filled with tradeoffs, and the world of information appliances is no exception. The virtues of the appliance model are many, but there are deficits as well. The major advantages derive from specialization, which allows the device to fit the task and the person who uses it, rather than requiring that the person adapt to the technology. Specialization also means that the physical structure and means of interaction can be tailored to the task. As a result, ease of use is directly related to the effort level of the task. Easy tasks can be done effortlessly; hard tasks may still be difficult.

The personal computer does have many virtues that are in danger of being lost in the transition to independent appliances. Here, the advantages are of several forms: cost, unexpected synergies, flexibility to support new uses and new usage patterns, and, finally, the ease of transferring information and documents from one task to another, often in unexpected or novel ways.

The remarkable power of the general purpose PC is that it can indeed do so many things. It automatically allows new combinations of tasks, for all the user has to do is buy the appropriate software and use the appropriate combinations at the same time. When new tasks arise, they can be supported by the development of new software, which can then be run on the same machine. The sharing of information is relatively easy, for everything is on the same device.

The appliance model seems to lack these advantages. Each device is deliberately designed to have a restricted, specialized set of activities. Change the activity, and the device no longer supports it. When new tasks arise, new devices will have to be manufactured and bought. Sharing of information seems difficult when relevant information resides on different machines. Yes, appliances seem to have the advantage of specialization and simplicity, but at the cost of flexibility and power.

Finally, the portable PC provides great convenience when travelling, even if at a cost in complexity. My laptop has my electronic mail system, a fax system, my calendar, address book, and writing program, as well as copies of all the things I have written over the past several years. It has restaurant recommendations and airline schedules, all in one device. If I had appliances, would this mean that I would replace my one portable device with multiple appliances? How many would I have to have? Wouldn't the total set be larger, heavier, and clumsier than the single PC? And what if I carefully assembled a set of appliances, only to discover during the trip that I needed something I had failed to bring along? With the portable PC, everything is always there.

Basically, the tradeoff is between ease of use and simplicity on the one hand and convenience on the other. This is a well-known tradeoff in life. Thus, when I travel, I carry a Swiss Army knife with me, complete with cutting edge, scissors, screwdriver, and tweezers. This small, compact knife has many times proved its usefulness, despite the fact that none of its tools is ideal. When I'm at home, I use a wide assortment of knives, scissors, screwdrivers, and tweezers. The superiority of the individual tools does not detract from the value of the integrated Swiss Army knife in particular situations.

The nice part about information appliances is that we need not make a choice; we can have it all. Some people will prefer appliances optimized for the task, others will prefer them optimized for all-in-one convenience, especially for travel. Manufacturers will provide a variety of types of appliances following a variety of design philosophies; as long as there are sufficient people willing to purchase them, manufacturers will produce these devices. After all, there is no correct answer for the configuration of an appliance; what is correct depends upon the task to be done, and the work habits and preferences of the user. I myself might vary my preferences depending upon my activity. At home or work, I will probably want a variety of specialized appliances. When I travel, I will probably prefer an "all-in-one" appliance that combines a number of separate ones, even if at some sacrifice in utility or usability.

As long as there is free and easy interchange of information among appliances, and especially if reconciliation of data can be made automatic, there is no penalty for owning a variety of appliances that cover the same activities. The user chooses the one preferred for the circumstances, and when the activity is complete, the information is effortlessly distributed and shared among all.

Families of Appliances Are Systems

Although any individual information appliance can function on its own, the real power comes from viewing appliances as a system of interconnected components. The power of musical instruments comes from interconnecting them together as a system; the total is far more powerful than the sum of the individual components.

The systems approach leads to the realization that we need not individual products but whole product families structured to work together smoothly and effortlessly. Consider the needs of a photographic family of appliances. A camera alone is not sufficient, not even if the camera has a viewer on the back to allow immediate examination of the pictures. The total system includes cameras, several kinds of viewing devices, including photograph-sized portable viewing appliances for use in the field, larger viewers for use in the home or office, and viewers as large as television screens for use with groups of people. Cameras will need to send their sounds and images to these viewing devices, to storage systems where they can both enhance the capability of the appliance by allowing for extended, almost unlimited amounts of storage and also safeguard the information by keeping it in dispersed geographical regions. There will need to be printing appliances, some portable for use while traveling, some larger and fixed in location. When I travel I will need a storage appliance to hold my photographs outside of the camera, the better to extend the number of pictures I can take. But I also want those photographs stored safely away so that were I to lose the storage appliance, or if my home or office burned down, my precious photographs would survive. The same holds true, of course, for much of the information that we generate and deal with. This provides a business opportunity: Offer a storage service to protect and store information. The ideal service will encrypt the information prior to transmission to the storage location, ensuring privacy; even if someone with access to the storage facility wanted to look at your private data, they would be unable to without access to the encryption key that you alone would hold.[2]

All information appliances partake in similar families of interrelated systems. For these to work smoothly requires an efficient, omnipresent, and invisible infrastructure. One part of the infrastructure has just been discussed: the need for a readily accepted international set of standards for information exchange. But the standards are not very useful without the appropriate communication networks and information servers.

I envision an entire industry set up to establish the infrastructure for information appliances. There will be a need for local communication networks. In offices and schools, it is often possible to run wires and cables, usually through false ceilings or even along the floorboards. In the home, adding new wires to existing structures is very difficult and resisted by most homeowners. Hence, home networks will probably be wireless, requiring very low power transmitters, probably in the various frequency bands in the gigahertz region already reserved for this usage.

There will be a need for information storage and servers, storage devices that hold the large amount of information, sounds, images, and videos required throughout the day, serving them up to the appropriate devices upon demand. Much of this information may be stored off the premises, so there needs to be a high-bandwidth communication link to outside information servers and storage utilities, plus the associated retrieval appliances that allow the user to specify just what information is to be retrieved. When large amounts of information are involved, especially when much of this involves sounds and images rather than words, the best ways of doing this are still unknown; this is a difficult problem that still requires a great deal more research before it can be implemented.

The Vision

The vision of information appliances is clear: Overcome complexity, introduce simplicity. Make it possible to share and combine the information of one device with that of another, thereby enabling new applications, new arts, new sports, new industries. It is easy to imagine information appliances for games, for music, for sports, for social interaction, for communication. Appliances for this, appliances for that. Let your own imagination add to the list. New technologies always spawn forth new uses that were unthought of prior to the introduction of the technology. The same will be true here.

The vision will not be easy to achieve. It requires the proper technology, proper attention to market forces, and proper sensitivity to the needs of the consumers who will actually use the technology. It needs a human-centered design rather than a technology-centered one. It requires that the technology be ready, so that appliances can truly be built at low cost to the consumer. Finally, it requires world-wide agreement on the appropriate infrastructure that will allow appliances to share their information with appropriate other appliances.

The free sharing of information is critical to the appliance vision. It has two major benefits: one, the power of serendipitous flexibility and, two, the avoidance of monopolistic control.

The Power of Serendipitous Flexibility

If each appliance is specialized, then although it is ideally suited for what it can do, it is also limited in its possibilities. One of the great powers of the computer is that it can combine outputs of a diverse set of applications, allowing creativity to reign. Appliances can have this power only if the output of one appliance can be shared with all others, regardless of their stated function, regardless of brand or manufacturer. Take a photograph and add it to a letter, report or greeting card. Or perhaps add sound to the photograph, or music to the spreadsheet. We will know that appliances are a success when people use them to create experiences the designers never thought about.

The power to create freely, to engage in a form of serendipitous flexibility, can only come about if the power to share information is free, easy, and unimpaired either by technical limitations, trade restrictions and proprietary protocols, or unnecessary complexity. Anything that gets in the way of effortless, unlimited sharing of information gets in the way of creativity.

The Avoidance of Monopolistic Control

The personal computer industry illustrates one of the problems of monopolistic control over an infrastructure. There are two kinds of economic goods, as I explain in chapter 6: substitutable and nonsubstitutable. Substitutable goods follow the laws of traditional market economics, where different companies divide up the market share. Nonsubstitutable goods are almost always infrastructures, and here the market division is most unfair: It is all or none. Such is the case with today's operating systems.

Today it is quite possible to share freely among all programs, as long as they are made by the dominant company. New entrants into software technology have a tough time; either they use the standards demanded by the controlling company or they are unlikely to attract a sizable following. And if they opt to use the dominant standards, they soon find they are no longer in control of their own destiny, for the giant owner of the standards can change it at any moment, without notice, and with, accidentally I am sure, benefit to itself.

If appliances are to avoid these problems, they must have free, open standards for information exchange, coordinated by an international standards committee, available to all. In this way, the technology inside an appliance will not matter to the user; it can use any chip, any operating system. All that will matter to the user is the overall performance of the appliance: Does it match the user's needs? As long as it can be guaranteed that any appliance can share its products with any other, no matter who makes it, no matter what technologies are inside, then customers are free of the tyranny of nonsubstitutable infrastructures.

Design Principles for Information Appliances

What will information appliances look like? Everything and anything. This is because their look is dictated by the activities they perform. In many cases, they won't even be noticeable, for they will become such an intrinsic part of the task it will not be obvious that they are there. They will be invisible like the embedded processors in the automobile or microwave oven.

The whole philosophy of the appliance is that it should fit the activity. As a result, there really won't be an information appliance company or product. A company can't manufacture an appliance; it has to manufacture appliances for something, appliances for specific activities, for specific product domains.

Nonetheless, here are some critical design principles that can help ensure the viability of appliances. Three human-centered axioms that speak to the overall philosophy, to the satisfaction of the customer, not to the demands of the technology.

Three Axioms for Information Appliances

Design Axiom 1: Simplicity The complexity of the appliance is that of the task, not the tool. The technology is invisible.

Design Axiom 2: Versatility Appliances are designed to allow and encourage novel, creative interaction.

Design Axiom 3: Pleasurability Products should be pleasurable, fun, enjoyable. A joy to use, a joy to own.

The first axiom, *simplicity,* is the major driving force for appliances: to break the complexity barrier. The second axiom, *versatility,* comes from experience with the personal computer. We have learned that much of the power of the personal computer comes from its ability to make previously unknown, novel interconnections and combinations of the many individual things that can be done. Appliances must be able to interact in novel, creative ways, letting each device do its specialized operation, but with the combination being rich, dynamic, and flexible, able to cover the entire panoply of needs. Information appliances comprise a family where all members can interchange information effortlessly, often invisibly with a minimum of effort by the user.

The third axiom, *pleasurability,* might seem out of place. After all, what has pleasure got to do with appliances? These are serious matters, serious devices for serious uses. Not games, not amusement or entertainment.

Good tools are always pleasurable ones, ones that the owners take pride in owning, in caring for, and in using. In the good old days of mechanical devices, a craftperson's tools had these properties. They were crafted with care, owned and used with pride. Often, the tools were passed down from generation to generation. Each new tool benefited from a tradition of experience with previous ones so, through the years, there was steady improvement, each new generation ever-better fitting the requirements of the task and the needs of the owner. Woodworking tools, gardening tools. Tools for painting and drawing, tools for baking and cooking. Gloves and bats for baseball, fishing rods, boats, cars. A pleasurable tool is one that is made with quality, that fits the mind and body, that makes it fun to do a task. Tools that help. Tools that do not get in the way.

Appliances should add pleasure to our lives. They can remove the drudgery of tasks and make them enjoyable, fun even. Hence "pleasurability" as a design axiom for information appliances.

4

What's Wrong with the PC?

If there is any device that characterizes modern technology, it is the personal computer (PC). It gives all of us computational power that earlier scientists and business people could only dream of in their wildest fantasies. The world has been transformed once again, this time through the power of technologies available to the individual: communications, computation, access to information of all sorts in multifarious shapes and forms, all available through our personal computers, the instrument of power. But despite this, the PC is hardly a technological blessing; it is as much a curse as a wonder, and it is attacked as much as it is praised.

What's wrong with the PC? Everything. Start with the name. The personal computer is not personal nor is it used to do much computing. Mostly, it is used for writing, reading, and sending things to one another. Sometimes it is used for games, entertainment, or music. But most of the time it is using us. When I prowl the halls of my workplace, I often see people on their hands and knees beside their computer. No, not praying, but installing new things, rebooting, checking the cable connections, or just muttering under their breath. The *personal* computer isn't very personal. It's big and clumsy, sitting there on the desk, occupying space, requiring more and more time to maintain, requiring lots of help from one's family, friends, and neighbors. Rather than being personal, friendly, and supportive, it is massive, impersonal, abrupt, and rude.

Rebooting. Even the word is strange technical jargon. The word *booting* is derived from *bootstrap,* a small loop at the side or rear of a boot to help the owner pull it on. To bootstrap is to pull yourself up by those straps, not that many people have them on their boots anymore. A computer, when first turned on, starts up with no knowledge. No matter that you have long been using it, when first turned on it is completely ignorant of the past. In order to get started, it must find its operating system, that massive program that is the infrastructure for all else. But the computer doesn't even know how to find the operating system; It has to start off with a tiny program that has been permanently implanted in its memory and use that to load a larger program that in turn lets it load even larger programs that let it load the operating system. And, of course, the whole purpose of the operating system is to give you, the user, some way of calling up the stuff you want to work on. This process of bringing in a program whose sole purpose is to load yet a larger program is called *bootstrapping.* But why am I telling you this? Why do you need to know? You shouldn't have to know or care.

Boot, RAM, DRAM, ROM, floppy disk, hard disk, megahertz, gigabyte: Why should we want to know any of these terms? Answer: We don't. We are told we need to know because we are driven by technology and technologists.

The personal computer tries to be all things to all people. It casts all the activities of a person onto the same bland, homogeneous structure of the computer: a display screen, a keyboard, and some sort of pointing device. This is a certain guarantee of trouble. Any single set of tools is a compromise when faced with a wide range of tasks. It's like trying to do all your cooking with a knife, a fork, a spoon, and one saucepan over an open fire. It can be done. Campers do it. In olden times, people managed with less. But the myriad cooking utensils, stoves, cooktops, ovens, and so forth are in the kitchen for a reason; they make life easier, they do a better job.

A second problem is that of complexity. Try to make one device do many things and complexity increases. Try to make one device suffice for everyone in the whole world and complexity increases even more. The single, general purpose computer is a great compromise, sacrificing simplicity, ease of use, and stability for the technical goals of having one device do all.

We humans are social beings. We work best with other people. The real promise of the new technologies comes with the merger of the communication and computing industries, keeping people in touch with one another, communicating, socializing, working together, playing together. Sure, there are times when we do things alone. Creative work requires solo, silent, concentrated periods. Reading is a solitary activity. But much of our time is spent in talking to others, whether by mail, on the phone, or in person. The exciting new services are social and interactive, yet here we are, trying to build them on a device whose first name is "personal."

How many hours a week do you spend keeping your computer working, updating hardware or software, reading instruction manuals, help files, or the monthly PC magazine? Too many. How many hours a day do you spend keeping your TV set or telephone or refrigerator working? Updating it? Reading instruction manuals and help files? Not very many. There is a lesson to be learned from that contrast.

Today's PC has gotten too big, too expensive, too complex, demanding more and more attention. It is a general purpose machine, which means it can do anything. This is not a virtue.

Take another look at the Swiss Army knife, one of those knives with umpteen blades. Sure, it is fun to look at, sure it is handy if you are off in the wilderness and it is the only tool you have, but of all the umpteen things it does, none of them are done particularly well. Yes, my Swiss Army knife has a screwdriver and scissors and corkscrew—it even has a knife blade—but when I am home, I much prefer to use a real screwdriver, a real scissors, a real corkscrew, and even a real knife. Not only are the simpler devices superior, but they are easier to use; with the Swiss Army knife, I invariably pry up the wrong blade until I find the one I am seeking.

Now take another look at the PC: It does everything, serves all masters, works all around the world. The end result is that it comes with large instruction manuals, multiple layers of menus and screen icons and toolbars. Each item presents me with options that I neither understand nor care about. Today, the PC has become more complex than the old main-frame computer it was intended to replace. Why is this? In part because of the business model of the personal computer business, in part because we have let ourselves be trapped.

But finally, and much more important, I don't normally need to compute anything, so why do I want a computer? Sure, I need to write, yes, I am a habitual user of email, and yes, I use my personal computer for all sorts of activities; but the machine itself is an imposing technology, and I don't want to be controlled by a technology. I just want to get on with my life, enjoy my activities and friends. I don't want a computer, certainly not one like today's PC, whether or not it is personal. I want the benefits, yes, but without the PC's dominating presence. So down with PCs; down with computers. All they do is complicate our lives.

Don't get me wrong: There have indeed been many important virtues of our new technologies. After all, it is things that make us smart, things that allow us to represent our ideas in a permanent manner, things that allow ideas to be transmitted from one generation to another, that allow people to collaborate over time and space. We shouldn't give up the virtues. Moreover, I'm technically savvy, well versed in the technology. In my home, where I write these words, I have four desktop computers, two laptops, two laser printers, and an ethernet network. The problem is that the clumsiness and flaws of the technology tend to overwhelm the virtues, at least for most people. So, what we need is to keep the virtues of the machines without the overhead, without the clumsiness. We need to move to the third generation of the PC, the generation where the machines disappear from sight, where we can once again concentrate upon our activities and goals in life. We are ready for the generation of information appliances.

The First Two Generations of the PC

We are now in the second generation of the personal computer. The first generation was the era of the Apple II and the IBM PC. Before that, computers were large and expensive. They were sold to companies, governments, and universities. Then, suddenly, for the first time, computers were available as small, relatively inexpensive machines that could be bought and used by average individuals. These were awkward machines, quite puny by today's standards, but they were able to perform some useful functions, primarily word processing, creating spreadsheets, and playing games. These machines were limited in capability, difficult to learn, and difficult to use. But these early machines made a difference, primarily because they empowered their users. For the first time people could do their own accounts and budget projections without waiting for information technologists in their company to get around to them. The first word processors enhanced the ease of writing and revising. Computer games started to evolve. And thousands of individuals developed educational tools for schools. For the first time people were in control of their computing tools.

The second generation of the PC was that of the Graphical User Interface—the GUI (pronounced "gooey"). This is where we are today. The first successful machine of this generation was the Apple Macintosh, which followed upon the unsuccessful Xerox Star and Apple Lisa. Soon, other companies followed, IBM with OS/2 and Microsoft with Windows. In the GUI generation, the primary philosophy is "ease of use," making the complex machinery of the personal computer relatively simple to operate. And therein lies the rub: The machine is indeed complex, and the GUI goal is to sugarcoat this complexity so that it won't be noticed. Alas, complex things are truly complex, and an attractive image on the screen doesn't overcome the fundamental problems. Rather than trying to make a complex machine easy, the better way would be to make a simple machine in the first place.

What's Wrong with the Graphical User Interface
The Graphical User Interface was right for its time, but wrong for today. Why? First, it has outgrown its usefulness. The basic interface design was developed back in the days when personal computers were small by today's standards. The essential design principle was to make everything visible, so that instead of memorization of archaic commands, one could see the entire array of possible commands, file names, and directory names. Second, the basic operation was by selection, dragging, and

direct manipulation. These principles worked well as long as the machines themselves were small.

The graphical user interface really worked. Buy a new computer program, take it home, stick the floppy in the computer, and use it right away. Don't bother to open the manual; why would you need to do that? Just pull down each menu and look at it, and you have seen all the commands. Don't understand some? Just try them out—you couldn't do any harm, and everything is reversible anyway.

But those were the "good old days." The computer had a really small memory (128K, or 128 thousand bytes), and a small floppy diskette (that could only hold 400K, 400,000 bytes), and no network or hard drive. The programs were small and simple. And you couldn't store anything permanently in the computer. So making everything visible worked, for there wasn't that much to be visible. And learning by trying out everything worked, because there wasn't that much to try out.

Today, machines have expanded in power thousands of times. Today, all machines have internal disk storage, and many are connected to networks that enable them to receive millions of documents from locations all over the world. My home computer has almost ten thousand files in it, most of which are meaningless to me. My company network has hundreds of locations all over the world, each with thousands or even millions of documents. The design philosophy of making everything visible fails miserably in this context.

What's the matter with the graphical interface today? The solution doesn't scale. Making everything visible is great when you have only twenty things. When you have twenty thousand, it only adds to the confusion. Show everything at once, and the result is chaos. Don't show everything, and then stuff gets lost.

But although the computer has changed dramatically since the 1980s, the basic way we use it hasn't. The internet and the World Wide Web give much more power, much more information, along with more things to lose track of, more places to get lost in. More ways to confuse and confound. It is time to start over.

Reality check: The early Apple Macintosh computer was small and convenient, but the screen was small, too—small and inconvenient. Tiny is more like it. No color, just black and white. And it was slow. S-L-O-W. And no hard disk, just floppies, so you had to store your stuff on piles of floppies. If you didn't label those floppies and then keep the labels up to date (and who could ever do that?) it was awfully hard to find the stuff again. And if you think they don't hold much today, well, they held a lot less then. No large capacity storage devices, no CD-ROMs, no DVD, no hard disk, no networking. But easy to use? Yup. Nice and easy. You truly did not need to read the manuals. Those were the good old days, which, like most good old days, are happier in memory than in reality.

Why You Really Don't Want to Use a Computer (even though you think you do)

Do you really want to use a computer? Do you want to use a word processor? Of course not. The fact that you think you do is the triumph of marketing and advertising over common sense. Now, maybe if you are a confirmed technology addict, or a computer programmer, sure you love using computers, but not the rest of us. We want to get on with our lives.

I don't want to use a computer. I don't want to do word processing. I want to write a letter, or find out what the weather will be, or pay a bill, or play a game. I don't want to use a computer, I want to accomplish something. I want to do something meaningful to me. Not "applications," not some bizarre complex computer program that does more than I ever want to know about and yet doesn't really do exactly what I need. I want computing that fits my activities. I want the technology hidden away, out of sight. Like electric motors. Like the computers that control my car.

Once upon a time, cars were difficult to use. They had all those controls and meters and gauges. Spark adjustment, fuel priming, choke, and throttle. And there was little standardization, so every car worked differently. Some were steered with wheels, some with tillers, some with levers. The speed of the engine was adjusted by foot, by hand, by pedals, levers, or knobs. In the real early days you had to take your mechanic along with you when you went for a drive. To start it you had to prime the fuel line, adjust the spark setting, set the choke, open the throttle, and then stand outside the car beside the engine and crank it over by hand, being careful that it didn't start at the wrong time and break your arm. There were gauges for all sorts of things.

Today, now that the cars are extremely reliable, all you really need is a speedometer to tell you how fast you are moving, a fuel gauge to tell you when you are running low, and that's about it. Anything else can be done with warning lights or messages that only come on when they are needed, ideally to warn you a bit before serious problems arise, when there is still enough time to take corrective action or get help.

Even the fuel gauge isn't what you want. You don't really want to know how much fuel you have left (no, honest, you don't); what you really want to know is how far you can drive. Some cars provide this information. The normal fuel gauge can't do this because it is a simple float that rides up and down on the surface of the fuel, allowing its level to be translated into how much fuel is left in the gas tank. To translate fuel level into how many more miles of driving is possible requires some computation. The fuel level has to be converted to the amount of fuel, either liters or gallons. Then, an estimate of the efficiency has to be made: How much gasoline have you been using per mile or kilometer recently? Multiply the efficiency by the amount of fuel and you have the predicted range. Do the same computation in kilometers and liters as well as in miles and gallons so you can accommodate inhabitants of both the more advanced countries that use metric measurements and lesser advanced countries that don't. These computations require a computer; hence the moral of this story.

Computers ought to be like the embedded ones that tell you how far you can drive with the amount of fuel remaining in the fuel tank: invisible, automatic, and useful. It's invisible, so you don't have to do anything to it. It provides valuable information. Drive more efficiently, and the remaining distance goes up; drive less efficiently and the distance goes down. It wouldn't be difficult to add a time estimate: "Twenty minutes to empty."

This is the way the fuel tank meter ought to be: Get rid of the current gauge that tells what fraction of the fuel tank still has fuel in it and replace it with one that says how far or how long we can go. Notice, too, that this computer-controlled gauge is very limited in its functionality; It tells the range of driving with the remaining fuel. Nothing more, nothing less.

This is the way computers ought to be, not just in the car, but in the home, at schools, and in the office. Useful for doing things, for getting answers, for having fun, presenting us with the information we need to know, information we can use directly without further thought. According to this model they will be far easier to use. They will be designed specifically to fit the task, to fit the needs of their users. This also means that they will be specialized, so we are apt to need many of them. No problem, because they will be like all our other appliances: We buy just the ones we want, just the versions that fit our lives. Their simplicity and utility make up for their specialization.

Why the Personal Computer Is So Complex

The major problem with today's PC is its complexity. The complexity of the PC is pretty fundamental; it is built into its foundation. There are three major reasons for the complexity: the attempt to make a single device do too many things; the need to have a single machine suffice for every person in the world; and the business model of the computer industry.

Make a single device do everything, and each task will be done in a manner that is adequate, but not superior. As I have explained before, a multiple purpose device cannot be optimized for any single task; it has to be a compromise. Its physical shape, the nature of its controls and displays, are all compromises. Imagine a musical instrument that combines the violin, guitar, flute, and piano keyboard. Can it be done? Oh yes, your handy-dandy music synthesizer program will produce the sounds of all these instruments from a typewriter keyboard. But will it be inspired music? Will a real musician use it? Of course not.

The second cause of the computer's inherent complexity is that computer companies make products intended to be used by hundreds of millions of people all around the world. "Know your user" is the mantra of good design, but how can you possibly know your user when it could be millions of people, of every age, every educational level, and every social and cultural group, while hoping to satisfy every conceivable need and style of work? Because each country, each culture, and for that matter, each individual, has different interests and needs, this means that the product has to have a large set of features and operations in order to satisfy everyone who might use it. No matter that any individual is apt to use only a very small number of features or commands; to satisfy the world market, the product must have everything. Making one device try to fit everyone in the world is a sure path toward an unsatisfactory product; it will inevitably provide unnecessary complexity for everyone.

Finally, there is the business model, the strategy that the computer industry follows in order to ensure that it can make a profit year after year. There is nothing wrong with this: A company that fails to make money soon goes out of business, and then it cannot be of use to anyone, even if its products were loved and respected. But the strategy adopted by the computer industry is also one that dooms it to an ever-increasing level of complexity in its products. Let us look at this issue in greater detail.

How the Business Model of the PC Guarantees Complexity

All companies need to make a profit in order to survive. It doesn't do anyone any good to make great products if the company fails for a lack of funds. Now, how do you make a profit in the computer business? By selling computers and software, right? Yes, but the problem is that the vast majority of people, if they need a computer at all, only need one.

And each user of a machine only needs one word processor, one spreadsheet, one email program.

Think about it. Suppose you could buy a computer and software that would make you completely happy. From your point of view, that's good. But, oops, from the point of view of the computer manufacturers, that's a problem. How would they make money if their customers were so happy that they wouldn't need to buy anything else? Horrors. There is only one solution to their dilemma: They need to make you unhappy with what you have and make you want something else. Isn't this wonderful: An industry whose business model is based upon the need to make their customers unhappy.

Every year, the computer companies have to convince you that this year's version of software has features in it that you simply can't live without, even though you have lived without them all your life up to now. Moreover, because you think you are already happy with your software, the new software has to do everything that the old software did, while adding those exciting new features that you can't live without. Each year the hardware manufacturers make their systems more powerful, with more memory capacity, and faster, better graphical display capability, all absolutely necessary, of course, if you are to be able to use that new software with all those new features you suddenly can't live without. Year after year after year there will be new releases of that original, perfectly adequate software, with new feature after new feature added. Year after year you will need faster, bigger, more capable hardware. The result: guaranteed complexity.

All industries have a problem of ensuring a continuing revenue stream from their customers. They need a business model: a plan for ensuring a continual stream of revenue. The business model for some industries is trivial. If you sell consumable goods such as food, people eat it, and therefore need to buy more. Similarly, in the newspaper business, fresh news continually arrives, so customers naturally seek your services to find out about the latest events. In other businesses the life of the product is made artificially short, by making it into a fashion. Once things become fashion, a whole new industry of trendsetters emerges to produce the social pressures that cause people to buy new items so that they will never appear to be old-fashioned, never appear to be out of fashion. This, of course, is the mainstay of the clothing industry, so much so that it is called the fashion industry.

Most industries use a combination of methods. Automobiles are both consumable and fashionable. Cars fall apart after a while, which makes them consumable. And through clever advertising, autos can also fall out of fashion. Government regulation also helps by mandating new emission controls, fuel efficiency, and safety features, thereby enhancing the value of newer autos and diminishing that of older ones.

In the computer industry, the answer is to convince users that whatever hardware and software they are now perfectly happy with is, in actuality, unsatisfactory. This is done through the introduction of new features. The strange thing is that this strategy appears to work. Every six months the hardware side of the computer industry comes out with new models, each better and faster, with more capacity and lower cost than the previous model. These are called *speed bumps,* where the same basic computer as before is being offered, only speeded up a bit. In similar fashion, the software is "improved" every year. And every year the software industry comes out with new products and new versions of existing products, each with brilliant new features that are essential for the health, safety, and well-being of the planet.

Creeping featurism, is what I called this problem in 1988,[1] the symptom of the dreaded disease of *featuritis.* By 1992 the word processing program Microsoft Word had 311 commands. Three Hundred and Eleven. That's a daunting amount, more than I dreamed was possible when I wrote my 1988 book. Who could learn over three hundred commands for a single program? Who would want to? Who would ever need them? Answer: nobody. They are there for lots of reasons. In part, they are there because this one program must cover the whole world, so, in principle, for every command, there is at least one user somewhere who finds it essential. In part, though, they are there because the programmers dreamed them up; if it was possible to do, it was done. But the most important reason is for marketing. My program is bigger than yours. Better. It can do more. Anything you have, I have too, and more besides.

Creeping featurism may be the wrong term: perhaps it should be called *rampant featurism.* Do you think 311 commands is a lot for a word processing program? Five years later, in 1997, that same word processing program, Microsoft Word, had 1,033 commands. One Thousand Thirty Three. That made the program easier to use?

The problem is made even more complex by the way the computer marketplace has developed. Computer magazines review the new products, and the major things they think of looking for are comparisons of speed, lists of features, and artificial performance measurements. The stores that sell PCs also have certain requirements they look for when they decide to order machines from a manufacturer: *Hygienic* features is what the industry calls them. How fast is the machine in megahertz, how many megabytes of RAM, how many megabytes of hard disk space? Once again, it doesn't matter that speed measured in megahertz is not only a meaningless number to the consumer, but that it doesn't really measure computer speed either. It doesn't matter that the old speeds were perfectly satisfactory. It doesn't matter that consumers have no idea what a hard drive is compared to RAM. What matters is the numbers game: Bigger is better, and if your numbers don't compete, neither will your products. To sell its products, a computer company has to sell to the stores that stock them and deal with stores' purchasing agents, the "channels." And these channels have their own opinion of what sells. In particular, they like features, the more the merrier, so they have a standard set of hygienic features that the company's products must have in order to be purchased, properly displayed, and sold by the store. If it fails in the hygienic tests, the company will fail in the sales channels. The fact that the hygienic features have little to do with usage is irrelevant.

Actually, it isn't true that the current speeds and memory capacities are sufficient. They aren't, because it isn't in the industry's best interest to let them be. Nathan Myhrvold, one of the senior executives and gurus of Microsoft, once proposed, only partially in jest, "Nathan's First law": "Software is a gas, it expands to fill its container." Moreover, he added, "It's a good thing for the computer industry that computer power expands so rapidly. This way we can build bigger and fancier software that require you to get a bigger and faster computer, so we can use up all that space too."[2]

Think about it. When you go into a store to buy a stove or refrigerator, television set or telephone, you are bombarded with rows of almost identical-looking items, each barely distinguishable by price, perhaps by appearance, and by a comparison list of features. Whether or not you can use the device, whether it really does the job for you is usually not a major decision point, even if it should be. You have been taken over by the channel.

Whatever happened to the consumer? Whatever happened to the notion that one should solve the consumer's needs, which are really expressed in such terms as having fun, doing homework, writing letters, and the like, and not in megahertz and megabytes? What happened?

The computer industry works under a peculiar view of the world. The goal is to manufacture a machine that can do everything, that fits all people with the same basic hardware and software, that provides applications that have little to do with real work, and that grow ever more complex over time. It's a great business to be in, but a horrible way to affect people's lives. There are better ways to serve the customer, better ways to make money.

Activity-Based Computing

With today's PC, we buy the hardware, the computer, in order to support computer programs, also known as *applications*. Applications: what a terrible term. What a terrible concept. Applications have little to do with the tasks that people are attempting to accomplish. Look. We don't do word processing; we write letters, or memos, or reports, or notes to ourselves. Some of us write books. I do not want to go to my computer to do word processing. I don't want to go to my computer at all. What I do want is to be able to write, with a tool that fits my needs. When I write, I need some way of getting my ideas onto paper or screen, some way of reviewing them, of outlining and restructuring. I need to be able to incorporate notes I have made and sometimes drawings or photographs.

When I write business memos, I need a different writing tool. I may want to insert some budget tables and calendar schedules. When I write a letter I may want the letters I am responding to, and perhaps a calendar, and maybe my address book. Each task has its own special requirements, each of which encompasses several different applications. Today's applications have far too much power for the use I make of them, yet lack all the necessary components for any given task.

On top of all of this, life is filled with interruptions. It is a rare event when I can finish a task at one sitting. At almost any task I am interrupted by other people, by the telephone, by the next scheduled event, or because I need other material and can't proceed without it. Sometimes more urgent matters intrude, and sometimes I simply need to stop and do other things, such as eat, or sleep, or socialize.

People do activities, and the software ought to support this. At Apple Computer, we called this approach "Activity Based Computing" (ABC), and together with a hardy band of souls[3] we tried to interest the company in the notion that software based upon ABC would fit the lives of our customers better than the traditional application model that we and our competitors were selling. (What happened? It's a long story, so see the endnote.[4])

The basic idea is simple: Make it possible to have all the material needed for an activity ready at hand, available with little or no mental overhead. Tools, documents, and information are gathered together into packages maximally designed for the particular activities in which they participate, without interfering with other activities. Of course, it must be possible to make changes in the choices and to switch rapidly and easily among the activities. Finally, items not needed for the current activity are hidden so they do not distract and do not take up valuable work space.

An *activity* is a goal-directed set of tasks. Activities, tasks, and actions provide a hierarchy; an activity is composed of tasks, which in turn are composed of actions. Examples include "doing one's mail," "doing the weekly home banking activity of paying bills and balancing the checkbook," "writing a technical report." Tasks are lower-level activities, aimed at fulfilling particular subgoals of an activity. The activity of doing the mail will have in it the tasks of "read the new mail," "write a new message," and "forward the mail from Sonia to Fred." Similarly, the activity of "banking" might have subactivities, such as "balance the checkbook," or "send payment to a merchant." Actions are a lower level of interest and refer to such things as selecting a particular menu command, or typing a particular name or phrase, or naming a file. In the scientific research field of activity theory,[5] of which this set of specifications is a special case, there are further distinctions. Thus, an *operation* would be the physical movement of the hand in order to move the mouse so as to highlight a menu, with yet another operation being to move the appropriate finger so as to depress the mouse button and select the item of interest. Operations make up actions. Actions make up tasks, and tasks make up activities.

Work within any single activity can take a long time. It may involve numerous people. As a result, it is necessary to allow different people to share the activity spaces, and to figure out how to coordinate the work so that one person's actions do not interfere with another's.

Because activities take place over extended periods, it is necessary to make it possible to return to the tasks without disruption. If you are interrupted while doing an activity, you should be able to resume at a later time, whether it be an hour or a month, and find the activity space exactly as it was left, with all the items and tools in the same place and same state. If the cursor was in the middle of a highlighted word, it is still in the same place, with the same highlighting still present. All this would aid memory, would aid the resumption of the task, and would be built to reflect the way people really work. In everyday life there are multiple interruptions and it is important to be able to resume work at some later time exactly where one left off. This requires restoration of the exact context of the activity.

Activity spaces could be shared with other people or copied from one machine to another. A company might wish to provide standardized activity spaces for its procedures, such as for filling out expense reports or purchase orders. Small software companies might provide specialized activity spaces, much as stationery stores provide a wide variety of forms and notebooks. Users could then further customize these spaces to meet their particular requirements.

This would be a very different way of doing software than the homogeneous, super-duper general purpose software packages we now must use. Instead of long menu commands, one would have a chest of tools from which to select, much like working on a project in the home, where you select only those tools needed for the task and have only those at the worksite; activity spaces would allow just the needed selection. But, just as in the home where it is possible to go back and get another tool, it is possible in an activity space to add or subtract tools as needed.

Activity spaces are not a magical cure to all that ails the PC. The "C" in ABC still stands for "computing." Many of the negative characteristics I have described for the PC would be unchanged. All activities would still be mapped onto the very same set of interface tools: a screen, a keyboard, and a pointing device. And the same machine would still be doing everything, with the extra requirement that it manage the variety of activity spaces and tools that each user would need. Activity spaces are probably difficult to implement in today's world of the personal computer, although there have been numerous attempts.[6]

A far better approach is to implement ABC without the "C"—without the computer. The goal is to make it so that the tools match the activities. There is an alternative way of getting to this state: Build special purpose devices, information appliances, where each device is tuned especially for an activity. With separate devices, some of the properties come automatically. If you are interrupted, just put the device away. When you wish to resume, pick it up and get to work. There would be no interference from other activities, no problem of keeping the original state. If we made special devices for activities, we could tailor them appropriately. The banking activity could have a special check printer and dedicated connection to the bank and to your stock broker. The letter writer could have a built-in address book and print letters and envelopes.

The main barrier to the introduction of technology that is aligned with people's real needs and desires, with people's real activities, is the mindset of the computer industry. This industry has grown up being dominated by technology. The result has been the development of powerful tools that have become essential to modern life. The computer industry feels vindicated: It has been highly successful. It has prevailed in the face of skepticism. And it did it all through the power of modern information processing technology. Why should it change?

The problem is that the resulting device is technology-centric. To make it usable by the vast majority of people who lack the detailed technical skills, the industry has been forced to add all sort of add-ons: wizards, help systems, telephone support lines, books, training courses, internet sites that feature the answers to "Frequently Asked Questions," whose numbers have grown so large that we now need help systems to navigate through all those answers. All these add-ons contribute to the complexity; now, in addition to the ever-increasing complexity of the computer applications, we must cope with the ever-increasing complexity of the help systems and support services. The computer industry is stuck in a rut from which it can't escape. Its very success has driven it further and further down a path of no return. Its business strategy is caught in the endless loop of added features, continual upgrades, and, as a result, ever-increasing complexity and every increasing help systems to let us cope. The only way out is to start all over.

There are many hurdles in the way of information appliances, but the goal is worth it: devices that fit the person, that fit the task. Devices that are easy to use, not only because they will be inherently simpler, but because they fit the task so well that to learn the task is to learn the appliance.

Now let us take a look at the fundamental issues, the better to understand how to do better. In the next chapter I look at problems with the PC and the attempts to overcome them. I conclude that these are all doomed to fail. The problems are too fundamental; there is no simple magical cure. In chapter 6 I point out that the infrastructure is wrong. In chapter 7 I examine the mismatch between the needs and abilities of people and the requirements of machines. People are analog and biological; information technology is digital and mechanical. Being digital may be good for machines, but it is bad for people. This sets the framework for chapter 8's examination of why things have become so difficult to use.

In the final chapters of this book I propose an alternative approach: a human-centered development process coupled with a set of disruptive technologies, the better to yield a family of information appliances designed to fit human tasks, tailored for human needs and abilities.

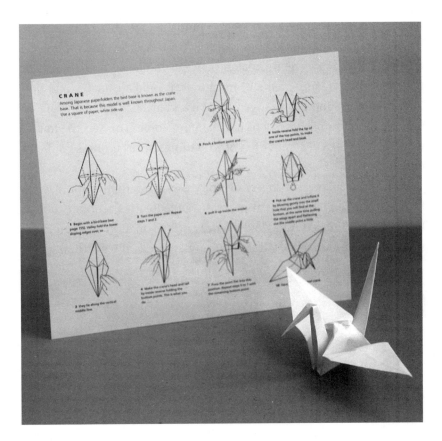

CRANE

Among Japanese paperfolders the bird base is known as the crane base. That is because this model is well known throughout Japan. Use a square of paper, white side up.

5
There Is No Magical Cure

Once upon a time, when vampires and werewolves roamed the land, the people sought a magical cure, one that would forever vanish the evils of these monsters. Eventually some were found. A vampire could be stopped by driving a wooden stake through its heart. Werewolves had to be shot with silver bullets. Ever since, the notion of a silver bullet has lingered on as a magical cure for all that ails. Find the silver bullet, say the pundits, and the problem, whatever it is, will go away.

Computers today are too difficult. Only the most addicted technology enthusiast would argue with this statement. The problem is that most people in the technology business either believe this to be inevitable, or they think, don't worry, there is a magical cure coming down the technological turnpike, a silver bullet that will kill the technological werewolves and make everything all right again. I am here to tell you that both points of view are wrong.

The notion that difficulty is inevitable is just plain silly. I'm willing to believe that the general theory of relativity in physics is difficult, and that there is no way of simplifying it. If I really want to learn the general theory I had better be prepared to spend time learning more mathematics and physics. OK, I can accept that. But I don't need to know relativity theory to use physical objects. Similarly, I shouldn't need to be an expert in computer science or engineering to use a computer, especially when all I might want to do is to write a letter, print a photograph, or send

Figure 5.1
An origami crane. Imagine trying to build this crane from a written textual description. Note that these instructions use illustrations. (Figure courtesy of Ori Kometani.)

some email. If we examine the difficulties in detail, we see that they are primarily caused by inconsistent design, by the attempt to cram too many features into one mass-produced product, by the business model that forces the software to grow increasingly burdened with new additions each year, and by a general lack of design elegance that leads to arbitrary methods of operation. Inevitable difficulties? No. Just a way of life for people who don't know any better.

The inevitable camp has another argument: This is only a problem for those of us in the older generation. Young children who grow up with computers, I am constantly told, have no problems. Nonsense. My children call on me for help. Sometimes when I had trouble with one of my computers, I would call in the very people who had designed them. I have watched the designers of these systems grow befuddled and confused. "Gee," they would say, scratching their heads in puzzlement, "I've never seen it act this way before." Not only were these the world experts on these computers (after all, they had designed them), but this was for the Apple Macintosh, a company that took pride in having a computer that was simple, easy, and well designed. This "old folks don't get it, but kids always do" argument is annoying. We got it. I get it. But we, including me, can't always make it work.

To me, the maddening point about those who have grown up with the technology is that they don't realize that there might be a better way. When I have problems, I fret and fume and suggest a dozen better solutions. When they have those very same problems, they shrug their shoulders. They have grown up believing that it is natural and correct to spend a large portion of every day redoing one's work, restarting systems, inventing "work-arounds." What a horrible heritage we have passed down to them.

The Mythical Man-Month

It is instructive to consider how large-scale computer programming is done to understand more about why computers are so difficult. In the field of computer science, the difficulties of programming have long been known to be a problem in search of a cure. The task of programming is notoriously slow. Writing computer programs is not just a matter of sitting down at the keyboard and typing. Today's large, complex system may have more than a million instructions; that's beyond the comprehension of any single individual. It takes teams to structure the problem, to lay out the attack, to write the specifications, and to do the actual programming. Programming starts with considerable thought, a set of design goals and specifications, and careful, systematic plans. The overall architecture is developed. Only then does the actual writing of the computer instructions, the code, begin, accompanied by testing and careful study, more testing and documentation. The structure is designed so that different groups can work independently, yet be guaranteed that their separate contributions will mesh smoothly. A whole set of techniques has grown up to ensure reliability, including code reviews in which fellow programmers critique each other's work, line by line, and careful and systematic tracking of the different versions of the material. Moreover, the work of one person must be coordinated with the work of the numerous others—sometimes in the hundreds, occasionally in the thousands—who are working on the same problem. Coordinating the work of all the people on the project may take as much effort as the actual writing of the program.

The typical programmer may average between ten and one hundred lines of code per day—ten to one hundred lines in a project that may ultimately require a million or more. At ten lines a day, that's 100,000 days. If a programmer worked typical business hours, with only 250 work days per year, it would take about 400 years. Most people can't wait that long for their programs to be finished, so they solve the problem by throwing more people at it. "Just think," muses the manager, "if one person would take 400 years, one hundred people could do it in four years, and four hundred could finish in one year."

Alas, programming, like any large, complex task, is not simply a matter of time and people. Throwing more people at the problem makes it worse, not better. In a justly famous book entitled *The Mythical Man-Month,*[1] Fred Brooks argued convincingly that the more people thrown at the problem, the more difficult it becomes. A widely quoted takeoff of the book goes like this: "If one programmer can write a program in one month, how long would it take two programmers to complete it? Answer: Two months." Why is this? Because as soon as two or more people work on the same problem, they need to coordinate their work to ensure that their work is not in conflict, and that they agree on the framework, the philosophy of approach, and the way in which the different components that each is working on will interact.

The size of the required administrative and support organization grows with the number of people working on the task, easily reaching 15 to 20 percent of the effort. Soon meetings are necessary to coordinate the activities of the many separate groups. Meetings to agree upon procedures and formal specifications. Meetings for code reviews, for testing, for discussing the user interface. Meetings to discuss the continually changing specifications as the results of the user testing come in, or to keep up with the claims of the competition and the customers' changes of mind. As with any large group of people, there will be absences and losses. New people will be continually entering the workforce, and they will all have to undergo considerable instruction to understand the organization, the procedures, and just what they will be doing, including trying to become familiar with the partially completed work that was done by the people they are replacing. Any change instigates widespread discussion to determine whether the change will have global impact. Any change in the specifications for the task must be passed down to all involved. In other words, the amount of overhead, the time and effort required just to do the synchronization, increases with the number of people at the task.

As you can see, writing the computer programs for any reasonably sized system is a complex task in which the administration can become more difficult than the technical issues. If management isn't careful, the entire effort ends up devoted to the administration and synchronization of efforts with no time left over for doing the work. And woe if someone leaves and has to be replaced: Teaching the new people the required history and structure of the project, getting them up to speed

---

Agency Chief Offers Little to Explain $44 Million Loss

GARY WEBB, Mercury News Sacramento Bureau
Lawmakers investigating the California Department of Motor Vehicles' $44 million computer fiasco voted Monday to hire an outside expert and launch an audit to find out why the six-year project flopped. . . .

Assemblywoman Valerie Brown, D-Santa Rosa, said after the hearing that Gov. Pete Wilson should "fire some people" for spending millions on a computer system the DMV admits will never work. . . .

Despite more than an hour of questioning by members of the Transportation Subcommittee of the Assembly Ways and Means Committee, DMV chief Frank Zolin provided few answers, other than to admit that the project turned out to be more complicated than anyone thought.

"'I'm sorry,' and 'I don't know' is about all I've heard since you've been here," Assemblywoman Doris Allen, R-Cypress, groused to Zolin. "It is not acceptable to say 'I don't know' when we're talking about $44 million."

[From the *San Jose Mercury News*, May 3, 1994, p. 3B. ©1998 *San Jose Mercury News*. All rights reserved. Reproduced with permission. Use of this material does not imply endorsement of the San Jose Mercury News.]

---

on the process, methods, and results, can slow down everyone's progress. And because turnover of personnel does indeed take place at a reasonably high rate, it can even be that adding more people slows down the project to the point where it is no longer possible to proceed. It is no wonder that large projects often falter, taking years longer than predicted or even being canceled because the funding has been used up.

Very large programming efforts have actually been canceled before completion after spending tens of millions of dollars, and in extreme cases, hundreds of millions. In many projects, the task is never completely understood, and in any event, the specifications keep changing as the project drags on. The costs of these projects, with large numbers of programmers working for years at the project, is high, and it is the rare organization that does not begrudge those dollars. Moreover, once the decision has been made to embark on the programming effort, the results are wanted rapidly; the result is continuing pressure on the programming team to do it faster, with dwindling resources. The unrelenting pressure tempts the team into shortcuts. Code reviews are tedious and time consuming, and so is testing. Human interface design, the task of ensuring that the system can be used by its customers, is almost always the first casualty. Code reviews and testing are often short-changed as well.

In almost all longterm programming projects, the specifications continually undergo revision. After all, if it takes years to complete the task, the technology will have changed, so the requirements will have changed as well. And as early test versions are released and tried out, they will rarely meet the real demands of the users, even if those very same users agreed to the specifications in the first place. It's like rearranging furniture: The only way you know if you are going to like the new arrangement is to try it out. But with furniture, it is relatively easy to move the pieces around. With software, once the framework is in place, change is extremely difficult and likely to lead to errors. Finally, the managers involved at the start of the project are apt to have changed, and the new management will have different goals in mind.

The wonder is that large software programs get written at all, and that so many turn out to be effective and valuable. It is no surprise that these large programs contain errors—bugs—that are only discovered through usage, if they are discovered at all. Once software is released to the community of users, the process of fixing these bugs becomes a drawn-out affair. Patches, bug fixes, and incremental revisions are common. The people who own the software must continually update it, hoping with each new fix that they have indeed caught the last important bug, hoping that the fix won't itself contain errors that will cause more difficulties. The hope is forlorn: with large programs, all the bugs can never be found, and the intricacies and interdependencies are so huge that a change in one section, even one that seems small and benign, intended only to correct a minor problem, can trigger unexpected consequences in other parts of the program. Software has simply gotten too complex.

For years, the computing profession has searched for the silver bullet, for the one potential cure for all these issues. Every year, some new magical cure is announced, some new method that will solve the problem, make it easy to change the program without introducing new problems, find methods that increase productivity, and bring sunshine, warmth, and blue sky to all. Yet each new proposal ultimately fails. Why?

Well, books and learned articles are continually being written on the ailments, the proposed cures, and the resulting deficiencies. One reviewer has suggested that each cure does its job, but that the aspirations of the users change even more rapidly, so that the cures can never quite keep up with the disease. Each year our aspirations grow larger, the requirements we put upon our computing systems increase, and as a result, the burden of managing the resulting large-scale efforts becomes ever more complex. I believe that, but I think the solutions fail because the proposals are always technical solutions, whereas the problems reside within the person; cognitive tools are needed to aid in the programming task, social and organizational tools are needed for the group problems. And these human problems are harder to solve than mere technical ones.

I have my own solution to the difficulty of writing large, complex software: Simply say no. In the early days of computing, larger was better. It was necessary to have everything in one place, on one computer, to ensure that all the required information was available when needed. This is no longer true. Today we understand distributed systems, systems made up of many small, interconnected parts. Each of the small parts can be relatively simple; their power comes from the way they interact. The information requirements can also be met through distributed systems, for with pervasive, high-bandwidth communication systems, it no longer matters where the information is located or where the computation is done.

Distributed systems have the virtue of separating the work effort into many small, understandable pieces instead of into a few, large, difficult to understand ones. The small pieces can also be constructed more rapidly and tested more thoroughly, and the bugs in early versions are easier to find and fix.

I have championed information appliances because they are better for people. By being relatively small and task specific, they fit into our lives and fulfill our needs in a superior way. But, hey, guess what? Being small and task specific also dramatically simplifies the software requirements. Now we can replace the large complex operating systems and applications with smaller, fundamentally simpler systems. Each appliance is relatively simple, requiring far less software, and of a far lesser magnitude than the massive programs attempting to fit all people, all needs. So here is an added bonus: Simplicity in intent leads to simplicity in design, which in turn leads to simplicity in construction, and then, simplicity in use.

Five Proposed Solutions to the Difficulty of Use Problem

That today's computers are too difficult for the average user is widely accepted. What is not so well known is the appropriate solution. Let's examine five proposed solutions to the difficulty of the PC: speech recognition, three-dimensional space, intelligent agents, the network computer, and small handheld devices. Each of these solutions does indeed have a valid use, each does offer considerable benefit. But neither any one alone nor all combined are sufficient to overcome the fundamental flaws of the one-size-fits-all personal computer.

Speech Recognition

"If only we could talk to our computers," goes a common belief, "all problems would be solved. We would finally have true ease of use." "If I could just tell my computer what I wanted without all those different commands and stuff," goes the argument, "then I would finally get useful stuff done."

I am a fan of the appropriate use of speech. Speech can be a great asset in many situations. Speech recognition allows documents to be dictated rather than typed, commands to be spoken. Speech recognition is valuable for those who can't type, either because their hands are otherwise occupied, because they have disabilities, or because they haven't yet learned how. It is valuable in many educational and training programs. Speech synthesis is even more useful, and although synthesized voices as yet do not have the natural rhythm and inflection (prosody) of human speech, they are good enough to be valuable in a large number of situations.

My quarrel is with those who extrapolate far beyond the limited capabilities of today's systems—in particular, those who confuse speech recognition with language understanding. The dream that speech recognition will somehow simplify the complexity of the computer is just plain silly.

We are very far from achieving language understanding   Everyone knows how perfect speech systems would work, anyone who has watched television science fiction shows such as *Star Trek* or movies such as *2001*, with HAL, the wondrous machine that truly converses with the astronauts. HAL doesn't even need the sounds: HAL can lipread. This is all wishful thinking: science fiction, not fact.

It is very important to distinguish between speech recognition and language understanding. Language understanding is a lot more than figuring out what words were actually said. Look, if the only problem were recognizing the spoken language, then why not simply type the action you wanted done?

"Computer, check this manuscript for typographical and grammatical errors, fix the formatting, and check that I have the correct references in the notes. Oh, and find the complete reference to that new book on software engineering."

Hah. I can't even correct the spelling properly when I sit in front of the screen and manually engage the spell-check program. And this is when I, the human being who knows exactly what was meant, tries to do it.

When words are typed, the problem of speech recognition goes away; the words are decoded precisely. But understanding is a different matter. No computer on earth could come even close to understanding the meaning of the sentences in this book, even though it could recognize each word and look up its dictionary definition. Someday it will be possible, but for now it is a fundamental research problem, best left to the university research laboratories.

There is yet another problem. Human beings are very good at selectively attending to one voice out of many; this is sometimes called the *cocktail party phenomenon*. When you are at a party or in a crowd you can select one voice out of the babble to listen to. It's often possible to switch attention to a different conversation without changing your physical position. Computers can't do this. Computers require high quality speech, with the microphone close to the lips and no distracting background noises or voices, unlike those depicted in television and movie science fiction.

Language understanding is a tough problem. It is made even more complex by the fact that when people communicate, most of what is meant is not even spoken; it is assumed to be understood because of the joint heritage and culture of the speakers. For example, a speaker of English from a small village in Northern Africa may find it difficult to converse with a teenager from Brooklyn, New York, even though both are speaking the same language. Their cultural backgrounds, experiences, and assumptions differ too much.

And even if we had perfect language understanding, that wouldn't be enough   Ever try to explain a task to another person, and fail? Language is not an appropriate tool for describing many of the things we do. A favorite teaching trick is to ask students to describe how to tie a shoelace or fold an origami object. That is, write a set of instructions that another person can read and follow to tie a shoelace or create the object, with no previous experience. Words only; pictures and diagrams are not allowed. If you have never tried this task, let me tell you that it is extremely difficult, perhaps impossible. (See figure 5.1, page 88.)

Tying shoelaces or folding origami figures are simple compared to most real problems. These two have well-known solutions. The difficult activities, the ones we need help for, are the novel ones. Even the non-novel tasks are often special. That is, most of the day, whether at work, school, or home, we perform activities that are closely related to ones we have done before, but with some variation. It is the variation that makes them challenging, usually because the nature of the variation is not known until we bump into it, and then the solution often requires quite a bit of trial and error.

How would you explain to a computer how to solve a problem before you even knew it existed? How would you explain what to do when you yourself didn't know? Computers cannot think for themselves, at least not yet; they can only solve the problems that they have been programmed to solve. Sure, they can then outperform many people, including the programmers who instructed them, but the behavior is very task specific. Thus, a chess-playing program may be world-class at chess, but it is very specialized. It took years of effort by scores of people to develop such capabilities in a machine, and the skill does not generalize to other games.

Anyone who has ever supervised another, whether it be a child or an employee, knows how frequently spoken instructions get misunderstood, or turn out to be inadequate or even wrong. Most tasks cannot be solved by talking. If they could be, life would be much simpler than it is.

"No, no," you tell your assistant, "that's not right, that's not what I meant, not what I had in mind."

And therein lies the difficulty: What we imagine systems of speech understanding to be is really mind-reading. And not just mind-reading of thoughts, but of perfect thoughts, of solutions to problems that don't yet exist. It is all very well to dream, it does the soul good. But it doesn't solve our problem.

Using today's computers is difficult for many reasons. Sure, the interfaces are horrid, making them confusing. They are badly programmed, requiring more effort than necessary. The applications don't fit the way people think and work, causing yet more problems. And the tools are seldom ideal for the task. All these factors make our jobs more frustrating than they need be. But a major reason that using a computer is difficult is that the tasks are difficult. Even if all the ailments of the interface were fixed, the tasks themselves would still be complex. Speech recognition won't solve the problem. Language understanding would help, but that is years away. As for mind reading, well, that's going to be a bit of a challenge. There is no silver bullet.[2]

Speech recognition systems are extremely valuable in their place. I have already mentioned dictation systems. Command and control systems are already useful for tasks in which the hands are occupied, such as in order taking, inventory taking, and airplane flying. The telephone company uses limited voice recognition for some of its automated services. My favorite is a telephone messaging system called Wildfire.[3] This system uses speech recognition to answer the telephone on your behalf. Wildfire takes messages, diverts calls, and tracks you down, no matter where you are, that is, if you have told her where you intend to be and given permission. (The Wildfire voice agent sounds like a pleasant woman.) It works well because the Wildfire company has done an excellent job of understanding the telephone activity. By knowing what tasks people need to accomplish, and the kinds of actions callers expect, it can overcome the deficiencies of the speech recognition program. That is the real secret to success: a deep understanding of the task that is to be supported.

Three-Dimensional Space and Virtual Reality

OK, speech recognition isn't the answer, but what about virtual reality, three-dimensional space? People are visual creatures, I am continually being told. If only we could have a three-dimensional view of the computer world, life would be simple. "Why," one earnest speaker propounded at a conference I attended, "people remember where on the page they have read a thought, where in their office they have placed a book. If we could provide the same three-dimensional facility to computers, the interface problem would be solved."

Wrong, wrong, wrong.

First, let me make a technical correction. The speaker confuses vision with space. The talents he is proposing are spatial, not visual. The blind possess an excellent spatial sense and ability even though they are deprived of vision. People do have a truly excellent spatial sense. The confusion between vision and space is critical to understanding where this set of proposals fails.

Second, most proposed solutions confuse pictures of three dimensions with actual spaces. And finally, the wondrous spatial abilities turn out to be widely overstated.

We do indeed posses powerful spatial abilities. People are spatial animals, and we can learn to navigate our houses, our town, our world. We are pretty good at remembering physical locations. But good is not perfect. And there are huge individual differences; what is easy for some is difficult for others.

The real problem, however, is that what many technologists seem to propose as the solution is *not* true spatial representation. What most technologists seem to want to do is present a picture of a three-dimensional world on the screen, letting us move the picture around so that the scenes that are visible are the ones we would see if we were moving inside the space. But there is no movement; the visual world moves, but we ourselves stand still. That is not at all the same as the real situation in which the world stays still and it is we who move. This is confusing visual images with spatiality.

These well-meaning but naive technologists confuse what people see when they move about the world with what they experience. If we look only at the visual information to the eye, there is no difference between moving the head to the left while the world stays stationary and moving the world to the right while the head stays stationary. The eye "sees" a moving image in both cases, but our experiences of the two cases are very different. When it is we who are moving, we perceive that our bodies are moving and that the world is stationary. Similarly, when it is the world that is moving, we perceive our bodies as stationary. It is possible to make the view on the display screen of the computer look just like the view that would be seen had the body moved, but the body is seldom fooled. The experience is not that of movement. (There are some well-known illusions where our perceptions become confused; when on board a stationary train, if the adjacent train starts to move we sometimes perceive it as stationary with us moving in the opposite direction. These instances are rare; human perception would be less effective were it fooled on a frequent basis.)

The body senses its own movement in two ways. First, to oversimplify somewhat, the mind knows that the body intends to move, as it has generated the neural commands to the various muscles that cause the movement. Second, the actual movement is sensed by the body, in part through the proprioceptive apparatus in each of the muscles and joints and the semicircular canals in the inner ear that act as accelerometers, sensing any change in velocity. In real motion, the sensory information received by the senses matches the intended motion and the proprioceptive cues. Whenever there is a mismatch either between the intended motion and the real one, or between the motion perceived by vision and that perceived by the proprioceptive receptors, it feels most peculiar—nauseating, in fact. This is the cause of motion sickness, whether it be in a boat, a car, or a spaceship. Discrepancies in the perceived and intended motions cause nausea. This is especially severe either when the motion is not controlled by the person, such as in the case of carsickness or seasickness, or when the body's motion and spatial receptors are not working properly because of illness, drugs (such as alcohol), or, in the case of outer space, because of the lack of gravity.

People also become nauseated when they view pictures that depict movement, but the body remains stationary. People can get sick in simulators that don't move or even in movies that show too much motion. Experienced military pilots can get sick in simulators of high performance jet aircraft even though they do not get sick in actual flight. Fixed-base automobile simulators, those that show the moving scene out the windshield without moving the car, often cause nausea in their drivers. Motion picture companies have learned not to show too many roller coaster shots taken from the front seat looking straight ahead, especially with wide screen movie projection; audience members get sick when the sight of motion does not coincide with actual motion. Individual tolerance for motion sickness varies considerably, with some people never experiencing the problem, others acutely sensitive to it. Any system that is to be used by everyone, without careful preselection of the participants, must be concerned with this phenomenon.

Moving things around the screen, no matter how realistic the depiction, is not true three-dimensional motion. If the depicted motion is too accurate, the result will be to cause nausea in some viewers. How about that: A system intended to help people remember things and get jobs done instead makes them sick. That is most certainly not a silver bullet.

But what if we could simulate real three-dimensional space, with the body actually moving? Wouldn't that be better than our current interfaces? Well, sure, and I look forward to having such a device. But don't think of it as a silver bullet. What if we used virtual reality? What if we wore helmets that projected a three-dimensional scene onto our eyes, changing the scenes as we walked about in space? No nausea there.

Virtual reality is already a useful training tool, and I expect its use and value to increase. But it is not going to solve the complexity problem of the personal computer.

The real world is three-dimensional, but that doesn't stop us from losing things, misplacing them, and, in general, getting confused. I lose my things. I can't find my book, or my keys. People lose their eyeglasses, their jewelry, their favorite items. And woe to the person who puts an important document in a "special place," the better to make sure that it won't get lost; as most of us learn through bitter experience, special places often turn out to be places we can't remember.

Yes, spatial location is a great aid to human memory. Yes, the Greeks used the method of places as a memory aid. But aids are not perfect solutions. Moving to three-dimensional space will be of assistance in some cases, but it is far from a cure. And moreover, it had better be movement to real 3D, not pictures of 3D. But if I lose things in my office, why will providing me with a realistic, virtual reality simulation of space solve the problem of misplacing items? Won't I have the same problems that I do in real space? And in computer space, we have millions—trillions—of items we need to find. Searching for them in three-dimensional space sounds like the high-technology equivalent of trying to find a needle in a haystack. The same problems that plague us in the real three-dimensional world will plague us in artificial ones.

Real life already has its many difficulties, such as messy offices and our inability to find sought-for things on demand. The new technologies should help us overcome these limits, not reproduce them.

Intelligent Agents

"Ah, don't worry," say the technologists. "You are right, speech isn't the answer, three-dimensional space or virtual reality isn't the answer—but wait, the answer is intelligent agents: intelligent systems that will understand what you want and deliver it to you. Sometimes they can even suggest things before you think of them: It's better than mind reading; they predict your mind."

Well, there are agents and there are agents.[4] Some are useful, some do indeed provide me with just the information I need even before I realized I needed it. Some can suggest useful books to read, interesting movies to watch, restaurants I might enjoy, all based upon matching my likes and preferences with those of thousands of other people, recommending to me things that like-minded individuals like, avoiding the things that like-minded individuals dislike, even if this goes against the mass opinion. That's good.

There are intelligent agents that monitor what I type, picking phrases and quietly looking them up in their files or even through internet search services. Then, while I continue to type, the agents quietly and unobtrusively make suggestions of related items I could examine in a small window at the bottom of the screen.

What is nice about the agents I just described is that they work inconspicuously in the background and then, when they surface, do so gently, offering suggestions that the human user can decide to explore or ignore. This assistance promises to be of great value, especially as it is always an option, the user is always in control. I find their goals attractive but, up to now, their performance unsatisfying. This is a branch of artificial intelligence that holds great promise at some, as yet unspecified, future time.

The danger comes when agents start wresting away control, doing things behind your back, making decisions on your behalf, taking actions, and, in general, taking over.

Will intelligent agents be useful? Yes. They already are. Will intelligent agents someday solve the complexity problem? No.

It is one thing to devise systems that are based upon careful task analyses and that can ferret out useful actions, information, and suggestions. This approach is bound to work well. I have already described how Wildfire, a combination of speech recognition and intelligent agent, does an excellent job of handling telephone calls. Systems of intelligent agents that follow this philosophy, that leave the user in control, can be and already are successful.

The hope for systems of such powerful, general intelligence that they will act as truly intelligent assistants, doing things for you better than you can do them, hiding the complexity of the computer behind their friendly, smooth exterior, is just that: a hope, a dream. It might even be a valuable dream if it pushes researchers to delve ever more deeply into the issues such a system poses, not only issues of general intelligence and of anticipating one's desires, but such issues as social responsibility. When is it appropriate for intelligent systems to take control? Is there a problem when intelligent systems mimic human beings, taking on their voices, appearances, and styles of interacting? What about people who might confuse an intelligent agent with a real person? Is this a social problem, or merely an amusing incident?

Just like the technologies of speech and three-dimensional displays, intelligent agents are a valuable technology that will add to our enjoyment and effectiveness. But they have to be used properly, and it is important to know not only their strengths, but also their weaknesses.

Help Systems, Assistants, Guides, and Wizards Specialized forms of intelligent agents are now common in applications aimed at the nontechnical market: intelligent help systems, assistants, guides, and wizards. To my mind, these are fundamentally misguided and patronizingly insulting. They are bandages on the surface problems of today's systems rather than attempts to eliminate the fundamental causes of the trauma.

Help systems are essential for today's computers. It is the rare individual who is expert enough to know all the details, settings, and interactions of all the various applications, device drivers, and hardware configurations required by today's machines. Help systems offer efficient ways of providing the required knowledge when it is needed, helping people track down problems or learn about new features.

Assistants, guides, and wizards are steps toward the automation of help. Here, agent technology is introduced that tries to infer the intentions of the users from their actions, providing suggestions and guidance. In some cases they take the action requested by the users and walk them through each step, requesting whatever information or decision has to be entered along the way. These forms of assistance can be helpful. They can also be annoying, pedantic, cloyingly cute, and condescending.

These systems are of limited use for two reasons. First, it isn't possible to infer intentions from actions. This is not just a matter of getting more intelligent technology; it is fundamental. There simply isn't enough information in a person's actions. After all, people are poor at the same task; think of how often we misunderstand another's intentions, even those of people with whom we have lived for many years. After all, the same action sequence can result from different thoughts, beliefs, and intentions; how is an observer to know, especially one as limited as is the computer system that cannot sense mood and emotion?

Sometimes assistants and guides will be correct, and when they are, they can indeed be useful. Actually, I think it is unfortunate that they can be so useful, for they mislead the technologist into thinking that they are on to an appropriate solution to the complexity problem. The problem is that when the systems are wrong, the attempts to help users do things they are not interested in doing are far worse than no help at all. In other words, when these systems are good, they are very very good, but when they are bad, they are horrid. The good is not enough to compensate for the pain of the awful.

The worst problems of these help systems, however, is that they are ointments applied after an injury to try to make everything better. The systems are fundamentally complex. The correct way to simplify the lives of the users is to eliminate the complexity. Attempts to deal with the complexity by means of explanations, hand-holding, and semiaccurate automation are never going to be as successful as solutions that tend to the underlying cause of the complexity. The way to create easier-to-use systems is to build in simplicity, not to add it on.

The Network Computer (NC)

In the 1960s and 1970s, before the rise of the PC, most companies and educational institutions had only a single computer, shared by all. Users were connected by so-called dumb terminals. These were display devices that contained very little intelligence or computing power. Their screens could only display the information passed to them by the central computer. This simplified the problems of maintenance; there was only one computer to keep up to date, one computer that needed all its various software kept compatible.

The PC changed all this. First, it allowed the computer to be used outside the workplace, in the home or school where there was no main computer. Even in large companies and universities that used central computers, the PC brought great flexibility and power to individual workers. Because people had their own machines, they tended to add their own software and special modifications. Soon, the workplace became a bedlam with large numbers of systems, growing more and more incompatible with each day. The virtues came at great cost.

The network computer (NC) is the modern solution to this problem of the proliferation of different, nonconforming systems. It attempts to combine the virtues of the old-fashioned central time-shared computer with those of today's powerful, flexible PCs. Basically, an NC is a PC without all the power, specifically without the capability of adding software locally. The software is located on the main computer and transferred as needed to the local machine where it is actually executed.

In the days of dumb terminals, the software was executed on the one shared machine and the results displayed on the local terminals. In the NC, the computations are all done locally, which makes for a more flexible, more responsive device. In this way, the local machine can use all the power of modern computers, especially for the rendition of graphics and sound. When the task is done, the software is removed from the local machine. Some NCs allow data to be stored locally; others require that all the data also be stored in the central machine, making it easier to ensure proper backup and safety of those data.

A major difficulty with today's computers is software maintenance, especially keeping up with the large numbers of new applications, updates, revisions, and corrections. New technologies are introduced, each with its own software requirements. Manufacturers discover problems with their software or unwarranted interactions when two different software applications are used at the same time. As a result, they are continually releasing new corrections to overcome the problems. The user must spend considerable time keeping the machine up to date, and sometimes fixing the problems introduced by the new software.

This problem is particularly severe in businesses and schools, where it is necessary to keep large numbers of machines working. All the machines must use compatible software to allow results to be traded from one machine to another.

The NC promises to make maintenance of systems easier. For this reason alone, it is a good idea; I recommend it to large companies and for many educational settings, especially ones plagued by people who tamper with machines and software. The NC ensures that everyone always has the equivalent tools, and safeguards the software programs and data.

But the NC does not solve the difficulty problem. The NC philosophy takes the same difficult computer we have always had, but instead of having many of them, one on each desk, we just have one, in some central location, plus lots of little display units on individual desks. The central computer has the same difficulties as before—probably even more, to enable it to handle the new job. The only difference is that it is maintained by professionals who are used to all the nonsense rather than by everyday folks like you and me. So, in this sense, it is a silver bullet—it spares us the everyday issues.

But at our end, we still have to contend with those same applications. We have to find them. And then they look the same, smell the same, and act the same. We still use one machine to do everything we need in life. The applications are just as complex as ever, still increasing in difficulty with every passing year, every new software release. Our only relief is that the maintenance is in some central place where it can't be seen.

The NC philosophy also takes away some of the powers of the PC— the ability to customize it to one's own preferences, to keep valuable data with their creator, where they can be looked at in privacy, their security guaranteed by their owner, not some distant service. Many people feel more comfortable when they are in control of their personal data and information. So, yes, the NC improves matters for the organization. It enhances the role of the system information manager and it eliminates the pain of keeping the PC continually up to date. At the same time, it takes away its power: It removes the "personal" from PC, both in letter and in spirit. Ah, the NC—a lead bullet, polished and shined, being passed off as silver.

The NC will help business and education, but it is an aid to the administration of large systems, not a solution to the fundamental problem.

Portable and Handheld Devices

The fundamental problems of difficulty have caused numerous vendors to try multiple approaches to the problem, often through the generation of small, specialized devices. Some are worthy of examination, others are simply the same complexity in a smaller package.

There are numerous portable computers, and they grow ever smaller each year. Most use simplified operating systems. The keyboards shrink in size or disappear, replaced with schemes for handwriting or, at least in the research labs, speech-recognition devices. The screens are also shrinking, some day to be replaced by tiny eyeglass displays, projecting a tiny image onto the viewer's eyes, optically designed so that the image appears to be a large, high-resolution image hanging in space some comfortable distance away.

These attempts to shrink the size of the PC are useful; they do enhance the power and flexibility of the machine. But they should not be seen as a means to simplify the device. When you take a difficult machine and make it smaller it remains just as difficult, except now it has an inferior pointing device, an inferior screen, and an inferior keyboard. Do I like these smaller machines? Yes. I use one. The small size makes them useful for travel. But the average person who has difficulties with the desktop PC will have the same difficulties with the small PC. Nothing fundamental has changed.

Some small devices do pass the test, devices that are true first steps toward appliances. These are specialized tools, sometimes called personal data assistants (PDAs). Some are quite valuable and, I'm pleased to report, are doing well in the marketplace, demonstrating that there is a demand for such devices, if properly designed.

One of the early PDAs, Apple's Newton, failed just after its introduction. Rightfully so. Its designers did not understand how it was to be used. They failed to provide utility to real people doing real work. Instead, the Newton provided a new form of general-purpose computer. It promised too much and delivered too little; however, the Newton did show the utility of small devices. The Newton made an excellent display for reference works such as maintenance manuals, city guides, and, in specialized markets, farm and insurance information. This is a legacy that should not be forgotten; it can still lead to a valuable product.

With time, the technology has improved and, with experience, some new powerful solutions for specialized tasks have arisen. Other devices, such as the 3Com Palm organizers, have learned from the experience of Newton and targeted a much more specific audience; they have become true information appliances. They are very successful in their applications.

Making the PC small does not change its basic nature. It still suffers from trying to do too much. Making small, specialized machines is another matter. These are valuable. These are the first steps toward the world of information appliances.

The Solution through Information Appliances

The problems of the PC are fundamental to its nature. The problems result from the very power of a general purpose machine and the attempt to make this single device, with a simple keyboard, display and pointing device, serve all needs. The result is not only ever-increasing difficulty, but inferior performance as well. Remember the Swiss Army knife; while it can fill an amazing variety of needs, it isn't particularly good at any one of them.

The solution is to break through the difficulty by using devices specialized for the task to be performed. The problem here is that if all these devices are independent, they lose many of the benefits of the computer, for in the computer, it is possible to combine the results of any two arbitrary applications. The computer's infrastructure, for all its complexity, provides a powerful tool for communicating, socializing, and working creativity. The combination of computation and communication infrastructures makes possible a large number of new activities.

Before we can go further, we must examine the existing information and communication infrastructures to understand their impact upon individuals. What we need is a human assessment of the impact of the infrastructure: an assessment of the economics and the impact upon individual life and social interaction. The next chapter provides this: a human-centered analysis of the all-pervasive infrastructure of modern technology.

6

The Power of Infrastructure

Insects wear their skeletons on the outside. What you see are the hard, supporting surfaces, the mechanical parts. Some buildings also wear their infrastructure on the outside. In the Centre Pompidou in Paris the skeleton and plumbing are fully exposed, dominating one's impression of the structure.

The term *infrastructure* refers to the basic services and foundations required for a system to function. Infrastructures are critical to the success of modern life, whether it be through the safe and reliable delivery of water, electricity, and mail or the efficient disposal of sewage and garbage. In the world of high technology, the computer chip and the operating system are fundamental infrastructures that provide the framework for the applications and communications of modern computing. In turn, the development of standardized protocols for the transport and structure of information provide the backbone for our communication networks, including the internet and its all pervasive services such as email, and the graphical structure, pages, and hyperlinks of the world wide web. It is the infrastructure that allows email, voice, and video to travel from sender to recipient. It is the infrastructure of the operating system that allows the output of a drawing program to be inserted into a word processor, that allows multiple programs to coexist and operate on the same machine at the same time.

Figure 6.1
The power of infrastructure. Horse-drawn public transportation, telephone and power lines in lower Broadway in New York City, 1889. (Photograph courtesy of Corbis-Bettmann.)

Infrastructures are seldom thought about, but like the skeleton of insects or the framework and plumbing of the Centre Pompidou, they are often quite visible. I look out of the window and I see wires and poles, roads and fences, radio and television antennas, satellite dishes. I go up a tall building and look down upon the roofs of the other buildings. Instead of the glorious architecture that can be seen from the ground level there are air conditioning ducts and heating vents, sewer vents, and drain pipes. Hanging laundry and water tanks. In an earlier era, the streets of major cities were a nightmare of wires and open gutters until they were finally put underground, out of sight, but not out of mind. Now, beneath the streets of the city lie pipes, sewers and water runoffs, gas lines, wires and cables for electricity, telephone, and television, and, here and there, special-purpose ducts for heating and cooling, even pneumatic tubing for sending packages. Add to the story the streets themselves, along with sidewalks, subways, and train rails, all part of the infrastructure that makes travel possible.

What do we make of this infrastructure? On the one hand, it is essential to life. It is a sign of the civilization in which we live. Without this complex infrastructure, life would not only be less pleasant, it would be less safe. Disease, discomfort, danger, and loneliness were common in cities before the advent of modern sewer systems, safe, drinkable water, gas and electricity for heating, cooling, cooking, and lighting, and the telephone, radio, and television for comfort, communication, and safety. We should be pleased to see the world covered with poles and wires, roads and fences, pipes and canals. On the other hand, they are ugly. They insult the senses. Infrastructure should be invisible. We should be proud of our accomplishments, but rather than copy the insects who have their infrastructure on the outside, perhaps we should copy ourselves, where the infrastructure is mostly hidden beneath the skin.

Infrastructures are essential to everyday life, but they are always the supporting player, never the goal. It is only when there is trouble that the infrastructure is noticed, and therein lies the problem. In many of our technologies, the infrastructure is in the way, it is always present, and it seems always to go wrong. Technology is our friend when it is inconspicuous, working smoothly and invisibly in the background, like a proper infrastructure should, to provide comfort and benefit. Technology is a pest when it is in the way, when it is intrusive.

Infrastructure can be the dullest of all topics. It can also be the most important. Infrastructure defines the basis of society; it is the underlying foundation of the facilities, services, and standards upon which everything else builds. Take away the infrastructure of daily life and we could not function: no water, electricity, transportation, communication. Infrastructures are largely invisible and unheralded, but critical, whether they be for an individual home or a society. So it is with our technologies: their infrastructure determines what can and what cannot succeed.

Infrastructure takes a long time to become established. It requires considerable agreements among all those affected, often at high cost. National and international infrastructures cost billions of dollars. Not all the countries of the world yet provide electricity, running water, or telephones to a majority of their inhabitants. Paved roads in good condition are rare in many of the developing nations.

If the lack of infrastructure is a major deterrent to progress, so, too, can be an existing infrastructure, especially as it becomes old and obsolete. Once a particular form of infrastructure has become established, it is very difficult, perhaps impossible, to make a change. As a result, organizations that take the lead in a technology and deploy expensive infrastructures can discover, to their dismay, that they eventually fall far behind, saddled with an expensive, obsolete infrastructure while others rush ahead with lighter, nimbler, more effective modern ones. Thus, countries that today lag behind the rest of the world in the deployment of telephone systems may soon overtake today's leaders by deploying the less expensive and far more powerful digital wireless telephone systems, ones that do not require running wires to every home in the country. When there are competing technologies, especially when their infrastructures differ, the cost and difficulty of establishing and switching infrastructures can determine the market leader, not the relative technical excellence of the opposing alternatives.

The United States has not been able to break the stranglehold of the English system of weights and measures, a pervasive infrastructure of measurement standards and culture, despite the arguments that overall trade and efficiency would be improved were the country to switch to the metric system. The telephone companies of the world are having great trouble dealing with the advent of data transmission and packet switching systems. This is partly because even the best intentioned of them cannot see how to get away from their huge investment in the existing technologies of circuit switching centers and wires from local switching offices to individual homes and businesses. Some human infrastructures, such as language and monetary systems, are so pervasive, so ingrained in human society that it is extremely difficult, foolhardy even, to suggest change, even where the benefits of change seem enormous to the outside observer. Witness the debates over language in Canada, the United States, and Belgium. Witness the fight over the switch to a single currency in the European Union.

Infrastructures are essential for any industry or society. But they are difficult and expensive to establish, and then, once established, difficult or impossible to change or remove.

Two Kinds of Market Economies: Substitutable and Nonsubstitutable Goods

The importance of a proper infrastructure goes beyond its impact upon usefulness and intrusiveness. It can determine the entire success and failure of a technology. The lesson of Thomas Edison and his choice of an incompatible infrastructure, both for electricity and the phonograph, leads to a more general lesson about the marketplace.

There are two kinds of economic markets: substitutable and nonsubstitutable. Substitutable goods are products like groceries, clothes, and furniture. Nonsubstitutable goods are invariably infrastructures. The two have very different properties. Most recent books about the business and marketing side of technology miss this distinction, but a company that provides a substitutable good must function very differently than one that provides a nonsubstitutable one.

In a substitutable marketplace, goods of one manufacturer can be substituted for goods of another. This is the classic market-driven economy, where competition prevails. This applies to food and newspapers, to automobiles and television sets. In this marketplace, standard market forces are at work and the market can be shared among competitors. Usually, one company has a substantial lead, but the others can coexist in relative stability. This is the classic case of free market competition.

The choice of one substitutable good makes no commitment for the future. The consumer can buy a Pepsi today and a Coke tomorrow: the first choice does not constrain the second.

In a nonsubstitutable market, the required infrastructure means that goods from one manufacturer cannot be substituted for goods of another. This is the marketplace that Edison found himself in with his use of DC electricity over the competition's use of AC. It was the same story with his use of vertically cut cylinders and discs when the competition used laterally cut discs. It is what happened with Beta videocassette recorders.

Once there is a nonsubstitutable market it doesn't matter how good the product is. Beta video was better than VHS, the Macintosh operating system was better than DOS, yet Beta lost to VHS and Macintosh lost to DOS. If purchasers switch between two competing brands in a substitutable market, the losing brand has a chance of getting the customers back when they make their next purchase. But if a user switches with a nonsubstitutable good, then there is essentially zero chance of ever getting the customer back. For this reason, the company that is behind in market share slowly dies. The competition is in an "absorbing" state.

In infrastructure markets, "good enough" suffices. It is far more important to get the lead in market share than to get the lead in technology. Woe to those technologists who think that technical superiority is the critical variable. Yes, it is important, but it does not stand alone. In the world's marketplaces, technical quality is only one of many variables.[1] Except in the early stages of an industry or for a tiny percentage of purchasers, technical quality usually is not the most important of those variables.

Nonsubstitutable goods are infrastructure goods. That is, usually the product itself is of little direct use; it provides the basis for a whole array of other goods and services. As a result, the choice of one makes a strong commitment for the future. A nonsubstitutable good usually implies an investment, and the more additional goods purchased that are compatible only with that infrastructure, the more the customer is committed to stay with that infrastructure. A customer who buys Microsoft Windows now cannot easily go out and buy Macintosh OS later; the customer will have too much invested in learning time, too much money invested in nontransferable hardware and software to make such a switch easily. Yes, it is possible to switch infrastructures, but only reluctantly, and at great cost in time, money, and effort.

The manufacturer of an infrastructure or nonsubstitutable good can achieve complete market dominance through a positive feedback mechanism. The more people who purchase the market leader, the stronger the case for others to do so and the stronger the case for secondary manufacturers to make goods that work in conjunction with the market leader. The more manufacturers who make goods for the market leader, the more attractive it becomes for new customers. Many customers feel compelled to purchase whatever brand their colleagues purchase, so they can share services and goods. The new customers, in turn, attract even more secondary manufacturers. This positive feedback cycle has only one stable point: full domination of the market by the major player.

In this kind of market, one manufacturer thrives while the others die. The one leading owns a special, but essential, part of the market, and within the sphere of coverage, the goods of other firms cannot be used. This market usually occurs when there is some essential infrastructure required for all in the market and one player has exclusive rights to that infrastructure. It is what happened in the computer industry with all the competitors to Microsoft's DOS and Windows (e.g., Apple's Macintosh

OS and IBM's OS/2). This is what is happening today between Microsoft's Windows NT architecture and Unix.

In the absence of government regulation, the winner-take-all impact of a nonsubstitutable good applies within any well-defined marketplace. The entire world does not have to use the same infrastructure. It is possible to have different standards in different markets, and alternative systems can survive in protected niches, where their lack of conformance with the dominant supplier does not matter. Any domain that is isolated from others can use its own unique infrastructure; difficulties arise only when domains intersect, when the goods produced for one infrastructure must mesh with the goods produced for another. But within each domain, nonsubstitutable goods lead to market domination by a single standard.

Thus, in any particular country, it would be disastrous if some automobile manufacturers made cars that drove on the right-hand side of the road (with the steering wheel on the left) and others made cars for the left side of the road (with the steering wheel on the right). However, different regions of the world can choose different standards. Thus, we do have different standards in the world for driving, for steering wheel placement, for electric voltage, frequency, and wall plugs, for telephone plugs, and for television and cellular telephone signals. But because telephone calls must work around the world, there is only a single set of standards for the information structure of the telephone call, for the routing information, for the transmission of voice and control information; these had to be standardized, or else world-wide telephone calls would be problematic.

If the differing international television standards (PAL, SECAM, and NTSC) all competed in the same country, one would dominate and the others die out, much as when VHS and Beta video recorders competed; one (VHS) survived. But PAL, SECAM, and NTSC are all defined by governments so that within any nation, only one of those standards applies. As a result, each survives in their national niches, dominating completely within their assigned countries. The same pattern can be seen in the width of major railroad tracks, in the choice of whether to drive on the left or the right side of the road, and whether to use 50 Hz or 60 Hz as the standard frequency for the delivery of electric power. In each case, several solutions survive, but within any single political region, all parties use the same system.

Nonsubstitutable goods leads to a winner-take-all market dominance. Because this can lead to monopolies, in many cases the government steps in to establish the standards and rules of the game, as governments all over the world have done with utilities and postal services. This works when the goods are key infrastructures. When the government assumes control of nonsubstitutable infrastructures, it stabilizes the foundation, allowing competitive forces of a substitutable kind to operate above the infrastructure. Examples of this would be the railroads, the interstate highway system, and the government regulation of standards for broadcast media. Imagine if one company had patented its form of TV transmission and other manufacturers had their own forms. The transmissions would be nonsubstitutable—the equipment that could receive one type of signal would not be able to receive the others. A battle to the death would have ensued among the companies. Instead, the government mandated the standards, thus avoiding the fight.

Standardization of infrastructure is often critical to the success of an industry. The lack of a clear market standard can cause an entire industry to fail. In the United States, the government specified a standard format for FM stereo broadcast. As a result, FM stereo is almost universal. FM transmitters and FM receivers are all designed to receive stereo. The audio sound reproduction industry has flourished. However, the United States government decided not to mandate a choice for AM stereo but, instead, to leave it for marketplace factors to decide. As a result, we do not have AM stereo. Several competing formats emerged, none of which survived. What happened was that no single format could get started; broadcasters wouldn't make the investment to start transmitting AM stereo until sufficient consumers had radios that could receive their signals. Consumers wouldn't make the investment to purchase AM stereo receivers until they knew that there were sufficient broadcasting stations that used the same standard as their choice of receiver. Radio manufacturers only wanted to manufacture to the standard that consumers were willing to purchase. As a result, most FM music is transmitted in stereo, but in AM stereo transmission is rare.

The same story is playing itself out in standards for cellular telephones. The United States government mandated a common form of transmission for analog cellular telephones, but left it to the marketplace to choose among the three competing digital formats. The Europeans decided upon a single digital standard, GSM. As a result, the same cellular telephone will work in most of the countries of Europe and even in much of Asia. This illustrates the power of standardization, which enables customers not only to use one telephone number and subscription service across a large, world-wide community, but also to reap the benefits of a superior digital technology that thwarts theft and ensures privacy.

Meanwhile, in the United States, the various competing standards are fighting to establish a stronghold, but the AM stereo story is being repeated. As a result, the United States still does not have a pervasive digital cellular system; instead, it has an inferior analog cellular system, one that has shorter battery life and heavier components than digital, and that allows easy eavesdropping and *cloning*—where an illegal set masquerades as a legal one. Letting the marketplace decide is not always the key to success for society, although it may please some of the participating companies.

The Impact of Nonsubstitutable Infrastructure in the World of the PC
The differences between the two different forms of economic goods, substitutable and nonsubstitutable goods, has major impact upon the deployment of the products of high technology. Today, the world of personal computers is settling upon a single standard, that of Microsoft Windows, a standard used by over 90 percent of the world's computers. This is truly a nonsubstitutable good. As a result, market factors force every major player in the world of computers to conform to these standards, force them to write their applications so that they fit within the style and manner dictated by this platform.

The restriction of choice has added to the complexity of the PC, in part because of marketplace requirements for continuity. The new versions of a product must remain compatible with the old. For the data of one product to be freely moved into that of another, each must abide by an increasingly complex set of agreements and internal standards. The internal communication language between computer applications and the operating system, called application programming interfaces (APIs), gets ever more complex, with substantial numbers of books devoted to documenting and explaining them. Meanwhile, the business arguments force deliberate obsolescence of products. Whether or not the customers were happy with the earlier software is of little concern; unless they upgrade to the new standards, they will soon find that their information structures are incompatible with those of their coworkers. It is a never-ending cycle in which users are trapped.

In striking contrast, the internet has established itself as a new vehicle for sharing information. Because of its strong heritage in the university community of the world, many of the internet standards are freely available without cost, freely accepted by all the major vendors. The internet promises to provide a substitutable marketplace for information, thereby overcoming the limitations of the existing nonsubstitutable information structure of PCs. On the internet, it doesn't matter what brand of computer is used, or what operating system. It could be Windows or Macintosh or OS/2 or Unix or Linux. This is the premise behind the introduction of the Java programming system. Once the information packet is formed and transmitted, the nature of the base machine does not matter.

The change from nonsubstitutable to substitutable market forces is clearly a threat to the dominant player and owner of the nonsubstitutable good. As a result, strong forces are at play within the internet to try to change the nature of the interaction, to try to force all information packets to rely upon the existing Windows infrastructure. The political maneuvering is intense. The battle is on. To a student of market economy it is a fascinating story being played out for all to watch. For the user of these technologies, it is a nightmare.

The Properties of Media

Let us temporarily leave the world of competing computer infrastructures and turn to the world of communication and its varied communication infrastructures or, as they are more commonly called, the *media*.

In the world of communication, there are numerous forms of media, each with its own characteristics. From the human side, each medium imposes its own strengths and weaknesses, its own particular qualities upon us and our lives. Not all media are equal. Each has its own special properties. In the world of high technology, the properties of communication media both enhance and constrain usage patterns.

Affordances of Media

Physical objects have affordances, a powerful, but little understood part of infrastructure. Physical objects can play a variety of roles. A rock can be moved, rolled, kicked, thrown, and sat upon—not all rocks, just those that are the right size for moving, rolling, kicking, throwing, or sitting upon. The set of possible actions is called the *affordances* of the object. An affordance is not a property, it is a *relationship* that holds between the object and the organism that is acting on the object. The same object might have different affordances for different individuals. A rock that affords throwing for me does not for a baby. My chair affords support for me, but not for a giant. My desk is not throwable by me, but might be by someone else.

The term affordances was created by the psychologist J. J. Gibson in his study of human perception. In my book *The Psychology of Everyday Things* I appropriated and extended the term for its application to the world of design. In the design of objects, real affordances are not nearly so important as *perceived* ones; it is perceived affordances that tell the user what actions can be performed on an object and, to some extent, how to do them. In the design of everyday things, proper uses of perceived affordances make the difference between objects that are understandable and usable and those that are quite unfathomable.

It's very important to distinguish *real* from *perceived* affordances. Design is about both, but the perceived affordances are what determine usability. I didn't make this point sufficiently clear in my book and I have spent much time trying to clarify the now widespread misuse of the term. "I added an affordance to this icon by putting shading around the sides," says the visual designer. I shudder at the misuse of the concept, however well intentioned. Worse, I imagine J. J. Gibson sitting up in his grave staring at me once again, and then, with a rich, dramatic gesture, shutting off his hearing aid and lying back down with a look of disgust on his face.

Perceived affordances are often more about conventions than about reality. The scrollbar on the side of a computer window does indeed afford movement vertically, constrained so as not to permit movement sideways. "Buttons" depicted on the screen do allow a person to "click" upon them to get a desired action accomplished. These control operations now have well-established conventions for the manner by which they are depicted on the screen. Shading and or other graphical techniques do influence the visibility of the parts that can be moved and therefore the understanding and usability of the system. But they don't affect the actual affordances, only the perceived ones.

Perceived affordances are not necessarily the same as actual ones. If I saw a realistic painting of a door on a wall, the perceived affordance would be that I could open the door and walk out of the room, and I might even try to do so, but the painting would not really afford those actions. Similarly, if a cupboard door has no perceivable handle, it may be impossible to figure out how to open it, even if the cupboard affords opening. Some objects have deliberately false affordances, as when parks and institutions place large vertical posts in the middle of roadways. To the uninitiated, the posts do not afford passage of vehicles, so people don't attempt to drive their cars that way. To the informed, however, the barriers are made of rubber, designed to bend and recover, so that cars can quite easily drive over them without damage to either car or barrier.

A communication medium is not a physical object, but nonetheless, media have affordances. The media of broadcast communications such as radio, television, and traditional publishing on paper afford one-way communication from performer to audience, but they do not afford communication in the reverse direction.

The act of creativity varies according to the demands of the media. Commentators or panelists on TV, radio, or even the internet, must respond to questions immediately, without much time for thought and reflection. Moreover, the demands of the broadcast media are to keep each utterance short, reduced to what is sometimes called a *sound bite*. Sound bites are pithy statements intended to be easy to understand, easy to repeat. But they also result in gross oversimplification of complex concepts.

Writing, on the other hand, does not take place in real time, and so it affords reflective contemplation. The writer can take time to construct the message and improve it until it conveys the intended meaning. Moreover, there is often space available for a detailed analysis of the concept, avoiding the sound bite constraint. The reader, in turn, can take time to reflect on the meaning, to skip some sections and to linger over others. The medium affords reflection.

Interactive written media, such as conventional letters, fax, or email, afford the recipient time to reflect on an appropriate answer. Real-time interactive media, such as telephone, computer, or talking in person, do not afford this reflective time between receiving an utterance and replying. The strength of real-time interactions is in their ability to afford a rich communication of emotions, affect, and intentions. Sarcasm and irony are often very effective in face-to-face communication but can be badly misunderstood in written interaction.

Cultural demands can interfere with the affordances of media. Electronic media, such as email, have developed a cultural expectation of immediate response. When I send a note to a friend, even one across the world, I expect a rapid response. An interchange of several messages in a period of an hour with a distant friend is normal. Such expectations, however, diminish the affordance of reflection, for fast responses do not lend themselves to well-considered ones.

Similarly, the lack of full two-way communication means that electronic communications afford interruptability. The person initiating a

telephone call may not wish to interrupt, but there is no way of knowing if the recipient is busy or free, receptive to interruption or not. Even
when the senders try hard to anticipate the likely activity of the recipient, the lack of full information means the attempt often fails. Thus,
most people try hard not to call when the recipient might be sleeping or
at dinner, and most business people hesitate to call someone at home or
on holidays. But these restrictions are only partially successful, and today, when a phone call thought to go to a person's office may automatically be redirected anywhere in the world, it isn't always possible to
know what day or time it is for the recipient.

Intrusive and Enhancing Technologies

Once upon a time, I never traveled without my camera. But eventually it
occurred to me that I was spending more time taking pictures than
enjoying the trip. Worse, after all the effort to get just the right angle,
just the right picture, once I got home, I was usually too busy to view the
developed prints and slides. So I had neither the benefits of the original
experience nor of the retrospective viewing.

In an earlier book, *Turn Signals Are the Facial Expressions of Automobiles,* I included an essay on this phenomenon, triggered by two key
observations:

▪ I attended a play put on by my son's elementary school. The audience
was packed with parents making videotapes, so busy with the parapher-
nalia of that technology that they hardly had time to see the play, let
alone enjoy it. Perhaps, I speculated, they were taping the play so they
could go home and watch the tape to see what they would have been
seeing had they been watching in the first place. Except, of course, for
those parents whose technology failed them. And indeed, in the days
that followed the play, we heard from a parent anxious to borrow a tape
because her video camera somehow failed to record the event.

▪ On my first trip to China, my hosts took me to the Yellow Mountains,
a famous and revered location, quite difficult to get to. For us, it was a
five-day trip: one day of driving to get there, three days of hiking to get
to the peak and return, and one day of driving to get back to our univer-

sity. For many, the trip to the top of Yellow Mountains was the pilgrimage of a lifetime. The Chinese had many cameras; they seemed to be everywhere, photographing everyone and everything. Because Westerners were so rare at this location, my family—and especially my young, blond-haired son—were the frequent targets of cameras. But on the magical morning on which we awoke at sunrise at the top of Yellow Mountains to look out over a sea of clouds with "islands" of mountain tops peeking out from the cloud cover, I was surprised to see not cameras, but drawing easels. Why, I wondered, would they sketch imperfectly when they could photograph with much more accuracy?

It took a while before I understood. A camera is an intrusive technology, one that gets in the way of the act. Drawing, on the other hand, is an enhancing technology, one that by its nature requires concentration, focus, and reflection upon the event being drawn. To sketch a scene requires a deep analysis of the experience, to savor it, to relish it, to reflect upon it. It is this act of reflection that is critical: Once the picture is drawn, the deed is done and the picture itself could be discarded, for the mental appreciation will last forever. Indeed, years after the event, those who photographed it may barely remember, whereas those who drew it will have an enhanced appreciation with more vivid memories. Perhaps their appreciation will have been distorted by the vagaries of human memory to be even larger than life, more fulfilling than the reality. But why not? Why not savor life's experiences with even greater satisfaction over time?

Photographs have their virtues and drawings their deficits, but my personal choice has been to stop carrying my camera while I travel, preferring to rely upon the unassisted mind instead. I haven't gone so far as to take up drawing, but maybe that, too, will come. For now, I am satisfied by taking "mental snapshots."

Note taking is somewhat akin to sketching. The average note taker cannot keep up with the speaker, so it is necessary to reflect upon what was said and capture only the highlights and the important moments. I know of many note takers, myself among them, who never ever look at their notes once they have been recorded. The process of note taking is what matters; it focuses the mind, minimizes the tendency to day-dream, and causes one to reflect upon the events being recorded so well that at the conclusion of the event, the notes themselves can be discarded; their purpose has been served.

Note taking during an event is also intrusive. The act of taking notes about one utterance prevents full attention to the next. The mechanics of the task add to the distraction. So although at times I take notes, more often than not I simply listen. Either I understand, in which case I will not need the notes, or I don't, in which case the notes won't help.

But what of those intrusive technologies, the telephone and the pager? If cameras are bad, these others are far worse, for at least with a camera, the user controls the activity whereas with a telephone and pager, the devices are in control.

No Moments of Silence

"There are no more moments of silence," the woman said to me. We were talking at breakfast, just before the start of a TED conference, one of those expensive, exclusive gatherings that the world of high technology is so fond of. "There are no more moments of silence," she said, "there is no chance to get away, to have time for one's self, to think, or perhaps just to be alone."

We both reflected upon the fact that more and more people seemed to be turning away from technology, not because they were opposed—many of these people are the leaders of major technological companies—but because the technology is more and more in the way: part of the problem, not the solution.

I find that paper notebooks are still used more frequently than portable computers in meetings that I attend, even though these are held in the conference rooms of the major high-technology companies of the world. The rooms are appropriately wired (with power outlets often conveniently located in the conference room tables), and the computers themselves are provided without cost to their users, paid for by company funds. So all these people own portable computers, but they don't use them in meetings. Paper notes are more convenient, much more flexible and expressive, and the act of note taking less annoying to others than the steady clatter of keys.

Electronic mail—*email*—once the efficient means of communication, is now a burden, so much so that many executives no longer have time to read their email. Instead they pass the task to their assistants, who print out the messages so the busy executive can scribble a response, which the assistant then sends out under the executive's name. Less important messages get answered directly, so the executive may never see them. The same procedure has long been followed with regular postal mail and, now, with faxes.

So, too, with telephone calls. It is the rare executive who answers the phone, not because of feelings of superiority or intolerance, but simply because of the lack of time to do so. I no longer answer my phone at work, but not because I don't want to speak to callers; I barely have time to get through my crowded schedule. Telephone calls, therefore, have to be scheduled on my calendar just like any other activity.

My electronic mailbox receives between 50 and 100 email messages a day. That is about ten an hour during the workday and over 20,000 per year. Add to that the telephone calls and visitors, and it is easy to see why there isn't time in the day to do one's job, much less to be alone or to think. Donald Knuth, a well known senior computer scientist, has disconnected his email, stating "I have been a happy man ever since January 1, 1990, when I no longer had an email address. . . . It seems to me that 15 years of email is plenty for one lifetime." As partial justification, he quotes the semiologist and author Umberto Eco, saying "I have reached an age where my main purpose is not to receive messages."[2]

Executives can free themselves of the tyranny of technology by assigning the responsibility to their staff. Ironic, isn't it? All those executives of high-technology companies, free from the need to use high technology because they can afford to hire people to shield them. Most businesspeople do not have this luxury. They lug portable computers, fax machines, pagers, and cellular phones wherever they go. In the car, at the airport, on the airplane, in the hotel room, there they are, sending and reading email and faxes, calling their companies and their customers, searching databases, continually changing their schedules. It used to be that during trips, computers could only be connected to company networks from the hotel room, which meant that email was restricted to mornings, evenings, and occasional returns to the hotel. But wireless connections for computers are now available, letting technology intrude anywhere, anytime. Wireless computers, wireless cellular telephones and pagers: There truly is no escape. There are no moments of silence.

Technology-Free Zones

Let's return to that picture of the electronically overwired business traveler. Once upon a time, not so very long ago, I always traveled with portable computer and cellular phone. So, too, did my colleagues. At business meetings, out would come the portable computers, their owners furiously clicking away at the keyboards. Every morning when I woke up and every evening before I went to bed I would dutifully dial the telephone number of my company's computer connection and spend an hour or so reading and responding to my email. I was not alone.

Today, however, more and more of us are stopping all that. I often travel without my personal computer, without my cellular telephone. At a recent conference I attended, of the more than 600 people in the auditorium, I could only find three portable computers.

One colleague, a senior executive at one of the largest telephone companies, told me he goes for a morning run every day while traveling. "How do you fit that in?" I asked. "When I wake up, I do my morning email, and by the time I finish, it's time to leave the hotel room."

"I don't do my email," he said, giving me a peculiar look. "What is more important—your health or your email?" I have since followed his example.

These modern technologies interrupt our lives, whether or not that is the intent of either sender or receiver. Worse, they disrupt the lives of nearby people, those innocent of any role in the activity but unfortunate enough to be located adjacent to it, where they cannot help but be disturbed. The result is the invention of what might be called *technology-free zones*. In actuality, they are not technology free, for it would be quite impossible for the modern human to exist for long naked, with no shelter, no knives, no blankets, no shoes, and no processed or cooked food. In most cases, the term *technology free* really applies only to intrusive technologies. We are beginning to see more and more restricted areas, where technology is prohibited in the effort to reduce disturbing others. Some examples include:

- Theaters prohibit cellular phones, pagers, cameras, and tape recorders.

- Some trains have cellular-telephone-free cars, where riders can be assured that their neighbors will not be discussing personal or business affairs for all to hear.

- Restaurants have similar exclusions. Tobacco-free zones. Cellular-phone-free zones. Some restaurants have television sets in the bar area, but the dining area is television free.

Some people create their own miniature technology-free zones. My family does it by not having a telephone near the dinner table and refusing to answer the phone if it rings while we are eating (an answering machine takes messages). The telephone number of my cellular phone is known only by members of my immediate family and my administrative assistant, and, in any event, I usually keep it turned off. I use it mainly to call others, not for others to call me. Other people have special workplaces either within their homes or in isolated locations where they do not allow telephones, television, or computers.

More and more business travelers are refusing to take their computers or cellular phones. And even when they do carry them, they restrict their usage, so that cellular phones are usually turned off, and computers are used only sparingly.

The Lessons of Infrastructure

This tour of the variety of impacts of infrastructure points out its critical nature for the development and establishment of a technology, for the impact upon society, and upon the success and failure of businesses. There are several important lessons.

First, the different infrastructures have very different properties. From the point of view of the person, the affordances are critical, for they determine the entire nature of the interactions that will take place with the devices, with the information being sought or used, and with other people.

Because an information appliance is specialized to single activities, it can exploit the powers of the positive affordances and mitigate against the problems of negative ones. The form of the appliance can be shaped to be appropriate to its desired usage pattern, if only attention is paid to the affordances and to the users' preferences. In many cases, the most effective component might be the "off" switch, allowing escape from the tyranny of continued accessibility, continued interruption. Better yet would be a "do not disturb" key, allowing the user to go about uninterrupted, but with the appliance quietly taking messages or otherwise performing actions in the background. This avoids missing items of interest, but at the pace and schedule of the user rather than the arbitrariness of the world's events.

Infrastructure is usually thought to be dull. Tedious. Few people wish to think about it until it is necessary, which is then often too late. Once established, it is expensive and often difficult to change. Moreover, infrastructures require standardization; They are too expensive and restrictive to allow multiple infrastructures to coexist, too important to society to allow the monetary interests of one company or industry to determine the underlying infrastructure for everyone. The establishment of international standards is yet another challenge, one I touch upon throughout this book, and in many cases, this challenge dominates all else.

Probably the most important lesson for the development of an information appliance industry is the importance of establishing an open, universal standard for exchanging information. If only we can establish world-wide standards for the sharing of information, then the particular infrastructure used within each appliance becomes irrelevant. Each appliance can use whatever best fits its needs. Each company can select whatever infrastructure makes most sense to its operations. Once the information exchange is standardized, nothing else matters.

The goal for appliances is simplicity and flexibility, along with universal interaction. These properties would allow appliances to interact and communicate when that is desired, to disconnect and remain unobtrusive when that is preferred. We could have an unobtrusive technology, we could have moments of silence. We might not need those technology-free zones once the technology comes under human control.

If only we can establish the proper infrastructure of international standards for universal communication. If only we can get away from today's domination and tyranny of the personal computer, and if only the manufacturers of the world are able to establish a viable economic marketplace for appliances that will allow them to emerge and survive.

If only.

7

Being Analog

We are analog beings trapped in a digital world, and the worst part is, we did it to ourselves.

We humans are biological animals. We have evolved over millions of years to function well in the environment, to survive. We are analog devices following biological modes of operation. We are compliant, flexible, tolerant. Yet we have constructed a world of machines that requires us to be rigid, fixed, intolerant. We have devised a technology that requires considerable care and attention, that demands to be treated on its own terms, not ours. We live in a technology-centered world where the technology is not appropriate for people. No wonder we have such difficulties.

Here we are, wandering about the world, bumping into things, forgetful of details, with a poor sense of time, a poor memory for facts and figures, unable to focus attention on a topic for more than a short duration, reasoning by example rather than by logic, and drawing upon our admittedly deficient memories of prior experience. When viewed this way, we seem rather pitiful. No wonder we have constructed a set of artificial devices that are very much not in our own image. We have constructed a world of machinery in which accuracy and precision matter. Time matters. Names, dates, facts, and figures matter. Accurate memory matters. Details matter.

Figure 7.1
Treating people like machines. The foreign service section of switchboard in the American Telephone and Telegraph Company, New York City, 1929. (Photograph courtesy of Corbis-Bettmann.)

All the things we are bad at matter, all the things we are good at are ignored. Bizarre.

Making Sense of the World

People excel at perception, at creativity, at the ability to go beyond the information given, making sense of otherwise chaotic events. We often have to interpret events far beyond the information available, and our ability to do this efficiently and effortlessly, usually without even being aware that we are doing so, greatly adds to our ability to function. This ability to put together a sensible, coherent image of the world in the face of limited evidence allows us to anticipate and predict events, the better to cope with an ambiguous, ever-changing world.

Here's a simple test of your memory:

How many animals of each type did Moses take on the ark?

What's the answer? How many animals? Two? Be careful: What about an amoeba, a sexless, single-celled animal that reproduces by dividing itself into two cells? Did he need to take two of these?

Answer: None. No animals at all. Moses didn't take any animals onto the ark. It was Noah.

Some of you were fooled. Why? Because people often hear what is intended, not what is said. In normal language, people ask real questions that have real answers and real meaning. It is only psychology professors and jokesters who ask trick questions. If you spotted the trick, it is because you were unnaturally suspicious or alert. We don't need such alertness in normal human interaction. Those of you who were fooled responded normally: That is how we are meant to be.

Your mind interpreted the question meaningfully, making sense of the information. It may have confused "Moses" with "Noah," but it was aided by the fact that those names have a lot of similarity: both are short, with two syllables. Both are biblical, from the Old Testament. In normal circumstances, the confusion would be beneficial, for it is the sort of error that a speaker might make, and it is useful when a listener can go beyond superficial errors.

Note that the ability to be insensitive to simple speech errors does not mean that people are readily fooled. Thus, you would not have been fooled had I asked:

How many animals of each type did Clinton take on the ark?

The name Clinton is not sufficiently close to the target: it requires a biblical name to fool you.[1] From a practical point of view, although a speaker might say "Moses" when "Noah" was intended, it is far less likely that someone would mistakenly say a nonbiblical name such as "Clinton." The automatic inaccurate interpretation of the original question is intelligent and sensible. The fact that the first question can fool people is a testament to our powers, not an indictment of them. Once again, in normal life, such corrections are beneficial. Normal life does not deliberately try to fool us. Take note of this example, for it is fundamental to understanding people and, more important, to understanding why computers are so different from people, why people and today's technology are such a bad match.

Why do accuracy and precision matter? In our natural world, they don't. We are approximate beings; we get at the meanings of things, and for this, the details don't much matter. Accurate times and dates matter only because we have created a culture in which these things are important. Accurate and precise measurements matter because the machines and procedures we have created are rigid, inflexible, and fixed in their ways, so if a measurement is off by some tiny fraction, the result can be a failure to operate. Worse yet, it can cause a tragic accident.

People are compliant: We adapt ourselves to the situation. We are flexible enough to allow our bodies and our actions to fit the circumstances. Animals don't require precise measurements and high accuracy to function. Machines do.

The same story is true of time, of facts and figures, and of accurate memory. These matter only because the mechanical, industrialized society created by people doesn't match people. In part, this is because we don't know how to do any better. Can we build machines that are as compliant and flexible as people? Not today. Biology doesn't build; it grows, it evolves. It constructs life out of flexible parts. Parts that are self-repairable. We don't know how to do this with our machines. We build information devices only out of binary logic, with its insistence upon logic and precision. We invented the artificial mathematics of logic the better to enhance our own thought processes.

The dilemma facing us is the horrible mismatch between the requirements of these human-built machines and human capabilities. Machines are mechanical, we are biological. Machines are rigid and require great precision and accuracy of control. We are compliant. We tolerate and produce huge amounts of ambiguity and uncertainty, very little precision and accuracy. The latest inventions of humankind are those of the digital technology of information processing and communication, yet we ourselves are analog devices. Analog and biological.

An analog device is one in which the representation of information corresponds to its physical structure. In an analog recording the stored signal varies in value precisely in the same way as sound energy varies in time. A phonograph recording is analog; it works by recreating the variations in sound energy by wiggles and changes of depth in the groove. In a tape recording, the strength of the magnetic field on the tape varies in analogous fashion to the sound energy variations. These are analog signals.

Digital signals are entirely different. Here, what is recorded is an abstraction of the real signals. Digital encoding was invented mainly to get rid of noise. In the beginning, electrical circuits were all analog. But electrical circuits are noisy, meaning they are susceptible to unwanted voltage variations. The noise gets in the way, mostly because the circuits are unable to distinguish between the stuff that matters and the stuff that doesn't.

Enter the digital world. Instead of using a signal that is analogous to the physical event, the event is transformed into a series of numbers that describes the original. In high-quality recording of music, the sound energy is sampled over 40,000 times each second, transformed into numbers that represent the energy value at the time each sample was made. The numbers are usually represented in the form of binary digits rather than the familiar decimal ones, which means that any digit can have only one of two states, 0 or 1, rather than the ten possible states of a decimal digit. When there are only two states to be distinguished between, the operation is far simpler and less subject to error than when it has to determine a precise value, as is required with an analog signal. Binary signals are relatively insensitive to noise.

As you can imagine, to record and playback a digital representation of sound waves requires a lot of processing. It is necessary to transform the sound into numbers, store the numerical digits, and then retrieve and restore them back to sound energy. Such rapid transformation wasn't possible at an affordable price until recently, which is why the emphasis on digital signals seems new. It is only recently that the technology was capable of high-quality digital encoding of audio and television signals, although the concept is old.

There are a number of common misconceptions about digital and analog signals. One is that *analog* means continuous, whereas *digital* means discrete. Although this is often the case, it is not the basis for the distinction. Think of *analog* as meaning *analogous:* analogous to the real world. If the real world event is discrete, so too will be the analog one. If the physical process is continuous, then so too will be the analog one. Digital, however, is always discrete: one of a limited number of values, usually one of two, but occasionally one of three, four, or ten.

A widespread misconception is that digital is somehow good, analog bad. This just isn't so. Yes, digital is good for our contemporary machines, but analog might be better for future machines. And analog is certainly far better for people. Why? Mainly because of the impact of noise.

We have evolved to match the world. If you want to understand how human perception works, it helps to start off by understanding how the world of light and sound works, because the eyes and ears have evolved to fit the nature of these physical signals. What this means is that we interact best with systems that are either part of the real world or analogous to them—analog signals.

Analog signals behave in ways human beings can understand. A slight error or noise transforms the signals in known ways, ways the body has evolved to interpret and cope with. If there is some noise in a conventional television signal, encoded in analogical form, we see some noise on the screen. Usually we can tolerate the resulting image, at least as long as we can make sense of it. Small amounts of noise have slight impact. People are analog, able to extract meanings despite noise and error. As long as the meanings are unchanged, the details of the signals do not matter. They are not noticed, they are not remembered.

In a digital signal, the representation is so arbitrary that a simple error can have unexpected consequences. Digital encodings use compression technologies that eliminate redundancy. Digital television signals are compressed to save space and bandwidth, the most common scheme being the algorithms devised by the Motion Picture Expert Group (MPEG). If any information is lost, it takes a while before the system resends enough information to allow recovery. MPEG encoding breaks up the picture into rectangular regions. Noise can make it impossible for the system to reconstruct an entire region. As a result, when the image is noisy, whole regions of the screen break up and distort in ways the human brain cannot reconstruct, and it takes a few seconds until the picture reforms itself.

The real problem with being digital is that it implies a kind of slavery to accuracy, a requirement that is most unlike the natural workings of the person. It is perfectly proper and reasonable for machines to use digital encodings for their internal workings. Machines do better with digital encoding. The problem comes about in the form of interaction between people and machines. People do best with signals and information that fit the way they perceive and think, which means analogous to the real world. Machines do best with signals and information that are suited for the way they function, which means digital, rigid, precise. So when the two have to meet, which side should dominate? In the past, it has been the machine that dominates. In the future, it should be the person. Stay tuned for chapter 9.

Humans versus Computers[2]

The ever-increasing complexity of everyday life brings with it both great opportunities and major challenges. One of the challenges, that the brain does not work at all like a computer, also provides us with an opportunity: the possibility of new modes of interaction that allow us to take advantage of the complementary talents of humans and machines.

The modern era of information technology has been with us but a short time. Computers are less than a century old. The technology has been constructed deliberately to produce mechanical systems that operate reliably, algorithmically, and consistently. They are based upon mathematics, or more precisely, arithmetic in the case of the first computing devices and logic in the case of the more modern devices.

Contrast this with the human brain. Human beings are the result of millions of years of evolution, where the guiding principle was survival of the species, not efficient, algorithmic computation. Robustness in the face of unexpected circumstances plays a major role in the evolutionary process. Human intelligence has coevolved with social interaction, cooperation, rivalry, and communication. Interestingly enough, the ability to deceive seems to have been one driving force. Only the most intelligent of animals is able to employ a sophisticated level of intentional, purposeful deception. Only the most sophisticated animal is capable of seeing through the deceit. Sure, nature also practices deception through camouflage and mimicry, but this isn't willful and intentional. Primates are the most skilled at intentional, willful deception, and the most sophisticated primate—the human—is the most sophisticated deceiver of all.

Note that some deception is essential for the smooth pursuit of social interaction: the "white lie" smoothes over many otherwise discomforting social clashes. It is not always best to tell the truth when people ask how we like their appearance, or their presentation, or the gift they have just given us. One could argue that computers won't be truly intelligent or social until they, too, are able to deceive.

We humans have learned to control the environment. We are the masters of artifacts. Physical artifacts make us stronger, faster, and more

comfortable. Cognitive artifacts make us smarter. Among cognitive artifacts are the invention of writing and other notational systems, such as
those used in mathematics, dance, and musical transcription. The result
of these inventions is that our knowledge is now cumulative; each generation grows upon the heritage left behind by previous generations.
This is the good news. The bad news is that the amount to be learned
about the history, culture, and techniques of modern life increases with
time. It now takes several decades to become a truly well educated citizen. How much time will be required in fifty years? In one hundred
years?

The biological nature of human computation, coupled with the evolutionary process by which the brain has emerged, leads to a very different style of computation from the precise, logic-driven systems that
characterize current computers. The differences are dramatic. Computers are constructed from a large number of fast, simple devices, each
following binary logic and working reliably and consistently. Errors in
the operation of any of the underlying components are not tolerated,
and they are avoided either by careful design to minimize failure rates or
through error-correcting coding in critical areas. The remarkable power
of the computer is a result of the high speed of relatively simple computing devices.

Biological computation is performed by a very large number of slow,
complex devices—neurons—each doing considerable computation and
operating through electrochemical interactions. The power of the computation is a result of the highly parallel nature of the computation and
the complex computations done by each of the billions of neural cells.
Moreover, the cells are bathed in fluids whose chemistry can change
rapidly, providing a means for rapid dispersion of hormones and other
signals to the entire system, chemicals that are site-specific. Think of it
as a packet-switching deployment of chemical agents. The result is that
the computational basis is dynamic, capable of rapid, fundamental
change. Affect, emotion, and mood all play a powerful—and as yet
poorly understood—role in human cognition. Certainly all of us have
experienced the tension when logic dictates one course of action but

mood or emotion another. More often than not, we follow mood or emotion.

Whatever the mode of computation—and the full story is not yet known—it is certainly not binary logic. Each individual biological element is neither reliable nor consistent. Errors are frequent—cells continually die—and reliability is maintained through massive redundancy as well as through the inherently error-tolerant nature of the computational process and, for that matter, the relatively high error-tolerance of the resulting behavior.

These last points cannot be overemphasized. The body, the brain, and human social interaction have all coevolved to tolerate large variations in performance under a wide-ranging set of environmental conditions. It is a remarkably error-tolerant and forgiving system. It uses both electrical and chemical systems of communication and processing. Conscious and subconscious processing probably use different computational mechanisms, and the role of emotions and affect is not yet understood.

Human language serves as a good example of the evolution of a robust, redundant, and relatively noise-insensitive means of social communication. Errors are corrected so effortlessly that often neither party is aware of the error or the correction. Communication relies heavily upon a shared knowledge base, intentions, and goals; people with different cultural backgrounds often clash, even though they speak the same language. The result is a marvelously complex structure for social interaction and communication. Children learn language without conscious effort, yet the complexities of human language still defy complete scientific understanding.

Biological versus Technological Evolution

We humans have evolved to fit the natural environment. At the same time we have learned to modify and change the environment. This process, in which we've changed to fit the world while simultaneously changing the world, leads to further evolutionary change. Until recently, this coevolution proceeded at a human pace. We developed language and tools. We discovered how to control fire and construct simple tools. The tools became more complex as simple tools became machines. The process was slow, the better to fit the new ways with the old, the new methods with human capabilities.

Biological evolution of humankind proceeds too slowly to be visible, but there is a kind of technological and environmental evolution that proceeds rapidly. We evolve our human-made artifacts to fit our abilities. This evolution is similar to, yet different from, the biological kind. For one thing, it has a history: It is Lamarckian, in that lessons learned in one generation can be propagated to future ones. Nonetheless, it is an evolutionary process, because it tends to be unguided except by rules of survival. Each new generation is but a small modification of the previous one.

A good illustration of how an evolutionary process shapes our human-invented artifacts is sports. Sports require an exquisite mix of the doable and the difficult. Make a game too easy and it loses its appeal. Make it too difficult and it is unplayable. The range from too easy to too difficult is huge, and fortunately so. One of our traits is the ability to learn, to develop skills far beyond that which the unpracticed person can do. Thus, some games, such as tic-tac-toe, which seem difficult when first encountered, are so readily mastered that they soon become boring. A successful game is one that has a wide range of complexity, playable by beginners and experts alike, although not necessarily at the same time. Successful games include soccer, rugby, tennis, basketball, baseball, football, chess, go, checkers, poker, and bridge. These are multidimensional, rich, and multifaceted. As a result, the beginner can enjoy part of their charm while the expert can exploit all the multiple dimensions.

Games work well when they do not use too much technology. The reason is simple: Games are suited to human reaction times, size, and strength. Add too much technology to the mix, and you soon move the game beyond the reach of human abilities. This is aptly illustrated in war, the deadly dueling exercises in which the armies of the world pit themselves one against the other. But here, the technologies are deliberately exploited to exceed human capability, so much so that it can take ten years of training to master a modern jet fighter plane, and even then the human pilot is rendered temporarily unconscious during violent maneuvers. These are games not fit for people.

Alas, the slow, graceful coevolution of people and environment, and of the tools, artifacts, and games that we have designed, no longer holds. Each generation benefits from the one before, and the accumulated knowledge leads to more rapid change. We benefit greatly from this cumulative buildup of knowledge, but the price we pay is that each succeeding generation has more and more to learn. The result is that the past acts both as a wonderful starting point, propelling us forward on the shoulders of giants, and as a massive anchor, compelling us to spend more and more time at school, learning the accumulated wisdom of the ages, to the point that one's motivation and energy may be depleted before the studies are over.

The Ever-Increasing Pace of Change

Once upon a time it was possible for people to learn a great deal about their culture. After all, things changed slowly, at a human pace. As they grew up, children learned about what had happened before, and from then on, they could keep up with the rate of change. The technology changed slowly. Moreover, it was mechanical, which meant it was visible. Children could explore it. Teenagers could disassemble it. Young adults could hope to improve it.

Once upon a time technological evolution proceeded at a human pace. Crafts and sports evolved over a lifetime. Even though the results could be complex, the reason behind the complexity could usually be seen, examined, and talked about. The technology could be lived with and experienced. As a result, it could be learned.

Today, this is no longer possible. The slow evolutionary pace of life is no longer up to the scale and pace of technological change. The accumulation of knowledge is enormous, increasing with every passing year. Once upon a time, a few years of schooling—or even informal learning—was sufficient. Today, formal schooling is required, and the demands upon it continually increase. The number of different topics that must be mastered, from history and language to science and technology to practical knowledge and skills, is ever-increasing. Once a grade-school education would suffice for most people. Then high school was required. Then college, postgraduate education, and even further education after that. Today, no amount of education is sufficient.

Scientists no longer are able to keep up with advances even within their own field, let alone in all of science. As a result, we are in the age of specialization, where it is all one person can do to keep up with the pace in some restricted domain of endeavor. But with nothing but specialists, how can we bridge the gaps?

The new technologies can no longer be learned on their own. Today, technology tends to be electronic, which means that its operation is invisible, for it takes place inside of semiconductor circuits through the transfer of voltages, currents and electromagnetic fields, all of which are invisible to the eye. A single computer chip may have ten million components, and chips with 100 million components are in the planning stage. Who could learn such things by disassembly, even were disassembly possible? So, too, with computer programs; a program with hundreds of thousands of lines of instructions is commonplace, and some have millions of lines.

Worse, the new technology can often be arbitrary, inconsistent, overly complex, and irrelevant. It is all up to the whim of the designer. In the past, physical structures posed their own natural constraints upon the design and the resulting complexity. But with information technologies, the result can be as simple or complex as the designer wills it to be, and far too few designers have sufficient appreciation for the requirements of the people who must use their designs.

Even when a designer is considerate of the users of the technology, there may be no natural relationship between one set of designs and another. In the physical world, the natural constraints of physical objects meant that similar tools worked in similar ways. Not so in the world of information: Very similar tools may work in completely different—perhaps even contradictory—ways.

Treating People like Machines

What an exciting time the turn of the century must have been! The period from the late 1800s through the early 1900s was one of rapid change, in many ways paralleling the changes that are taking place now. In a relatively short period of time, the world went through rapid, almost miraculous technological invention, forever changing the lives of its citizens, society, business, and government. In this period, the incandescent light was developed and electric power plants sprung up across the nation. Electric motors were developed to power factories. The telegraph spanned the American continent and the world, followed by the telephone. With the phonograph, for the first time in history voices, songs, and sounds could be preserved and replayed at will. At the same time, mechanical devices were increasing in power. The railroad was rapidly expanding its coverage. Steam-powered ships traveled the oceans. The automobile was invented, first as expensive, hand-made machines, starting with Daimler and Benz in Europe. Henry Ford developed the first assembly line for the mass-production of relatively

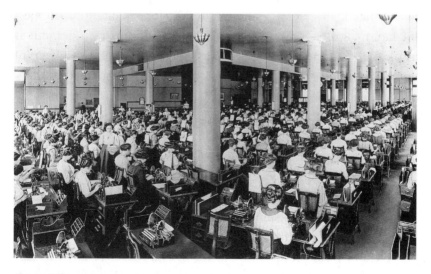

Figure 7.2
Typical pre–World War I office in a large American mail-order house, c. 1912.
(Photograph courtesy of Corbis-Bettmann.)

inexpensive automobiles. The first airplane was flown and within a few decades would carry mail, passengers, and bombs. Photography was common and motion pictures were on the way. Radio was soon to come, allowing signals to be sent all across the world without the need for wire. It was a remarkable period of change.

It is difficult today to imagine life without these products of technology. At night the only lighting was through flames: candles, fireplaces, oil and kerosene lamps, and in some places, gas. Letters were the primary means of communication, and although mail delivery within a large city was rapid and efficient, with delivery offered more than once each day, delivery across distances could take days or even weeks. Travel was difficult, and many people never ventured more than 30 miles from their homes during their entire lives. But in what to a historian is a relatively short period, the world changed dramatically in ways that affected everyone—not just the rich and upper class, but all levels of society.

Light, travel, entertainment: All changed through human inventions. Work did too, although not always in beneficial ways. The factory already existed, but the new technologies and processes brought forth new requirements, along with opportunities for exploitation. The electric motor allowed a more efficient means of running factories. But as usual, the largest impact was social and organizational: the advent of time-and-motion studies, of "scientific management," and of the assembly line. These developments analyzed human work patterns into a series of small actions. The belief was that if each action could be standardized, each organized into "the one best way,"[3] then automated factories could reap the benefits of even greater efficiency and productivity. The consequence was dehumanization of the worker. Now the worker was considered to be just another machine in the factory, analyzed like one, treated like one, and asked not to think on the job, for thinking slowed down the action.

The era of mass production and the assembly line resulted in part from the efficiencies of the "disassembly line" developed by the meatpacking factories. The tools of scientific management took into account the physical properties of the human body but overlooked the mental and psychological ones. The result was to cram ever more motions into the working day, treating the factory worker as a cog in a machine, deliberately depriving work of its meaning, all in the name of efficiency. These beliefs have stuck with us, and although today we do not go to quite the extremes advocated by the early practitioners of scientific management, the die was cast for the mindset of ever-increasing efficiency, ever-increasing productivity from the workforce. The principle of improved efficiency is hard to disagree with. The question is, at what price?[4]

The work of Frederick Taylor, some people believe, has had a larger impact upon the lives of people in this century than that of anyone else. He thought there was "the one best way" of doing things. His book, *The Principles of Scientific Management*,[5] published in 1911, guided factory development and workforce habits throughout the world, from those in the United States to Stalin's attempt to devise an efficient communist workplace in the newly formed Soviet Union. He is primarily responsible for our notions of efficiency and of the work practices followed in industry around the world, and even for the sense of guilt we sometimes feel when we have been "goofing off" instead of attending to business.

Taylor's "scientific management" was a detailed, careful study of jobs, breaking down each task into its basic components. Once you knew the components, you could devise the most efficient way of doing things, devise procedures that enhanced performance and increased the efficiency of workers. If Taylor's methods were followed properly, management could raise workers' pay while increasing company profit. In fact, Taylor's methods required management to raise the pay, for money was used as the incentive to get workers to follow the procedures. According to Taylor, everybody would win: The workers would get more money, the management more production and more profit. Sounds wonderful, doesn't it? The only problem was that workers hated it.

Taylor, you see, thought of people as simple machines. Once management found the best way to do things, it should have its workers do it that way, hour after hour, day after day. Efficiency permitted no deviation. Thought was eliminated. According to Taylor, the sort of people who could shovel dirt, do simple cutting, lathing, and drilling, those who perform the lowest-level tasks, were not capable of thought. He regarded them as "brute laborers." Furthermore, if thought was called for, there must be some lack of clarity in the procedures or the process, which signaled that the procedures were wrong. The problem with thinking, explained Taylor, was not only that most workers were incapable of it, but that it slowed the work down. That's certainly true: Why, if we never had to think, just imagine how much faster we could work. In order to eliminate the need for thought, Taylor stated that it was necessary to reduce all work to the routine:[6] That is, all work except for people like him who didn't have to keep fixed hours, who didn't have to follow procedures, who were paid hundreds of times greater wages than the so-called brutes, and who were allowed, even encouraged, to think.

Taylor thought that the world was neat and tidy. If only everyone would do things according to procedure, everything would run smoothly, producing a clean, harmonious world. Taylor may have thought he understood machines, but he certainly didn't understand people. In fact, he didn't really understand the complexity of machines or of work. And he certainly didn't understand the complexity of the world.

The World Is Not Neat and Tidy

Not only don't things always work as planned, but the notion of "plan" itself is suspect. Organizations spend a lot of time planning, but although the act of planning is useful, the plans themselves are often obsolete even before their final printing.

There are many reasons for this. Those philosophically inclined can talk about the fundamental nature of quantum uncertainty, of the fundamental statistical nature of matter. Alternatively, one can talk of complexity theory and chaos theory, where tiny perturbations can have major, unexpected results. I prefer to think of the difficulties as consequences of the complex interactions that take place among the trillions of events and objects in the world, so many interactions that even if science were advanced enough to understand each individual one there are simply too many combinations and variations possible ever to have worked out all possibilities. All of these views are compatible with one another.

Consider these examples of complex situations in which things habitually go wrong:

- A repair crew disconnects a pump from service in a nuclear power plant,[7] carefully placing tags on the controls so that the operators will know the particular unit is temporarily out of service. Later, as the operators attempt to deal with an unrelated problem, they initially diagnose it in an erroneous, albeit reasonable, way. Eventually, the problem becomes so serious that the entire plant is destroyed in the worst accident in the history of American nuclear power. Among the factors hindering the correct diagnosis of the situation is that the tags so carefully placed to indicate the out-of-service unit hang in front of another set of indicators, blocking them from view. Could this have been predicted beforehand? Maybe. But it wasn't.

- A hospital x-ray technician enters a dosage for an x-ray machine, then corrects the setting after realizing the machine is in the wrong mode.[8] The machine's computer program, however, wasn't designed to handle a rapidly made correction, so it did not properly register the new value. Instead, it delivered a massive overdose to the patient. Sometime later, the patient died as a result. The accident goes undiagnosed, because as far as anyone can determine, the machine had performed correctly. Moreover, the effect of overdosage doesn't show up immediately, so when the symptoms were reported, they were not correlated with the incident, or for that matter, with the machine. When the machine's performance first comes under suspicion, the company who manufactured it explains in detail why such an accident is impossible. The situation repeats itself in several different hospitals, killing a number of patients before a sufficient pattern emerges, so that the problem can be recognized and the design of the machine fixed. Could this have been predicted beforehand? Maybe. But it wasn't.

- The French air-traffic controllers seem to be forever complaining, frequently calling strikes and protests. American air traffic controllers aren't all that happy either. And guess what the most effective protest method is? Insisting on following procedures. On normal days, if the workers follow the procedures precisely, work slows up, and in the case of air-traffic control, airline traffic around the entire world is affected. The procedures must be violated to allow the traffic to flow smoothly. Of course, if there is an accident and the workers are found not to have followed procedures, they are blamed and punished.

- The United States Navy has a formal, rigid hierarchy of command and control, with two classes of workers—enlisted crew and officers—and a rigid layer of formal rank and assignment. There are extensive procedures for all tasks. Yet in their work habits, especially in critical operations, rank seems to be ignored and crew members frequently question the actions. Sometimes they even debate the appropriate action to be taken. The crew, moreover, is always changing. There are always new people who have not learned the ship's procedures, and even the veterans often don't have more than two or three year's experience with the ship; the Navy has a policy of rotating assignment. Sounds horrible, doesn't it? Isn't the military supposed to be the model of order and structure? But wait. Look at the outcome: The crew functions safely and expertly in dangerous, high-stress conditions. What is happening here?

These examples illustrate several points. The world is extremely complex, too complex to keep track of, let alone predict. In retrospect, looking back after an accident, the problem seems obvious. There are usually a few simple actions that, had they been taken, would have prevented the accident, precursor events that, had they been perceived and interpreted properly, would have provided sufficient warning. Sure, but this is hindsight after we know how things turned out.

Remember, life is complex. Lots of stuff is always happening, most of which is irrelevant to the task at hand. We all know that it is important to ignore the irrelevant and attend to the relevant. But how does one know which is which?

We humans are a complex mixture of motives and mechanisms. We are sense-making creatures, always trying to understand and give explanations for the things we encounter. We are social animals, seeking company, working well in small groups. Sometimes this is for emotional support, sometimes for assistance, sometimes for selfish reasons, so we have someone to feel superior to, to show off to, to tell our problems to. We are narcissistic and hedonistic, but also altruistic. We are lots of things, sometimes competing, conflicting things. And we are also animals, with complex biological drives that strongly affect behavior: emotional drives, sexual drives, hunger drives. Strong fears, strong desires, strong phobias, and strong attractions.

Making Sense of the World

If an airplane crashes on the border between the United States and Canada, killing half the passengers, in which country should the survivors be buried?

People try to make sense of the world. We assume that information is sensible, and we do the best we can with what we receive. This is a virtue. It makes us successful communicators, efficient and robust in going about our daily activities. It also means we can readily be tricked. It wasn't Moses who brought the animals aboard the ark, it was Noah. It isn't the survivors who should be buried, it is the casualties.

It's a good thing we are built this way: This compliance saves us whenever the world goes awry. By making sense of the environment, by making sense of the events we encounter, we know what to attend to, what to ignore. Human attention is the limiting factor, a well-known truism of psychology and of critical importance today. Human sensory systems are bombarded with far more information than can be processed in depth; some selection has to be made. Just how this is done has been the target of prolonged investigation by numerous cognitive scientists who have studied people's behavior when overloaded with information, by neuroscientists who have tried to follow the biological processing of sensory signals, and by a host of other investigators. I was one of them: I spent almost ten years of my research career studying the mechanisms of human attention.

One useful tool to deepen our understanding of the cognitive process of attention comes from the notion of a "conceptual model." This idea has great importance in chapter 8 when I discuss how to design technology that people can use. A conceptual model is, to put it simply, a story that makes sense of a situation.

I sit at my desk with a large number of sounds impinging upon me. It is an easy matter to classify the sounds. What is all that noise outside? A family must be riding bicycles and the parents are yelling to their children. And the neighbor's dogs are barking at them, which is why my dogs started barking. Do I really know this? No. I didn't even bother to look out the window. My mind subconsciously, automatically created the story, creating a comprehensive explanation for the noises, even as I concentrated upon the computer screen.

How do I know what really happened? I don't. I listened to the sounds and created an explanation, one that was logical, heavily dependent upon past experience with those sound patterns. It is most likely correct, but I don't really know.

Note that the explanation also told me which sounds went together. I associated the barking dogs with the family of bicyclists. Maybe the dogs were barking at something else. Maybe. How do I know they were on bicycles? I don't, but it is a common activity near my home, which means it is reasonably likely. The point is not that I might be wrong, the point is that this is normal human behavior. Moreover, it is human behavior that stands us in good stead. I am quite confident that my original interpretations were correct, confident enough that I won't bother to check. I could be wrong.

A good conceptual model of events allows us to classify them into ones that are relevant, and ones that are not, dramatically simplifying life. We attend to the relevant and only monitor the irrelevant. Mind you, this monitoring and classification are completely subconscious. The conscious mind is usually unaware of the process. Indeed, the whole point is to reserve the conscious mind for the critical events of the task being attended to by suppressing most of the other irrelevant events.

On the whole, human consciousness avoids paying attention to the routine. Conscious processing attends to the nonroutine, to discrepancies and novelties, to things that go wrong. As a result, we are sensitive to changes in the environment, remarkably insensitive to the commonplace, the routine.

Most of the time people do brilliantly. People are very good at predicting things. Experts are particularly good at this because of their rich experience. When a particular set of events occurs, they know exactly what will follow.

But what happens when the unexpected happens? Do we go blindly down the path of the most likely interpretation? In fact, this is the recommended strategy and will usually lead to a correct diagnosis. Most of the time we can then find a solution. You seldom hear about those instances. Headlines appear when things go wrong, not when they go right.

Look back at the incidents I described earlier. Consider the role played by conceptual models in the nuclear power incident, the famous Three Mile Island event that destroyed the power-generating unit and caused such a public loss in confidence in nuclear power that no American plant has been built since. The operators' conceptual model of the events led them to misdiagnose the situation, leading to a major calamity. But the misdiagnosis was a perfectly reasonable one. As a result, they concentrated on items they thought relevant to their diagnosis and missed other cues, which they thought were just part of the normal background noise. The tags that blocked the view would not normally have been important.

In the hospital x-ray situation, the real error was in the design of the software system, but even here, the programmer erred in not thinking through all of the myriad possible sequences of operation, something not easy to do. There are better ways of developing software[9] that would have made it more likely to have caught these problems before the system was released to hospitals, but even then, there are no guarantees. As for the hospital personnel who failed to understand the relationship, well, they too were doing the best they could to interpret the events and to get through their crowded, hectic days. They interpreted things according to normal events, which was wrong only because this one was abnormal.

Do we punish people for failure to follow procedures? This is what Frederick Taylor would have recommended. After all, management determines the one best way to do things, writes a detailed procedure to be followed in every situation, and expects workers to follow them. That's how we get maximum efficiency. But how is it possible to write a procedure for absolutely every possible situation, especially in a world filled with unexpected events? Answer: It's impossible.

Procedures and rule books dominate industry. The rule books take up huge amounts of shelf space. In some industries, it is impossible for any individual to know all the rules. The situation is made even worse by legislatures that can't resist adding new rules. Was there a major calamity? Pass a law prohibiting some behavior, or requiring some other behavior. Of course, the law strikes at the factor easiest to blame, whereas in most complex situations, multiple factors interact and no single one is fully responsible. Nonetheless, new rules are written, controlling sense and reasonableness in the conduct of business.

Do we need procedures? Of course. But procedures must be designed with care and attention to the social, human side of the operation. The best procedures will mandate outcomes, not methods. Methods change; it is the outcomes we care about. Remember the striking air traffic controllers who brought things to a halt following procedures? The same condition exists in most industries. If the procedures are followed exactly, work slows to an unacceptable level. In order to perform properly it is necessary to violate the procedures. Workers get fired for lack of efficiency, which means they are subtly, unofficially encouraged to violate the procedures. Unless something goes wrong, in which case they can be fired for failure to follow the procedures.

Now look at the Navy. The constant critiques and arguments are not what they seem to be. The apparent chaos is a carefully honed system, tested and evolved over generations, that maximizes safety and efficiency in the face of numerous mistakes, novel circumstances, and a wide range of skills and knowledge among the crew. Having everyone participate and question the actions serves several roles simultaneously. The very ambiguity, the continual questioning and debate keeps everyone in touch with the activity, thereby providing redundant checks on the actions. This adds to the safety, for now it is likely for errors to get detected before they have caused problems. The newer crew members have a lot to learn, and the public discussions among the other crew serve as valuable training exercises, not in some abstract fashion, but in situations where it really matters. And by not punishing people when they speak out, question, or even bring the operations to a halt, they encourage continual learning and performance enhancement. It makes for an effective, well-tuned team.

New crew members don't have the experience of older ones. This means they are not efficient, don't always know what to do, and perform slowly. They need a lot of guidance. The system automatically provides this constant supervision and coaching, allowing people to learn on the job. At the same time, because the minds of the new crew members are not yet locked into the routines, their questioning can sometimes reveal errors. Their fresh approach challenges the official mindset, asking whether the generally accepted explanation of events is correct. This is the best way to avoid errors of misdiagnosis.

The continual challenge to authority goes against conventional wisdom and is certainly a violation of the traditional hierarchical management style. But it is so important to safety that the aviation industry now has special training in crew management, where the junior officers in the cockpit are encouraged to question the actions of the captain. In turn, the captain, who used to be thought of as the person in command, with full authority and never to be questioned, is now trained to encourage crew members to question every act. The end result may look less disciplined, but it is far safer.

The Navy's way of working is sensible. Accidents are minimized. Despite the fact that the Navy is undertaking dangerous operations under periods of fast pace and high stress, there are remarkably few mishaps. If the Navy would follow formal procedures and a strict hierarchy of rank, the result would very likely be an increase in the accident rate.[10] Other industries would do well to copy this behavior. Fred Taylor would turn over in his grave (efficiently, without any wasted motion).

Human Error

Machines, including computers, don't err, in the sense that they are fully deterministic, always returning the same value for the same inputs and operations. Someday we may have stochastic or quantum computation, but even then we will expect them to follow precise laws of operation. When computers do err, it is either because a part has failed or because of human error, either in design specification, programming, or faulty construction. People are not fully deterministic; ask a person to repeat an operation, and the repetition is subject to numerous variations.

People do err, but primarily because they are asked to perform unnatural acts: to do detailed arithmetic calculations, to remember details of some lengthy sequence or statement, or to perform precise repetitions of actions, all the result of the artificial nature of invented artifacts. They err when attempting to alter habitual behavior, forgetting to mail a letter on the way to work or stop at the store on the way home. Slips of the tongue are common, although often the intended meaning is still conveyed sufficiently well that the errors are not even noticed by either speaker or listener. People leave jackets on airplanes and babies on buses. They lock themselves out of home and car. People are expert at making errors.

Human error matters primarily because we followed a technology-centered approach in which it matters. A human-centered approach would make the technology robust, compliant, and flexible. The technology should conform to the people, not people to the technology.

Human languages provide an excellent example of how systems can be tailored for human capabilities, providing a rich structure for communication and social interaction while being extremely tolerant of error. Language is so natural to learn that it is done without any formal instruction: only severe brain impairment can eliminate the capability of learning language. Note that "natural" does not mean "easy"; it takes ten to fifteen years to master one's native language. Second language learning can be excruciatingly difficult.

Natural language, unlike programming language, is flexible, ambiguous, and heavily dependent on shared understanding, a shared knowledge base, and shared cultural experiences. Errors in speech are seldom important: Utterances can be interrupted, restarted, even contradicted, with little difficulty in understanding. The system makes natural language communication extremely robust.

Today, when faced with human error, the traditional response is to blame the human and institute a new training procedure: blame and train. But when the vast majority of industrial accidents is attributed to human error, it indicates that something is wrong with the system, not the people. Consider how we would approach a system failure caused by a noisy environment: We wouldn't blame the noise, we would instead design a system that was robust in the face of noise.

This is exactly the approach that should be taken in response to human error: redesign the system to fit the people who must use it. This means avoiding the incompatibilities between human and machine that generate error, making it so that errors can be rapidly detected and corrected, and being tolerant of error. To blame and train does not solve the problem.

Humans and Computers as Complementary Systems

Because humans and computers are such different kinds of systems, it should be possible to develop a strategy for complementary interaction. Alas, today's approaches are wrong. One major theme is to make computers more like humans. This is the original dream behind classic artificial intelligence: to simulate human intelligence. Another theme is to make people more like computers. This is how technology is designed today; the designers determine the needs of the technology and then ask people to conform to those needs. The result is an ever-increasing difficulty in learning the technology, and an ever-increasing error rate. It is no wonder that society exhibits an ever-increasing frustration with technology.

Consider the following attributes of humans and machines presented from today's machine-centered point of view:[11]

The Machine-Centered View

People	Machines
Vague	Precise
Disorganized	Orderly
Distractible	Undistractible
Emotional	Unemotional
Illogical	Logical

Note how the humans lose: All the attributes associated to people are negative, all the ones associated with machines are positive. But now consider attributes of humans and machines presented from a human-centered point of view:

The Human-Centered View

People	Machines
Creative	Unoriginal
Compliant	Rigid
Attentive to change	Insensitive to change
Resourceful	Unimaginative

Now note how machines lose: all the attributes associated with people are positive, all the ones associated with machines are negative.

The basic point is that the two different viewpoints are complementary. People excel at qualitative considerations, machines at quantitative ones. As a result, for people, decisions are flexible because they follow qualitative as well as quantitative assessment, modified by special circumstances and context. For the machine, decisions are consistent, based upon quantitative evaluation of numerically specified, context-free variables. Which is to be preferred? Neither: We need both.

It's good that computers don't work like the brain. The reason I like my electronic calculator is that it is accurate; it doesn't make errors. If it were like my brain, it wouldn't always get the right answer. This very difference is what makes the device so valuable. I think about the problems and the method of attack. It does the dull, dreary details of arithmetic—or in more advanced machines, of algebraic manipulation and integration. Together, we are a more powerful team than either of us alone.

The same principle applies to all our machines; we should capitalize on the difference, for together we complement one another. This is useful, however, only if the machine adapts itself to human requirements. Alas, most of today's machines, especially the computer, force people to use them on their terms, terms that are antithetical to the way people work and think. The result is frustration, an increase in the rate of error (usually blamed on the user—human error—instead of on faulty design), and a general turning away from technology.

Will the interactions between people and machines be done correctly in the future? Might schools of computer science start teaching the human-centered approach that is necessary to reverse the trend? I don't see why not.

OPERATING INSTRUCTIONS FOR AERIOLA SR.

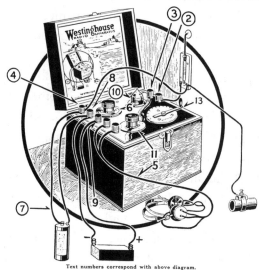

Text numbers correspond with above diagram.

No. 7. Connect to positive (center) terminal of the single 1.5 volt dry cell.

No. 8. Connect to negative (outside) terminal of the single 1.5 volt dry cell and negative terminal (—) of 22.5 volt plate battery.

No. 9. Connect to positive terminal marked (+) of 22.5 volt plate battery.

No. 10. Insert Aeriotron Vacuum tube in receptacle provided. Note that the four holes in base which receive prongs of tube are not all alike, one being larger than the rest, thus permitting insertion of tube in but one way. Be sure prongs register with holes and then press in firmly.

Numbers Corresponding to Diagram

No. 1. First, refer to accompanying sketch, then erect antenna and place protective device in position as described on page 56.

No. 2. Connect a wire leading from terminal marked R on protective device to binding post indicated by arrow for stations below 350 meters.

No. 3. For stations between 350 and 500 meters, connect the above wire to this post.

No. 4. Connect this post with terminal G of protective device.

No. 5. Connect telephone receivers to these two posts.

No. 6. Turn rheostat as far as it will go toward tail of arrow.

No. 11. Place "Tickler" pointer at zero point of scale.

No. 12. Turn rheostat (6) toward point of arrow until vacuum tube shows dull red. Do not try to burn too brightly as this materially reduces the life of the filament.

No. 13. Rotate tuning handle slowly over the scale, meanwhile listening until sound is heard in the telephone receivers. Adjust to best position, then increase "Tickler" (11) until maximum strength of signal is obtained. If tickler is turned too far toward maximum position, signals will lose their natural tone and reception of telephone signals may become difficult.

Note: This terminal is also connected to terminal G of the protective device.

Complete Aeriola Sr. Broadcasting Receiver, Model RF, 190-500 Meters, with One Aeriotron WD-11-D Vacuum Tube, One Filament Dry Cell, One Plate Dry Battery, Head Telephone Receivers, Antenna Equipment and Full Instructions **$75.90**

Aeriola Sr. Broadcasting Receiver, Model RF, As Above, Less Batteries and Antenna Equipment **$65.00**

Dimensions: 7 in. x 8½ in. x 7¼ in.

Weights: Net, 6 lbs.; Shipping, 12 lbs.; with Antenna Equipment and Batteries, 25 lbs.

NOTE: For Prices of other Complete Receiver Combinations, see page 35.

8
Why Is Everything So Difficult to Use?

"Everything that can be invented has been invented."
— Charles H. Duell, Commissioner, U.S. Office of Patents, 1899

We are fond of believing that today's world of technology is special, that the rapid pace of change, the fights among companies in the battle for supremacy, and, especially, the story of the personal computer and tele-communications revolution mark this as a special time in history. Well, sort of. If this is a special time in history, it is because every time is special. Every era is unique, having its own particular quirks and foibles. Today's technological revolution is sparked by the convergence of sev-eral industries, especially information technology, communications, and entertainment, but even here, what is happening today follows a century-old historical pattern.

In many ways, the changes during the latter part of the nineteenth century and the start of the twentieth were far more dramatic and far-reaching than what we are currently witnessing at the start of the twenty-first century. In the early 1900s, there were radical changes in lifestyles. Rapid travel was not possible before; now it was starting to be commonplace, first by means of the train and the ocean liner, then with the automobile and airplane. Talking to someone at a distance had not been possible; now, with the invention and deployment of the tele-phone, it was. Instant records of events, both the sights (via photogra-phy) and the sounds (via the phonograph) never were possible, now they were.

Figure 8.1
The first radios were not easy to use. From *Radio Enters the Home.* (New York: Radio Corporation of America, 1922.)

Today, the "revolution" in which we live consists mainly of improvements in what has already existed. These, of course, are important; they are changing the fabric of everyday life and the structure of society and government. But compared to the dramatic changes at the start of the twentieth century, they seem more incremental than revolutionary. Today we are amused by the statement made in 1899 by the Commissioner of the U.S. Office of Patents that "everything that can be invented has been invented," but given the remarkable list of accomplishments and discoveries in that era, we should also feel sympathetic.

If the late 1800s and early 1900s was an era of dramatic revolution in technology, it was also the era of increased complexity of life and of a regimented work style.[1] Henry Ford's assembly line philosophy ("Fordism") and Frederick Taylor's principles of scientific management ("Taylorism") specified work practices throughout the world.[2] They led to the dehumanization of work, although this trend had started prior to Ford and Taylor in the textile factories of both England and New England. Feeding, clothing, and entertaining the people of the world is a huge enterprise, one in which the foot soldiers (factory and field workers) are often sacrificed. For the steadily increasing middle class and the upper class, it was a great time to be alive.

Today, we are fond of making similar claims. We live in interesting times. Information technology has reached its prime, or, at least, so we think. We sit in front of personal computers and communicate with the world. In a few seconds I can do research on the history of technology by examining locations around the world: Europe, the United States, Canada, Australia. Indeed, I am not always sure where the information resides that I am examining, and often I don't care. National boundaries do not matter. Today, two technologies provide a powerful infrastructure: communications and computation. Put them together and it changes the face of personal interaction, business, education, and government. The financial and business sectors are breaking away from governmental boundaries and controls. The world is changing in ways difficult to forecast.

The Double-Edged Sword of Technology

The double-edged sword is a technology, and technology is like a double-edged sword. It can enhance and diminish our lives. I have long been a fan of technology—even when I was a professor and long before I worked for the computer industry. In *Things That Make Us Smart* I made the case for technology, arguing that properly built, properly deployed, technology makes people smarter than we would otherwise be. The problem lies in that word "properly." Modern-day technology enslaves us as much as it empowers us.

The modern-day culprit is the computer, but I can make the point even better by looking at the telephone. When the telephone was first invented, in the late 1800s, everyone knew it was important, but nobody knew why. "Every city in the United States will have to have one," the pundits said. The thought was that people would gather round the phone in the town square and listen to news and concerts. Little did they realize that it would change the fabric of business and home. In the early days, great concern was given to privacy, to the question of who would be allowed to use the telephone. One telephone company took the phone away from a hotel: why, it was allowing mere guests to use it. What would happen, the telephone company asked, if anyone could simply call up anyone else? Horrors.

Those early concerns were soon brushed away; today they seem quaint. But perhaps they were also correct. The telephone today is abrasive and intrusive. A caller has no way of knowing whether the person being called is busy or idle, in a good mood or foul. The person getting the phone call has no way of knowing if the message is important or a bother, whether it will be a short conversation or a long one.

The telephone answering machine has improved life to some extent. It allows us to decide whether we wish to answer. The answering machine itself is a double-edged technology, one with an interesting history. When it first appeared, it was mainly used by business, in particular small businesses without anyone who could answer the phone and take messages when the intended recipient was not there. When the first answering machines appeared in homes, most callers considered them to be rude; people were annoyed to get an automated response on a machine when what they wanted was a person.

Today, at least in many countries of the world, the answering machine is taken for granted. In some places, it is considered rude not to have such a machine, for then it isn't possible to leave messages when the person is either away from the phone or otherwise not answering. Not only that, but there are times when we simply wish to convey a short message without a lengthy conversation. In this case, we sometimes prefer just to get the answering machine. How many times have you called someone and been annoyed to get a person rather than the machine, especially when the person who answered the phone was not the one for whom the message was intended? "Let me call back and just leave a message on the machine," you request of the person.

The transition of the answering machine from that of a rude, inconsiderate technology to the class of an essential, convenient one, is similar to the path followed by other devices. Most technologies go through a cycle of initial rejection, followed by experimentation and transformation as their true value is discovered. The original answering machines played aloud the caller's voice as their message was being recorded. I don't know if this was purposeful or not, but surely the original designers of these machines—who had business users in mind—could not have anticipated that this feature would be used in homes to screen calls, to decide if the caller was somebody anyone at the receiving end wished to speak with at that moment.

But there is more to come. Wireless telephones and pagers are increasingly popular, not just among business people but also in the home, especially with teenagers. Today, some information technologies are so important that they get fastened to the body: the watch, eyeglasses, and hearing aids. Soon, the telephone will join the watch, always with us, always available. But what then of privacy, of peace and quiet? Of time to ourselves? The tremendous convenience of continual access carries with it an invasion of privacy and personal space.

Will the telephone really join the watch? I think it will supersede the watch and join the pacemaker. The watch has become jewelry, worn on the wrist as much for fashion's sake as for telling the time. But a phone? Why not permanently implant it in the head? After all, wiggle the skin just below the ear, at the jawbone. Feel that extra slack? Just enough to make a tiny cut, implant a tiny telephone, put the microphone and earpiece on the bone near the ear, and there you have it: a telephone always available, no matter where you are, no matter what you are doing. Every so often it will be wonderful. Every so often it will be a nightmare come true.

Complexity and Difficulty

There are two faces to the complexity of a device, one internal to the machinery, the other external to the world and to the user. The complexity that concerns me is the second kind: the external complexity that determines how easy or difficult the device is to use. To distinguish between these two meanings of complexity, let me use *complexity* to refer to the internal mechanisms of the device and *difficulty* to refer to the factors that affect ease of use.

Along with advances in technology come the dreaded curses of technology: difficulty in operation and diminished control over our lives. Technology can be confusing, maddening, infuriating. Technology is its own master. It has its own requirements and own rules of operation. The complexity, difficulty, and demands of technology have long been a source of complaint. That people must conform to technology seems to be the basic premise, and the notion that it is technology that should conform is a modern invention. In many ways, the conformance of technology wasn't even possible until recently, for up until recent times, it was remarkable enough that the complex mechanical and electrical devices would work at all, let alone be designed to be accessible and usable by the average person. This is the reason for the paradox that today's technology is largely built from a machine-centered point of view even though it is designed and built by humans.

Early technology was not only difficult, it was dangerous. Missing fingers, even limbs, are still common among farmers, construction workers, and miners. At the start of the industrial revolution,[3] hunger and poverty were prevalent. Disease was everywhere, and plagues could kill entire communities. The working conditions within many industries were hazardous, and there was slight regard for safety—that was the responsibility of the worker. Clothes could be caught in machinery, resulting in death or serious injury. It is only in recent times that we have started to care for the welfare of the workers and put the blame on the design or the work procedures rather than on the worker.

It is still common to hear managers say that if someone gets injured on the job, that individual must have been doing something wrong. This is the "blame and train" philosophy. This philosophy makes the managers' lives easier, and it is one with which even the injured workers will often agree.

"That was stupid of me," they say, shaking their heads. "How did I stick my finger into that fan blade?" the worker says. "I knew it was there, I knew it was dangerous."

True, but why was the fan blade designed so that a finger could be stuck into it? Why was it located where the finger could reach? Just because people are willing to blame themselves for their injuries does not mean they are correct to do so.

The new technologies are designed to be used by people, ordinary people, people who grow fatigued, whose attention wanders, whose mind is preoccupied. It does no good to legislate against such properties of human nature. It does no good to complain that if only workers would keep their minds focused on the task, they would not be getting injured. Everyone's mind wanders, everyone daydreams, gets fatigued, workers and management alike. Proper design takes this into account.

A great deal of effort is aimed at preventing analogous problems in machines. Engineers and designers take account of metal fatigue and random electrical noise. They need to do the same for human functioning. It's not easy. The "blame and train" philosophy seems deeply ingrained within our consciousness, in part a relic of the Fordism and

Taylorism of the early 1900s. This is a philosophy that avoids the true source of the problem: badly designed technology, badly designed procedures.

The dilemma has been with us a long time, and I suspect it will be with us yet for a long time. This is yet another legacy of the era of scientific management, where the human is treated as a machine and then found to be deficient. Someday the values might change, letting it be acknowledged that we are complementaty to machines. When we evaluate human skills and abilities according to human values, it is people who are found to be superior, machines deficient.

The Origins of Technological Difficulty

Others have speculated on why today's technology seems so much more difficult and complex than that of earlier years. One author thought it was due to covering up the working parts. He suggested that:

If the discovery of electricity changed the face of the earth, it also altered the look of every tool, appliance, or piece of machinery that it touched. You cannot see the workings of any electrical device. All that mysterious stuff is placed within a housing of some sort—out of reach, out of sight, and beyond control. This 1905 chopper shows the way things used to be. The works, blades, gears are all there for all the world to behold. People had to know how things worked, so when things stopped working, they could be fixed.[4]

There is much to be said for this idea, but it isn't entirely true. Many mechanical devices were difficult to use even though (or perhaps because) all of the moving parts were visible. Electricity is not the culprit. Difficulty seems to go hand-in-hand with technology, from early mechanical devices through today's information-based ones.

How long has technology been so difficult? Perhaps forever. The joint evils of poor manuals and overcomplexity resulting from "creeping featurism" attacked the common farm tool, the plough, almost 500 years ago.[5] Where is the difficulty in something as simple as a plough? The problem was that those sixteenth-century technologists kept adding features and adjustments. There was a coulter to cut roots in front of the share and a mouldboard to deflect the sod as it was cut. Sometimes there was a wheel, depending upon the type of soil. The curvature of the mouldboard was adjustable (and it was also twisted). The blade could be wood or iron covered. The plough then had to be adjusted for the kind of soil, the amount of water (muddy versus dry soil), the condition of the soil, the amount of existing vegetation, and the kind of plant being prepared for.

The real boom in difficulty came with the industrial revolution as continual improvements in farming, mining, manufacturing, and transportation were introduced. The late 1800s and early 1900s saw the emergence of the electrical industry, starting with communications (the telegraph, stock ticker, and telephone), along with devices for light, heat, and power (light bulbs, heating devices, and electric motors). These moved into the home and office. Today the phonograph, the telephone, and typewriter are considered simple; not so when they were first introduced.

For example, the earliest phonographs were completely mechanical, driven by a hand crank and by the acoustic energy of the source. The spring-driven and the electric motor came later, but they didn't necessarily make the device simpler. The phonograph took weeks to master and, in the end, led to the failure of the first generation of products. Early users were asked to persevere:

"If the first trial . . . is not pleasing, try it again and persevere at it. . . . stick to it. Give the Phonograph a thorough trial of two weeks."[6]

"Why should we spend time and money to learn telegraphy, shorthand and typewriting and then have an idea that no time is required to learn the Phonograph; the most delicate of all and one of the most useful.

"The use of the Phonograph must be learned, the same as anything else. . . . [One needs] a few days to learn everything about it and only a few weeks practice to acquire all the dexterity in its use."[7]

To be fair, the difficulty was to enable the phonograph both to record and play back sound, but even playing back was a trial. The point is that difficulty in the use of our technology has been with us for a long time. Many of those early technologies were difficult and, worse, dangerous.

The steam engine kept exploding, with numerous deaths and government investigations before it was tamed. The automobile was viewed with alarm. Drivers had either to be expert mechanics or be accompanied by one. Vehicles were difficult to control, and governments passed restrictive legislation. The telephone was a special technology that took time to master and, for that matter, to figure out what it was good for.

Robert Pool argues that difficulty follows almost inevitably from the need to improve.[8] The earliest steam engines, those of Thomas Newcomen, were extremely simple, but inefficient. James Watt improved the efficiency considerably, but at the cost of added complexity. Watt's version required extra valves, parts, and critical timing. The piston had to fit more snugly into the cylinder, so the manufacturing process had to be held to much closer tolerances. The engine ran at a higher temperature—increasing the temperature of the piston was one of the means of increasing efficiency—so new lubricants and seals had to be developed that could withstand these changes. The more efficient machines produced greater power, not just in the downward direction, which is all Newcomen's machine could do, but in both the downward and upward cycles. This increased the stress upon the parts. Further efficiency required raising the pressure of the steam, which increased the danger of explosion, leading to even more complexity in the attempt to add safeguards.

Most technology goes through cycles of development and change in both internal and external complexity. Often the very first device is simple, but crude. As the device undergoes the early stages of development, its power and efficiency improve, but so does its complexity. As the technology matures, however, simpler, more effective ways of doing things are developed, and the device becomes easier to use, although usually by becoming more complex inside.

Early radios used a simple "cat's whiskers" and earphones: a metal contact (the "cat's whisker") upon a germanium crystal. With the introduction of vacuum tubes, the sets became much more powerful but required multiple controls to modulate the amplification level and tuning of each stage. Some required adjustment of filter bandwidth, depending on what kind of signal was being received and how much background noise could be tolerated by the listener. As the illustration at the opening to this chapter shows, the instructions for operation of these early radios could be rather intimidating. The user of early radios was expected to know "the five fundamentals of radio reception":[9] intercepting, tuning, detecting, amplifying, and reproducing. Today's radios are trivial to use, sometimes having only an on-off switch, a volume control, and a set of buttons to choose the station. The external simplicity comes with a greatly increased internal complexity within the electronic circuits themselves, a complexity that would astound the electrical engineers who worked on the early vacuum-tube sets. (See figure 2.1, page 22.)

A similar cycle is followed by most technology. The modern automobile is simpler for the driver than ever before, but the auto itself has greatly increased in complexity. It has thousands of parts from several technologies—mechanical, hydraulic, and electronic—so many that probably no single individual understands them all. The modern airplane is simpler and safer for the pilots and passengers than those of only a few decades ago, but it contains millions of parts that take hundreds of designers to construct. Even small devices have been modified in the years since their initial development for increased efficiency, improved performance, increased safety, smaller size, less power consumption, and less environmental impact. The result is enhanced performance and ease of use, but increased internal complexity.

I once argued that modern technology is difficult to use because its operations are invisible.[10] Information is abstract, conveyed by electrons and voltage levels. The workings of modern devices are hidden inside the sealed parts. We are left to the mercy of whatever conceptual model the designer decides to impose upon us, and the result is often confusion and misunderstanding. In the old days, I argued, the user had a hope of figuring out how a thing worked by manipulating it and watching what moved. Well, I was wrong. The difficulties with the plough, with the mechanical phonograph, and with other older technologies show that this explanation is too simplistic. Some of those early mechanical devices were extremely difficult, with such a variety of mechanisms that they were incomprehensible. The first digital computer was entirely mechanical, as were early analog computers, and they were dauntingly complex and difficult.

It is the designer's responsibility to overcome the difficulties, to provide coherence and understanding for the user. If the designer makes the operations vague, ambiguous, and hidden from sight, provides controls with no obvious meaning, and provides little or no feedback, then the result is guaranteed to be confusing. When the user lacks a clear conceptual understanding of the device, the result is difficulty of use.

The same principles apply whether the device is mechanical or electronic. The only difference is that many mechanical devices offer the possibility of being self-explaining, of having the purpose and function visible, of offering continual and immediate feedback for each action. Electronic information devices, on the other hand, by their very nature control invisible, symbolic events, and so the possibility of a clear conceptual understanding is entirely up to the competence of the designer. When it comes to the ability of engineers to design things so that the average user can understand them, the level of competency is low indeed. This is not meant to be an indictment of engineers. After all, they are trained in engineering, not in human-centered design. To change things requires a design philosophy that focuses upon ease of use, upon providing an appropriate conceptual model, making it visible, and making all actions and displays consistent with that model.

What Makes Things Easy to Use?

When is something easy to use? My studies convince me that even the most difficult of things becomes easy when users feel they are in control, that they know what to do, when to do it, and what to expect from the device whenever they perform an operation: in other words, when they have acquired understanding. What makes something understandable? Technical knowledge is not required, just functional. What is critical is to have a good conceptual understanding of the device. Few of us understand the technologies of the automobile, radio, or television, yet we feel comfortable with these devices because each control has a known function, we can tell when the device is working properly, and we know what to do when there are problems. We feel uncomfortable when we are out of control, when we do not know how to respond, or when our actions do not lead to the results we expect.

A feeling of control, a good conceptual model, and knowledge of what is happening are all critical to ease of use. The controls must be recognizable, it must be easy to remember their function and operation, and they must provide immediate and continual feedback about the state of the system.

When is something difficult? When the controls and actions seem arbitrary, when the system can get itself into peculiar states, peculiar in the sense that the person using it does not know what it is doing, how it got there, or how to recover. When there is a lack of understanding.

Understanding comes about when the system presents a clear conceptual model of itself, making the possible actions apparent. I called this state "knowledge in the world"[11]—when the world itself helps tell you what to do, so no instructions, no courses, no manuals are necessary. A solid wall tells you that you can't walk in that direction. A door signals passage. A properly constructed door even specifies whether it is to be pushed or pulled, slid or lifted, by the construction of its handles, no labels or words required. If you have to add a sign that says *push* or *pull,* then this indicates that the door is not as simple as is possible; its design is faulty.

Did you ever look at an unfamiliar tool or appliance and try to figure out what it was for and how it might work? Usually the tool makes no sense. Once you are told what it is used for, however, the previously puzzling construction of weird parts suddenly all fit together wonderfully. At first, the device presents itself as a bunch of apparently unrelated affordances. This part can stick into something, this part permits turning, this part cuts. But any object has a large number of affordances, and an assemblage of parts has a huge number of alternative combinations. What is lacking is a cohesive story to fit them together for some

Figure 8.2
Without a conceptual model, without knowing what a device is to be used for, it can appear mysterious and confusing. Know that this is an apple peeler, know that an apple is placed on the prongs and, as the handle is turned, the apple rotates under the blade, and now the structure is clear. Produce a good conceptual model, and no manual is necessary. (Photograph courtesy of Corbis-Bettmann.)

purpose—a conceptual model. In the case of the kitchen appliance, the name alone is often sufficient to provide coherence.

"That's an apple peeler? Oh, I see. So the apple must fit here, and these prongs go into the core, holding the apple and this crank turns it. This cutting edge must be the peeler, and this crank turns the apple in front of the blade. And this is the blade that moves along the outside, cutting off the skin. Oh yes, now I see. It's obvious."

Even if you know what a tool is for, unless you understand how it works, its use is limited. It's possible to use things without understanding by just following instructions. This works until either something goes wrong or there is a need to do something unusual, something not covered by the instructions. In either case, the result can be frustrating; there is no hint of what to do next. Once there is understanding, it's possible to explain the problems and predict what to do. It's possible to invent new applications and to make corrections when things go wrong. With understanding comes a feeling of control.

Given a chance, people are wonderfully good at making sense of the world. People see faces and objects in clouds. They see patterns in tea leaves. They give explanations of people's behavior, even people they don't know. We human beings are sense-makers, making sense of the way we experience the world, but only if there is something to go on, some hints and clues as to what is happening, and why.

When I encounter a new situation, how do I know what to do? I look, listen, and copy. I try to understand what is happening. I see if I can find anything that looks familiar, and if I do, then I'll perform the actions that work in the familiar situation. Is it a new restaurant? I have to decide whether I seat myself or whether I wait for someone to seat me. If the latter, I have to decide who it is that helps me, where I should stand while waiting. To answer these questions, I look around and try to find clues. If I'm supposed to wait, is there a place that looks like a waiting area? Is there a table or stand that looks like it belongs to the head waiter, or a host who will guide me to my seat or tell me how long I must wait? I look for any clues I can find.

When I encounter a new piece of technology I do the same thing. I look at it and try to see if anything looks familiar. I look to see if there are any clear indications of what to do. And when I do something that causes a reaction, I try to understand why whatever I did led to that result.

In other words, in new situations we look for familiar patterns, we look for any signs that might direct us, and we try to make sense of whatever happens. In general, people make up explanations, stories of events that help us make our way through novel and complex situations until they become understandable and comfortable.

The Conceptual Model

The use of a good conceptual model is so fundamental to good design that I would like to discuss it here in greater detail than presented in chapter 7. What does it mean to understand how something works? Do I really have to understand automobile mechanics to drive my car, or to understand solid state physics and computer programming to use my computer? Of course not. But what I do need is a good conceptual grasp of what is going on, an understanding of the different controls and alternative actions I can take and what their impact is on the device. I need a story that puts together the behavior and appearance of a device in a sensible, comprehensible pattern. Good designers present explicit conceptual models for users. If they don't, users create their own mental models, which are apt to be defective and lead them astray.

The word processor on which I am typing this chapter makes visible an excellent conceptual model for its operation. There is a ruler on the top of the page with several sliding pointers. What is particularly nice about the design is that I can experiment by moving each slider in turn and seeing what happens. As a result, I have formed a good conceptual

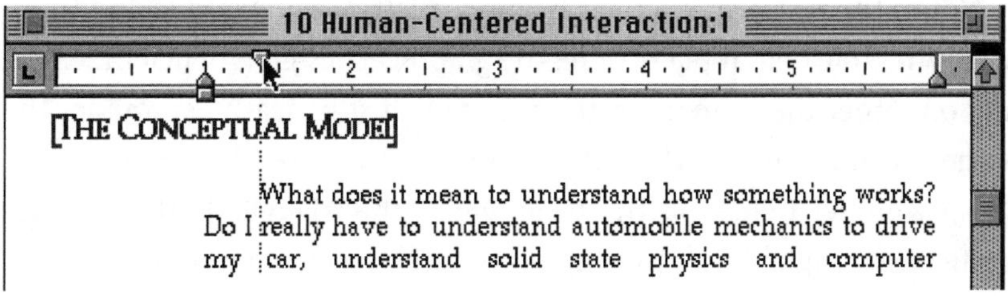

Figure 8.3
Microsoft Word's excellent conceptual model for adjusting margins. The ruler, along with the triangular and rectangular sliders are clear indicators of margin adjustments. The ruler starts and ends at the edge of the printed region of the document. Moving the mouse pointer to the downward-facing triangle and depressing the mouse button produces a vertical dotted line, helping define this triangle as the indentation for the first line of a paragraph and also aiding the user in adjusting it to the desired value. The difference between the rectangular slider and the upward-pointing triangle is not so well indicated.

model of the role the sliders play in the composition of the page. As soon as I move a slider, a dotted vertical line drops down over the text, confirming the conceptual model that the slider adjusts the location of the margins on the page, as well as letting me see just where the slider is positioned relative to the existing text. The leftmost slider sets the left margin. The next slider over, the upper slider, sets the left indentation for the first line of each paragraph (as shown in the illustration). The rightmost slider sets the right margin.

That's a useful conceptual model. I don't know how the word processor really works, deep inside its intricate programming structures. I don't know anything about all the gory programming details that couple the pointer movements to the part of the page where the action takes place. Part of my conceptual model is that the action only takes place on the line or paragraph where the cursor is located, unless I have highlighted a section of text, in which case it applies to everything that is highlighted. With this understanding I feel empowered to adjust the formatting of the page. I am in control. Notice how skillfully the graphical design conveys the model: The most clever component is the vertical dotted line that appears only when the slider is activated. It is really the vertical line that conveys the conceptual model.

Notice the rectangle that sits below the leftmost upward-facing triangle. What role does it play? Here, the graphical design is deficient. Clicking on either the triangle or the rectangle just beneath it provides the same visual result: a vertical dotted line. Moreover, if I try moving the item, whether I click on the rectangle or the triangle, both move together as a single unit. This implies that the rectangle has no function. Could it be just a design element to distinguish that first triangle from the others? A more careful examination shows that the outcome of moving the rectangle differs from that of moving the triangle. When the triangle is moved, it affects the paragraph left margin, but leaves the indentation for the first line unchanged. This lets me adjust the following lines to be left of, equal to, or right of the first line. When I move the rectangle, both the margins for the first line and the rest of the paragraph move simultaneously, as if they were locked together. This lets me widen or narrow the paragraph, leaving the amount of indentation of the first line unchanged. Too bad the graphical design doesn't support this conceptual model.

The proper graphical design would show an explicit linkage between the rectangle and both sliders. One way of doing this would be to make the rectangle extend in length between the two controls: If I move a control, only that part of the margin is affected, and the rectangle would grow or shrink accordingly. If I moved the rectangle, it would move in position without changing its length, thereby reinforcing the conceptual model of the operation. As it is, the relationship is more difficult to discover and remember than necessary.

This point may seem like a minuscule detail, and in some respects it is. But usability often lies in the details. How many users of this word processor never discover the operation of the rectangle? Worse, how many are confused because of what they believe to be capricious results? Sometimes when they attempt to move the left margin, they change both the first line and the others, sometimes only the others. Will they be astute enough to recognize that the exact region of the slider they touched was what mattered, the triangle or the rectangle beneath it? Details matter, especially when they impact the user's conceptual model and, thereby, the user's understanding.

The basic principle is this: Start with a simple, cohesive conceptual model and use it to direct all aspects of the design. The details of implementation then flow naturally from the conceptual model.

To summarize, a conceptual model is a story. It doesn't have to discuss the actual mechanisms of the operation. But it does have to pull the actions together into a coherent whole that allows the user to feel in control, to feel there is a reason for the way things are structured, to feel that, when necessary, it's possible to invent special variations to get out of trouble and, in general, feel mastery over the device.

The job of creating a good conceptual model is in the hands of the designer. The model has to be coherent, understandable, and sufficiently cohesive that it covers the major operations of the system. It is successful if the users can tell a story, can explain to others how it all works. It is successful if the users can then use the system in ways the developers never imagined. Above all, the user should be able to discover and learn how to use it with a minimum of effort. In the ideal case, no manual would be required. It is unsuccessful if users simply follow instructions with no understanding; they will be unable to go beyond the instructions, unable to perform novel activities, unable to get out of trouble.

Telling a coherent, consistent story that is readily understood by the wide range of users is not an easy task. It is a task best left to experts. Task-centered development, human-centered development, conceptual model-guided development: These are the secrets of success. There are more, but these are essential starting points.

Why Metaphors Should Be Avoided

A myth has grown up in the land that good interface design requires the development of a metaphor: "What metaphor shall we use to design this device?" I am often asked. "If only we would have the correct metaphor, then people would find it easy to use, right?" Wrong.

A metaphor is always wrong, by definition. After all, what do we mean when we design by means of a metaphor? We mean that we try to pick something else to guide the design, something that already exists and that we believe the users of our devices will be familiar with. The word processor is like a typewriter. The display on the page is like a piece of paper. The background of my computer screen is like a desktop, and the files and icons that are displayed upon it are like file folders, piles of paper, and physical objects on my real desk.

No, they are not. The objects on my computer screen aren't at all like the real objects with which they share a name. Metaphors are an attempt to use one thing to represent another, when the other is not the same. But if it is not the same, how can the metaphor help?

True, where the properties of the metaphor and the new thing are closely related, the metaphor helps in acquiring those properties. But when they differ, the metaphor can get in the way of learning; it either provides the wrong model or it slows up acquisition of the correct one.

Basically, those who espouse the use of metaphors are giving human-centered development a bad name, almost as bad as those who believe in "user-friendly" systems. User-friendly systems invariably aren't. They are cloying, annoying, in-your-face systems that force the user through a sequence of steps, whether or not these are appropriate, whether or not the user is at a far more advanced level than the steps assume.

It is true that use of a metaphor is appropriate in the initial stages of learning. But while those first stages are only there temporarily, the metaphor is with us forever. After those first few steps of learning, the metaphor is guaranteed to get in the way, because by the very nature of metaphor, the thing being represented by the other isn't the same. The result is conflict. The "window" in the computer interface has a quite different meaning than the word "window" in a home. A real window does not have a "scroll bar," nor a way to change size. When the window at home is shut, it doesn't go away, out of sight. What value is added to the computer image by thinking metaphorically? For every point that the metaphor helped in understanding, it confuses at all the other points where the computer version differs from the real one.

Designers of the world: Forget the term "metaphor." Go right to the heart of the problem. Make a clean, clear, understandable conceptual model. Make sure the user can learn and understand it. Make all the actions consistent with that conceptual model. Provide feedback and interaction consistent with that model, the better to reinforce it. Forget metaphors—they will only get in the way.

Making Computers Easy to Use

Computers are general-purpose devices, designed to do everything. As a result, they can't be optimized for any individual task. Their controls are arbitrary, often limited to what can be typed on the keyboard or pointed at on the screen and clicked by the mouse. There is no possibility of using the physical construction itself to present the conceptual model of the device or of the actions, since the range of functions is so large.

With a special purpose device, everything about it can shout "Here is how I work, this is what I do." The shape of the case, the layout of the controls, even the shape and form of operation of each control indicates something significant. The displays and feedback can be precise and to the point: explaining to the user what is going on, why the actions are needed, what they are for.

Good design is not necessarily self-explanatory: Some tasks are inherently too complex. The notion that design can render anything "intuitively obvious" is false. In fact, intuition is simply a state of sub-conscious knowledge that comes about after extended practice and experience. With minor exceptions, things that we call intuitive are simply skills that we have practiced for so many years that we no longer recall how difficult it was to learn them in the first place. Skills such as using a pencil, driving an automobile, speaking and understanding language, reading and writing: All these are intuitive to the skilled adult, yet all took years to learn. Difficult tasks will always have to be taught. The trick is to ensure that the technology is not part of the difficulty.

Devices for complex tasks must of themselves be complex, but they can still be easy to use if the devices are properly designed so that they fit naturally into the task. When this is done, learn the task and you know the device. One goal is that each operation fit so elegantly within the structure of the task that it need be explained only once. If users say "Of course, I see," and never have to be told again, there is success. If users say, "Uh, I guess," and discover that with each usage they must once again ask or consult a manual, then the design is faulty.

The goal is to let you pick up a device and use it. The goal is for the device to be built for the job and be no more difficult than it needs to be. Does this come at a cost? Of course. Among other things, it means that there must be one device per activity, which means a multitude of devices. It means that the devices are separate, so something extra must be done if you want to combine the output of several activities. All of these problematic situations can be overcome, as will be shown. The solutions require careful consideration of what things go together, of just what is meant by an activity. The solutions require a universal communication scheme so that the products of one device can be sent effortlessly to another with no more thought than if they resided on the same machine—and considering the complexity of sharing material on today's machines, the separate devices might even make sharing easier than today's overloaded systems. Life is full of tradeoffs, with each choice being better for some things, worse for others.

The ultimate goal is simplicity. Make things fit the task, make the difficulty of our tools match the difficulty of the job to be done.

How do we make things less difficult? Sorry, but the causes of today's difficulties are too fundamental for simple change. As we have seen in chapter 5, there is no magical cure that will make everything all right, letting us proceed essentially as we are now doing. What is the answer? The most promising hope is a new process for product development that focuses upon human comprehension, a human-centered development process. Read on!

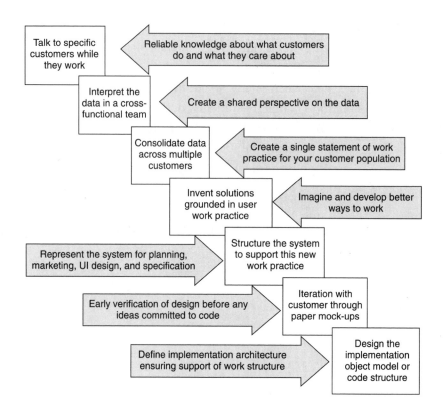

Talk to specific customers while they work

Reliable knowledge about what customers do and what they care about

Interpret the data in a cross-functional team

Create a shared perspective on the data

Consolidate data across multiple customers

Create a single statement of work practice for your customer population

Invent solutions grounded in user work practice

Imagine and develop better ways to work

Represent the system for planning, marketing, UI design, and specification

Structure the system to support this new work practice

Early verification of design before any ideas committed to code

Iteration with customer through paper mock-ups

Define implementation architecture ensuring support of work structure

Design the implementation object model or code structure

9

Human-Centered Development

What is human-centered product development? The answer is simple: It's a process of product development that starts with users and their needs rather than with technology. The goal is a technology that serves the user, where the technology fits the task and the complexity is that of the task, not of the tool. At its core, human-centered product development requires developers who understand people and the tasks they wish to achieve. It means starting by observing and working with users, writing a simple instruction manual—no more than one page long, if possible. It means constructing and evaluating physical and software mock-ups of the device to see how its potential users employ it for its intended activities, allowing all to judge whether the design meets their requirements. Then, after a period of iterative evaluation and redesign, it means building a technology that fits the mock-ups. All of this means completely reversing today's technology-centered process.

Human-centered development is a *process*. It starts with a multidisciplinary team that includes representatives from marketing, technology, and user experience. The first task is to determine what the product should be. Although this seems obvious, it is the task most often ignored and most often done too quickly, poorly, and superficially. How

Figure 9.1
Contextual design. The tasks start with market definition, the uppermost boxes, continue through strategy definition and requirements engineering, finishing with the bottom right boxes of design adoption. User interface design (UI design) doesn't start until the fifth box and software and hardware coding and design do not begin until the seventh box, the final and last one in this process. (Diagram from the home page of InContext Enterprises, http://www.incontextenterprises.com/. Reprinted with permission.)

does one define the product? Study prospective users: Watch them as they go about their daily lives. Understand what role the proposed product will play. Find activities that are as close as possible to the one the product is intended to support. The goal is to understand the users' true needs, what they care about. Then compile, refine, and analyze the observations to determine what the product might be, what role it would play, what actions it should perform. Go beyond the problem that is given to develop solutions that truly meet the customers' needs.

In all of this, take a systems approach. Go beyond the specifics of the product to understand how it is to be used in the full context of a complete activity. How does the work session start, how does it end? How often is it interrupted, and how do the resumptions occur? What other activities are required? Can you support those as well? Should you?

If the product is to be an enhancement of one that already exists, watch how customers use the existing product. Use these observations to drive the new ideas. Test the new ideas through mock-ups and simulations with the existing customers; use their reactions as feedback for further refinement. Are there potential target customers who are not using the existing product? Visit them, watch them. Why are they not using it? Is there something you could do that would benefit them as well? It's always a good idea to improve matters for existing customers, but it's even better if you can also attract new ones.

If this is a new product, make rough, crude prototypes with which to test the original ideas. Use rapid prototyping tools such as paper-and-pencil sketches, software prototyping tools, and foam models. Show them to sample users and get their reactions. Make them use the prototypes in real situations, play-acting the performance of the devices if necessary. Use the feedback from these sessions to refine the early ideas. At this stage these early prototypes and studies are not tests of the design; they are tests of your understanding of the issues, of your ability to put together a system that users feel comfortable with and that they believe will simplify their lives. Keep doing this, continually refining and testing. When the development team and the customers are happy, then it is time to translate the mock-ups into design specifications, time to start building.

These are the basic steps of the development process. But these steps are seldom followed. This method of procedural stages is new to product development. It is not taught in schools, nor is it well documented. Those who advocate these procedures are still in the early phases of developing them. There is not yet much written material available to give guidance. One method that I particularly like is called *contextual design*,[1] diagrammed in figure 9.1 (page 184).

In contextual design, the human-centered product team goes through considerable analysis and testing of their conceptual ideas before reaching any of the traditional stages of development. User interface design doesn't start until the fifth stage of the process; software coding and hardware construction don't start until the last, seventh stage of the process. Proponents of this approach argue that although it leads to a longer time from product conception to initial coding and building, the total time to product completion is shorter. User testing of the final product is also faster and easier. The goal at this point is to find only minor difficulties, with all the major conceptual and structural issues already having been determined in the initial stages of the process, when it is relatively easy and inexpensive to fix them. My recommendations mirror this process.

Taking Human-Centered Development Seriously

What does a human-centered development team look like? How does it do its job? The answer really depends on the circumstances, on the company, and on the product itself. Will this be a new product, breaking new ground? Is this a continuing sequence, where the current product is an iteration of a previously released line of products? Is the target customer well defined, or is the product aimed at a large, undifferentiated collection of people? Will the same product be sold to millions of people with different backgrounds, cultures, and educational levels? Will it be an international product?

The pitfalls of current products and suggested solutions are well known and well documented. There are numerous books on the subject;[2] I've written a few of them myself. There are university courses and degrees, lectures, and consultants. There are societies and journals. The interested reader who has not yet been exposed to these topics can readily become knowledgeable. I provide some starting points in the chapter notes, and numerous consultants are ready and eager to help.

Although each company will have its own way of doing things, there are certain immutable principles that should apply to all human-centered development processes.

1. Start with an assessment of user needs, through both traditional marketing methods and customer visits. Watch the users as they perform the activities the new product is intended to assist. Use a structured interaction process, such as the contextual inquiry of the contextual design approach. Do not offer advice to the users if they run into trouble. Your goal is to learn.

2. Study the market. What other products exist? What is the likely customer segment the product is aimed at? If this is a new product, who will the original purchasers be? How do they differ from the eventual target group? What price range can they afford? Where is the product to go? What must it look like? What size constraints exist? Learn, learn, learn.

3. From the results of items 1 and 2, put together a description of the users' needs. Each need should be validated by observations, data, and market surveys.

4. From item 3, the team should create some mock-ups of sample products: physical mock-ups out of foam and other rapid-prototyping tools; paper drawings; mock-ups of electronic displays. Take them back to the customers and get their reactions. Have them play-act, using them like props in real activities. Use the customers as design assistants. Iterate steps 1–4 until satisfied.

5. With the final mock-ups and description of users' needs, write the manual if one is needed. Make it as short and simple as possible. Reward

the technical writing team on the smallness of the manual. One page is the goal; five pages are better than ten. Assume the users won't read even a one-page manual.

6. Start the design process, working with the manual, the physical prototypes, and the mock-ups. Ask the technologists to meet the challenge of making the product live up to the manual and fit inside the prototypes.

7. Continually test and revise. Representatives from user experience, marketing and technology attend the tests, watching but not touching. No talking, no aiding. When potential users have difficulties, this is a challenge to the development team, not an indictment of the developers, not a reflection of low intelligence by the users. Challenge the development team.

The resemblance of my list to the suggestions of contextual design (figure 9.1) is not a coincidence. Anyone who has been involved with product development will recognize that both proposals reverse the normal scheme of things. That's deliberate. After all, we are making the shift from technology-centered development to human-centered development. It's only appropriate that the traditional order in which we start with the technology be replaced with the new order in which we start with people.

The goal is a harmonious team consisting of several disciplines, all working smoothly together. If this is done right, after a short time, people forget from which discipline the others come and instead rely on each one's individual expertise. If done wrong, there will be squabbles and jurisdictional fights.

The Six Disciplines of User Experience

User experience (UE) is not a single discipline. At least six skills are needed, and they are almost never found in the same person. There are few places that provide education in this area. In any event, the six skill sets cut across traditional academic disciplines. Here is what it takes:

- **Field studies**   People to observe potential users in their normal settings, the better to determine real user needs. Training for this discipline is most apt to come from anthropology and sociology, where the skills of careful, systematic observation are taught.

- **Behavioral designers**   Those who can create a cohesive conceptual model for the product, a model that is consistent, is easy to learn and understand, and will form the basis for engineering design. The behavioral designers work from a detailed task analysis of typical action sequences that are required for the tasks to be supported. They must ascertain that the solution provides support for the work flow, not just for each isolated action. Behavioral design has to mesh the task requirements with the skills, knowledge, and capabilities of the intended users. Skills in behavioral design are most apt to come from cognitive science and experimental psychology, especially from programs in human-computer interaction.

- **Model builders and rapid prototypers**   Those who can rapidly build product mock-ups, pretend systems that can be tested immediately, even before the real technology is ready. It often takes three people to cover the capabilities required by this task: programming, designing electrical circuits, and building mechanical models. Here the skills typically come from computer programming, electrical and mechanical engineering, and model building of the sort usually taught in schools of architecture and industrial design.

- **User testers**   People who understand the pitfalls of experimental tests, who can do feasibility and usability studies quickly and efficiently with one-day turnaround time. These rapid user-testing studies of the prototypes allow for rapid iteration of designs, the better to meet the real needs of the users. The results will be approximate rather than exact,[3] which is usually sufficient, since in industry we are looking for big effects, not the small phenomena of interest to the scientist. These are the skills of experimental psychology, although what is needed in practice has to be much faster, much less labor-intensive than the traditional laboratory experiments.

- **Graphical and industrial designers**   Those who possess the design skills that combine science and a rich body of experience with art and intuition. Here is where "joy" and "pleasure" come into the equation: joy of ownership, joy of use. This part of the design must satisfy many constraints. It must merge the conceptual model and behavioral aspects of the product with the various size, power, heat dissipation, and other requirements of the technology, yet produce a device that is aesthetically pleasing ("a joy to own"), cost-efficient, and consistent with the demands of manufacturing. These skills are most frequently taught in schools of art, design, and architecture.

- **Technical writers**   People whose goal should be to show the technologists how to build things that do not require manuals.

Technical writers traditionally have the cleanup job. When all is finished, they are called upon to make it look like the entire design was carefully orchestrated as a systematic whole. They are the cleanup artists, and often they get the least respect of all.

Technical writing is a difficult skill. It requires understanding the audience, understanding what activities the user wants to accomplish, and translating the often idiosyncratic and unplanned design into something that appears to make sense.

To a user-experience architect, the technical writers should be the key to the entire operation. Have them write the simplest, most elegant manual imaginable. Reward them for brevity. (Would you believe that some technical writers are rewarded for the length of the manual, as if a long manual is somehow more valuable than a short one? That is certainly perverse.) Test the manual to make sure people can follow it. Then build the device to fit the manual. The technical writer should be a crucial part of the development team. Indeed, if the technical writer is completely successful, the device will be constructed so well, with such a clear conceptual model, that no instruction manual will be required.

This list leaves out the sacred test method of marketing: the focus group. A focus group is a gathering of typical users to evaluate an existing product or a new concept. They are asked to describe their impressions, express their opinions, and offer suggestions, usually in a discussion-group setting led by an experienced facilitator. I am not a fan of this method of evaluation.

Focus groups are fun. They provide a lot of information. Any interaction with potential customers is always informative. But focus groups can be very misleading. They tend to reveal what is relevant at the moment, not about what might happen in the future. Users have great trouble imagining how they might use new products, and when it comes to entirely new product categories—forget it.

There is a more fundamental problem with focus groups: They tap the conscious, rational part of human behavior, which is not necessarily consistent with actual behavior during the course of a day. It will be difficult to convince you with words alone, for after all, you are reading this as conscious, rational human beings. But students of human behavior know that observations often reveal vast discrepancies between what people say they do and what people actually do. The truth is in the observations.

Much of our skilled behavior is not conscious: we are primarily aware of our acts when they go wrong or when we have difficulty. Moreover, focus groups tend to reveal what people assume they should think rather than true underlying beliefs. Mind you, this is not deliberate; within the setting of the focus group, pleasant interaction is the norm. In psychology this is called a *demand characteristic*. People respond to these subconscious demand characteristics by behaving in whatever manner is deemed appropriate: polite, formal, respectful. These are all essential to polite society, but not necessarily indicative of what really goes on in the familiar settings of their workplace, school, or home.

People can describe what they are doing and what conscious thoughts are in their minds, but when it comes to explaining the reasons for their own behavior they often make up folk theories. Professional psychologists are apt to be more cautious, more realistic, more accurate. It may seem counterintuitive that an outsider can explain a person's behavior better than the actual person, but this is a common finding in experimental psychology. Experimental and cognitive psychologists can generally do better than the person giving the explanation. After all, this is their field; they know the scientific studies and findings. They often know why people do things and what they need better than the people themselves.

Consider how typical users explain their jobs. They can describe their activities in great detail. The observer carefully writes down the descriptions and checks to ensure they are accurate. But then, if a user is watched on the job setting, lo and behold, the actions are usually not a good match for the description.

"Why did you do that?" asks the observer. "Didn't you say earlier that in these situations, you would do things differently?"

"Oh," says the person, "my original description was correct. This is just a special case."

True, but guess what: Most of the day is made up of special cases. The description is of an ideal that is seldom met.

I'm a fan of observation in actual settings. Don't ask people how they do their work. Watch them. Don't ask people what they want. Watch them and figure out their needs. If you ask, people usually focus on what they have and ask for it to be better: cheaper, faster, smaller. A good observer might discover that the task is unnecessary, that it is possible to restructure things or provide a new technology that eliminates the painstaking parts of their procedures. If you just follow what people ask for, you could end up making their lives even more complicated. That's one of the reasons our computer applications have so many confusing features: Every one was requested by a user.

Approximate Methods

Designers need answers in hours, not months. This means that the UE community must learn to do its observations and tests quickly. But UE is a new discipline, one not yet fully established, one that derives from such academic disciplines as the social and behavioral sciences—cognitive science, experimental psychology, anthropology, and sociology—from computer science, and from the design disciplines of graphical and industrial design. None of these disciplines has developed an appropriate methodology for applied observation and testing.

Applied science does not need the precision of the traditional scientific method. In industry, it is good enough to be approximately right. Speed comes before accuracy. When designing a product, designers need to know how to proceed when questions arise. They need answers rapidly. The answers can be estimates, and some of the time they can be wrong. The cost of an occasional wrong answer is small compared to the benefit of many fast answers. Moreover, because we seek big phenomena, a "wrong" answer is usually less effective than the "correct" answer, but still quite usable and reasonable.

Experimental psychology has a well-established, rigorous procedure for answering questions about human behavior by controlled experiments. Following the strict rules of the standard scientific method, the psychologist carefully selects the people to be tested and counterbalances and controls the tests so as to eliminate bias and artifacts of the testing procedure. These techniques are important when the phenomena to be studied are small and delicate. It is obviously important to use when testing experimental products of pharmaceutical and medical companies. But human-centered development is concerned with big, robust phenomena, effects that apply across a wide range of conditions. As a result, careful and laborious experimental methods are not required; big effects can be found with simpler methods.

Ethnography is the branch of anthropology that deals with the scientific description of human cultures. The ethnographer seeks to live among the culture of interest, observing and recording the behavior, the rituals and ceremonies, the symbols, beliefs, and actions of the society. Ethnographers try hard to keep out of the way, to learn through their observations without disturbing the behavior they seek to record. But ethnography also includes long, laborious, detailed studies, sometimes requiring painstaking analysis of video and audio tapes on the frame-by-frame, utterance-by-utterance basis required by the scientific analyses. Ethnography is a specialized skill of the social sciences. However, its basic philosophy supplies what is needed in the applied area of product development.

What human-centered development needs is a variant of traditional ethnography, one that I call *rapid ethnography*. This is an observational technique for going to the prospective users of a product and observing the activities they perform, their interactions, and the subculture in which they live, work, learn, and play. Rapid ethnography is critical to the invention of new product classes. New product concepts come from observation of the needs of prospective users, devising tools that will simplify and enhance their lives. The goal is to make the people who are being observed become participants in the discovery process of learning just what their real needs are—not the artificial needs proscribed by the way they do things today, but what the goals are, what they are striving for. This is the role of rapid ethnography.

Much progress has been made in the development of methods of estimation that fit the needs of the product development process. A series of methods has been developed, called *usability heuristics* or *cognitive walkthroughs,* that speed up the test process. One description of what a rapid ethnography might look like is provided by a special form of rapid observations called *contextual inquiry* by the proponents of contextual design.[4]

Is a Special Discipline of UE Really Necessary?

Mature technologies are always easier to use than youthful ones. Do we really need a special discipline for ease of use and overall user experience, or will the necessary improvements occur naturally as the technology matures?

Technologies usually start off simply, growing in complexity and difficulty as they age, until they reach some peak of difficulty. From then on, as they mature, they get progressively simpler to use. In the early days of a technology, devices are usually technically simple, but limited in performance. The technical simplicity is often offset by the difficulty and skill required for its use. The first airplanes were simple, with few controls, but it took a skilled pilot to fly one safely. The first radios were crystal receivers with few controls but, again, it required skill and dexterity on the part of the user to receive and tune a station. Early devices often require considerable skill to master and to use well.

In the early stages of technologies, difficulty increases with time. New functions are added, along with more controls and adjustments. But eventually, as the technology matures, the difficulty starts to decrease as technologists learn to simplify the mechanisms, improving accuracy and precision so that numerous compensatory controls are no longer required, and automating many of the operations. The difficulty continues to decrease.

Figure 9.2 shows the change in the number of controls in airplane cockpits over time, continually increasing for over 50 years but then starting to decrease with the advent of automated systems. Today's displays and controls are simpler because of the power of sophisticated computers inside the aircraft that automate many of the functions. The numerous independent mechanical meters have been consolidated into integrated, cohesive graphical displays. As figure 9.2 shows, the peak of complexity for commercial aviation was the Concorde. Since that time, cockpit automation and advances in instruments have led to much simpler aircraft from the pilot's point of view.

The early automobile had manual cranking to start the engine, as well as manual spark advance, choke, and transmission. Today, engine starting, spark advance and choke are handled automatically, and the majority of cars have automatic transmissions. In some brands, automation has so much taken over that manual transmission is an extra-cost option. Even the seat controls are automated. Early radios had multiple controls for tuning, sensitivity, and frequency bandwidth; today, the radio can find its own stations, and all that is left for the user is to set the listening level. Television circuits have become increasingly complex, the better to simplify the interactions required by the user. So, too, with all technologies. In all these cases, the simplicity for the user has come at the cost of greater complexity of the device itself.

The usability of all technologies is poor whenever the power and performance of the technology fall below the level required by the users. Here is where the device is difficult, for the user needs numerous controls and adjustments to compensate for the impoverished technical abilities of the device. As the technology matures, however, it can simplify the activity from the user's point of view, even if at a cost in complexity for the technology itself.

The big question today is whether computers will follow this same cycle. Perhaps they are just now reaching their peak in difficulty for the user. Perhaps as software engineers become better able to automate the functions, the difficulty of the actions required by the user will decrease, just as it did for other technologies.

Personally, I am counting on this phenomenon. The success of the information appliance can only come about if the underlying technology is sophisticated enough to work effortlessly, with no need for control or advice from the user. The personal computer can probably never reach this level of simplicity because the attempt to have one device do many tasks guarantees difficulty, even if any single task can be made relatively simple. Moreover, any task requires a minimum level of control that is governed by the nature of the task itself.

Look at writing. Writing still requires the writer to fashion the words, in part through trial and error, making multiple corrections. The visual component of writing conveys much of the emotional or information content, and so it will always be necessary to allow a writer control over format, heading, and type font, as well as, of course, wording. Some forms of writing require footnotes and figures, with references, headings, and tables of contents and indexes. Even as they get replaced by live links to text, hyperlinks to other texts, and live documents, the need for human selection of the links, content, and manner of presentation remains, for writing exploits the human ability to manipulate emotions, to describe, to tell stories, to inform and educate. These pose minimum levels of complexity and activity on the part of the writer, thresholds that cannot be decreased.

Aircraft provide an excellent example of the role of automation in simplifying the task. Although the new, integrated instruments that comprise the modern automated "glass cockpit" have dramatically simplified the job of the pilot, the instruments and the automation themselves are the results of many studies by researchers in the field of aviation psychology and human factors. Some of the aviation automation has increased the risk of problems, because it has taken the pilots "out of the loop," so they are not always aware of the state of the airplane. As a result, when things go wrong, pilots may take longer to grasp

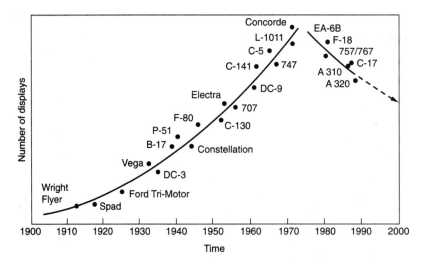

Figure 9.2

The rise and fall of complexity of aviation cockpits. In the early days of aviation, cockpits were pretty simple, with few instruments. As airplanes added multiple engines, radios, and navigation equipment, the cockpits grew in complexity and difficulty of use—reaching a peak with the Concorde. There were so many dials, instruments, and controls on the Concorde that the designers seriously considered eliminating all windows to leave space for the displays. After the Concorde, complexity and difficulty of use started decreasing with the advent of computer-controlled displays and the so-called "glass cockpit," the substitution of computer display screens for multiple mechanical instruments. Increased automation further reduced the need for so many displays. Today's aircraft have reached the point where even I have flown such advanced airplanes as the Boeing 777 (in simulators at NASA and the Boeing Company), mainly because all that is needed for takeoff and landing is to push the correct button, and sometimes not even that. (Chart above, reprinted from Sexton 1988 with permission of Academic Press; top photograph, the Concorde, courtesy of Air France; bottom photograph, the Boeing 777, courtesy of Boeing.)

the situation and respond than had there been no automation, so that they would have continually been engaged with the system. Mindless automation can be more dangerous than no automation, a topic I have explored elsewhere.[5] Advanced technology and automation can simplify the tasks in dramatic fashion, but the manner in which this is done is enhanced by the expert judgment that a human-centered development process can provide.

Automation has decreased the user's level of difficulty in many technologies. It will—and already has—with the digital computer. But the simplification is made more certain and beneficial if it is done with care and concern for the abilities of the human. Do we really need a special discipline of designers specialized for ease of use? Yes, we do.

Forming the Successful Triad of Technology, Marketing, and User Experience

When products reach the mature cycle of their life where customers are demanding convenience, a high-quality user experience, and other consumer attributes, product development has to become human-centered with three equal supporting components: technology, marketing, and user experience. Good development cannot come about without all three. Moreover, all three legs must rest upon a common foundation: the business case for the product.

Note the complementary role of marketing and user experience. The two should form a strong bond, for they are the ones who understand the customer. Marketing knows what customers are asking for, what drives their behavior at the point of sale, what they will pay for, and what determines their purchasing habits. User experience knows what customers actually do, what makes a product simple or difficult, usable or not, likely to require handholding via expensive telephone calls to the service help lines or not. Alas, marketing and UE are often in conflict, for each likes to think it "owns" the customer, each feels its insights are superior. No component is superior: marketing, technology, and user experience have to work together as a team, like three equal legs of the tripod that supports product success.

User experience consists of designers and observers who know what people actually do, what their real needs are as opposed to their stated needs. UE understands behavioral design, the better to make the product work smoothly and easily. On the other hand, user experience people seldom understand market pressures and what drives sales. This is the expertise of marketing. They are expert at point of sale issues, the kinds of concerns customers bring to bear when they buy. Marketing people seldom are designers, capable of translating the lessons they have learned from customers into a product that works. Together, marketing and UE should make a great team, if only they could bridge the gap of differences in background and language.

In similar fashion, engineers are experts at the technology and at engineering design, both hardware and software. They are not behavioral designers; they are not trained to understand the needs of real users, to understand the psychological principles and science underlying human-centered development. Engineers also often fail to understand market pressures. In turn, neither marketing nor user-experience experts possess the knowledge of engineers. These three disciplines are all essential for the success of the product, but each speaks a different language, comes from a different starting point, and focuses on different things. The challenge is to bring their practitioners together and help them learn how to cooperate as equal members of a team.

Proper development does not come about by accident. Human-centered development requires a focus and commitment to the users of the product. It requires the skills of the appropriate professionals. But most important, it requires the proper organizational structure within the company so that human-centered development permeates everyone's thinking from product conception through manufacture and sales.

It isn't easy to put together a human-centered development team in a company without one. This is especially true in technology-driven companies, where the history and culture emphasize technical excellence, often at the expense of usability and convenience. When a company makes the transition to the world of consumers, when it tries to cross the chasm from early adopters to late, conservative and pragmatic ones, it has to learn to change its development process. Does the company want human-centered development? It may have to reorganize.

Designers Concept

What Marketing
Specified

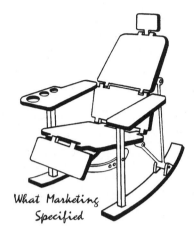

What Health
& Safety
Required

What
Manufacturing
Produced

Engineering
Design

brian h clark 98

What the Customer
Requested

10

Want Human-Centered Development? Reorganize the Company

What do you want for your product?
Good quality? Inexpensive? Quick to get to the market?
Good, cheap, quick: pick any two.
— Old engineer's saying.

Development is a series of tradeoffs, often with incompatible constraints. Multiple factors compete for attention, each factor often demanding a solution incompatible with that required by the others. Marketing, engineering, and usability experts all champion their favored approach, each correct in their assessment but, nonetheless, each voicing conflicting concerns. How do these inconsistencies and incompatibilities get resolved? Tradeoffs. That is what the product process is all about.

In high-technology companies, the problem is exacerbated by the fact that success in the early stages of the technology marketplace favors technology-centered, feature-driven products. Customers clamor for

Figure 10.1
Design tradeoffs. The designer, top left, wanted a unique, sophisticated chair that would differentiate it from all others—a signature chair. The Health and Safety committee demanded that hands, feet, and head be positioned to prevent injury; rocking was prohibited. Engineering provided a rugged, sturdy, practical design. Marketing conducted focus groups and came back with a list of features: adjustments, accessories, and cupholders. Manufacturing wanted simple materials, cut with simple tools, assembled with tabs and glue. As for the customers, they wanted a simple, comfortable rocking chair, bottom right. (Original artwork created and supplied by Brian Hall Clark of clarkcooper design, 205 Santa Clara Street, Brisbane, California 94005. © 1997 Brian H. Clark. Reprinted with permission. All rights reserved.)

more and better technology; engineers become experts at providing a stream of continual improvements in power and increased features, all at decreased cost. In this world, engineering rules the show. Engineers reluctantly cede a place for marketing, and the reluctance is quite visible. Marketing, moreover, becomes primarily feature driven. Query the existing customers for the features they desire most and pressure the engineering team to add them to the product, often with little regard for their impact on the coherence and integrity of the product. Mind you, this feature-driven emphasis is probably correct; early adopters are not overly concerned about the total user experience. Coherence in the product is of secondary importance, if it is noticed at all. These are technology-driven customers, customers who purchase their products on the basis of technological accomplishments, novelty, and lists of features.

In the latter stages of a technology, the game changes considerably. As we saw in chapter 2, as the technology matures, it becomes less and less pertinent. It is taken for granted. New customers enter the marketplace, customers who are not captivated by technology, but who want reliability, convenience, and low cost of purchase price and upkeep. New factors such as the total user experience play a major role; customers want convenience and lack of hassle. This new entry, user experience, is not well established. Nobody knows quite how to deal with it.

The engineering team thinks it already understands user experience. After all, their previous customers were happy. The engineers themselves have no trouble with the product. Who are these new customers who need so much hand-holding? What's the matter with them, anyway?

The marketing group thinks it already understands user experience. After all, marketing is in close touch with the customer; it knows first-hand what they want. Do they want ease of use? Sure, add it to the list of features. Do they want an attractive product? Sure, hire a graphics designer to make it look pretty. Each item gets added to the list of things to be accomplished, as if the total user experience were simply another feature like "more memory" that can be added on to an established design.

This assumption that user experience is just another add-on is fairly consistent across the industry. Consider how the problem of ease of use is handled. First we build it, say the engineers, then we bring in those user-interface folks to add some graphics and menus and make it easy to use. After all, how can you make a product easy to use before it has been built? The same goes for the technical writers. How can you describe how to use a product until it is all finished, so there is actually something to write about? The writer's job has to come at the end.

The traditional sequence of product design is technology driven. First, marketing provides a list of essential features; then, the engineers state what neat new technical tricks and tools they are ready to deploy. Next, the engineers build the device, putting as many new technologies to work as they can within their allotted time and budget, squabbling with marketing along the way over time and cost, arguing about which of those features really matter the most and which don't. Then after all is finished and the product is ready to ship, the technical writers are called in to explain it to the customers. The graphics and industrial designers are asked to make it look pretty, and the user-interface experts are urged to make it usable.

Guess what: This process doesn't work. For proof, we simply have to look around us at those high-technology products and ask why so many telephone help lines, so many lengthy, expensive phone calls, are required to use the product. We simply have to go to the bookstore and look at how many shelves are filled with books trying to explain how to work the devices. We don't see shelves of books on how to use television sets, telephones, refrigerators, or washing machines. Why should we for computer-based applications?

The high-technology industry is at a crossroads. The basic technology is now good enough for most purposes. It is at the transition point, in the gap between a technology-driven marketplace and a consumer-driven one. The customers have already made the transition to consumer products. They want convenience, they want simplicity. The high-technology companies, however, have not crossed over the chasm. They are still mired in technology-driven product development, feature-driven marketing.

It is difficult for a company to make the transition to a consumer-driven marketplace. It requires an entirely new approach to products, starting with an understanding of customers and their needs, their real needs, not the feature sets so loved by marketing. It means using social scientists to collect, analyze, and work with the data—moreover, social scientists on an even footing with engineers and technologists. It means structuring the whole product process differently than before. It may well mean reorganizing the company.

In chapter 9 I suggested that development start with the study of the true needs of customers determined through observation and structured interaction, observations using psychologists and anthropologists, skilled social scientists who know how to observe and learn without disturbing the phenomena they are there to record. Analyze what has been observed. Do quick tests of design concepts. Do rough, quick mock-ups and try them out in the context of the customer's location, be it home, office, school, or athletic field. Try different industrial designs. Try different interaction models. Then write a simple manual. Test as you go along on different populations, all representative of the target customer. Then, and only then, start with the technological factors and the design details.

"Start with psychologists and social scientists instead of technologists?" I can hear the rumblings throughout the company, "Hey, bringing in marketing was bad enough, but who are these people? What's happening to our company?"

The remedies I propose are certainly not easy to implement. They call for restructuring of the established process of product development. They call for changing the company culture, which is the hardest part of a company to change.

A company's culture is that nebulous, ill-definable set of knowledge, history, folklore, and spirit that determines how it goes about its daily activities, how it treats its employees, customers, partners, and competitors. It is seldom written down, although written mission statements and company policy procedures are a major part of the culture. Company culture is often established in the early days of a company by its founders, then nourished until it establishes the deep roots of commitment that are difficult to see, to describe, and to change.

The Structure of the Product Team

Today in the high-technology industry most existing products are revised once or twice a year as determined by a marketing analysis of the competition and the features requested by the buyers and customers. The result is products that are technology-driven, feature-driven, defined by lists of critical features: items that are necessary, items that are desirable. The engineering teams struggle to get them into the product, and when schedule deadlines loom, a vast cutting exercise ensues in which the desired but not essential features are cut.

Design by feature-lists is fundamentally wrong. Lists of features miss the interconnected nature of tasks. Any given feature is apt to be insignificant in isolation, but critical when viewed as a whole, or seemingly important and critical when viewed in isolation, but insignificant or unnecessary when viewed in context.

The proper way to make design tradeoffs is to understand why each of the various elements of a system exists, what role each serves for the customer, or marketing, or technological performance. Then the tradeoffs can be made, pitting each element of the system against the costs in usability, marketability, and schedule. Cutting or prioritizing must be done with a good understanding of the gains and losses from an overall point of view; the evaluation must involve looking at each item in context. A system-wide approach of the design in full context of its use, sale, marketing, and construction requires a new kind of product process, one that starts with the user and ends with the technology. And if this is taken seriously, it means a very different structure to the company.

The Design Police

Companies that are having difficulties with their products sometimes resort to heavy-handed bureaucracy. Is the design flawed? Are the products too difficult to use? Are service calls and help-line support rising? Call in the design police.

Years ago, other disciplines faced the same problems. It wasn't long ago that marketing was also scorned, thought of as something tacked on at the end. In a similar way, quality was controlled at the end of manufacturing by testing the finished product. Both cases proved wrong. A lot can be learned by studying how marketing and quality control centers restructured the product process.

The same lessons that applied to marketing and quality control apply to user experience. Leave out marketing from the product conception, and the wrong products get built. Leave out quality considerations and no amount of testing will bring quality back in. Leave user experience factors out of the initial development constraints and by the time they are ready to be considered, it is too late: The die is cast. The user experience team becomes the design police. But calling in the police after the crime has been committed is not the best way to solve a problem.

Calling in the police is a standard approach to remedying any flaw: legislate and police. This solution doesn't work very well. The only way to get real, long-lasting improvement is to attack the root cause of the problem. Sometimes this means better training or changing the reward structure of the company or of society. In the case of good design, it means both of these things, plus one more: reorganizing the company.

The first step in undertaking a cure for bad design is to determine the underlying causes. After all, poor design is not deliberate. The reasons are manifold, including ignorance of the principles of good development, lack of understanding of the people for whom the product is being designed, and, occasionally, a lack of empathy. But even when these factors are eliminated, the organizational structure of the company can often prevent good development practices from coming into play.

An abbreviated account of the history of reliability and quality of products is instructive. Quality used to be achieved by a hit-or-miss approach. Employees were urged to work harder, to produce better products, without, of course, deviating from their assigned target rates of production. This approach works no better than a parent telling a child "be careful."

Nobody is intentionally careless in conducting daily activities. Nobody deliberately sets out to produce an unreliable product. Nobody wants the product to be difficult to use. These things happen because they are not the primary focus of activity. Quality, ease of use, and even personal safety are the results of a process. These goals are met only if attention is paid to the process that leads to unsafe practices, to poor quality and design. Only after the processes have been discovered and new ones put into practice can one hope to see any changes. And these new processes are onerous to develop and implement.

In the field of quality control, the next step after exhortation was testing, continual testing of the product as it went through the manufacturing process. This had several virtues. It allowed defects to be discovered before the product was shipped. It also allowed quantitative assessment to be made of any problem discovered by the tests. Proposed solutions could then be tested against the requirement of actual improvement in the measured results instead of the intuitive assessment practiced earlier.

Enforcement of quality through testing is a clear case of design by legislation, with the dreaded quality police looking over everyone's shoulder. Although it can reduce incidents of failure and improve quality, it's a bad way to proceed. It is seldom sufficient to produce true products of quality.

Once upon a time I was a reliability engineer. During my college years I had a summer job at Univac, a major computer manufacturer back then. My job was to determine how to test circuit components for reliability. Engineers would design the circuits, both their electronics and the layout of the printed circuit boards. A few prototypes would be made and submitted for approval to the reliability group. Note the phrase "submitted for approval." It was our job to approve the work that had already been done, not to find problems.

Not only were the electronic circuits submitted to us after all the work had been done, but by that time, the work was always behind schedule and frequently above cost. If we were to say "approval denied," everyone would be angry at us: the engineers, the managers, the company administration. Redoing the circuits would take too much time. Sometimes it would be impossible, for other circuits had also been constructed that depended upon the configuration of the one we were expected to approve. If we changed the physical dimensions, the pin layout, or almost anything else, the whole product would have to be redesigned. This was a product that cost a million dollars, back in the days when a million was real money. In other words, things had to be pretty bad for us to deny approval and not suffer repercussions. We were supposed to approve everything.

Guess what: This method of quality maintenance doesn't work. The reward schedule of the company was wrong. We were not rewarded for doing our job; in fact, we were punished. Withholding approval delayed schedules and cost the company extra money. The engineers were not rewarded for attention to quality: after all, that was our job. The whole process of testing for quality at the end, coupled with the reward structure of the company, guaranteed the failure of this method.

The effective way to get an acceptable product is through a cooperative process with all the concerned parties participating at every step of the way. If a company wants its engineers to design reliable circuits, the proper way is to teach them the principles of reliability engineering so they will be embedded throughout the development process. Let the reliability specialists serve as consultants, playing a role from the very start of the development and remaining available to help when perplexing development problems arise. This transforms the role of the reliability experts from the dreaded law enforcement officer to that of being trusted colleague, advisor, and friend. Reward the design engineers for quality improvements. If service calls or the need for replacement parts decrease, reward the development engineers. Ask the development engineers to spend time with service representatives, with maintenance, with customers, to understand the way their products get used, and the kinds of problems that exist. Make quality everyone's job. We shouldn't be surprised if the result is a superior product.

Over and over again, experience shows that the only way to satisfy the many complex factors that must be considered throughout a project is through cooperative, interactive, and iterative development where all interested parties play a role on the team. Development is a series of tradeoffs. There is no single correct design—the whole process consists of compromises among a large number of conflicting requirements. Aesthetics, cost, usability, functionality, ease of manufacturing, ease of maintenance, ease of use, reliability, size, weight—all are legitimate, important factors, often at odds with one another. Make it less expensive and reliability might decrease. Add all the features customers require and usability and reliability might decrease while cost increases. Provide a portable system with the power and battery life customers demand and the weight and cost will increase, just the opposite of what the customers have requested. On and on it goes.

The traditional method of development is to follow a linear sequence, from specifications, through design, manufacture, sales and delivery, usage, and then repair, service, and assistance. Marketing provides the specifications, the engineers design to meet them, then pass the design on to the manufacturing experts. Somewhere along the way, the industrial designers and human-interface teams are asked to do their jobs, and when all is finished, the technical writers are called in to write a cohesive, intelligible set of instructions or user manual. Finally, the sales teams are asked to sell the finished package and the service and maintenance people are trained on its operation and on the kinds of problems that are expected. This is a time-tested method of development. It has led us to the complex, messy, unsatisfactory situation we are in today, especially in high-technology products, where customer satisfaction is low, the cost of help lines and service high.

How else can we proceed? Once again, as discussed for the Univac engineers, have all the affected parties participate together in the development process. This is a foreign approach for most engineers. But this is how to achieve human-centered development. This is how many companies have succeeded in getting high quality into their products: ease of manufacturing, ease of installation, ease of use, and ease of maintenance. The moral is simple: Don't test it in, design it in. This occurs when each of the experts in the many different disciplines that are relevant to the end product have a say throughout the entire process of product development, from conception to final delivery.

Today, many companies have restructured their development and manufacturing processes, the better to make products of high quality. The transformation was often painful, taking years, requiring several changes of organizational structure and, most difficult of all, encouraging the growth of a new culture. But once everyone focused on quality as a high-level development goal, once it was realized that quality experts should be thought of as consultants and colleagues, the overall process won acceptance. Companies have discovered that producing higher quality products by attending to the issues from design all the way through the development and manufacturing process ends up being cheaper and faster than the old way of doing business.

The outcome will be similar with the other issues of concern to companies; ease of use, ease of manufacturing, ease of maintenance. It requires a reevaluation of the company, a restructuring, and a commitment to these principles. And it also requires working much more closely with customers, for it is from them that one gets the essential feedback to assess how well the process is going.

Putting Together the Product Team

There are numerous ways to form a product team, none of which is necessarily the one best way. Different types of products, industries, and even corporate cultures might dictate various styles of work. A new product, especially a potentially disruptive one, requires a very different process than a sustaining product, one that continues a long-existing product line through incremental improvements and changes.

Remember the story in chapter 7 of how the United States Navy performs its work? The Navy has two different organizational structures at work simultaneously. One is a rigid, formal organization that handles the general assignment of personnel, their ranks, promotions, and administrative requirements. This is the formal rank structure of the Navy. But in the conduct of the daily work the organizational structure is very different. Now rank is not so important. Instead, crew members of various levels of skill and knowledge work together in functional teams, keeping track of the activity of the entire group, listening, critiquing, discussing, and learning.

This is an excellent model to follow. Although the exact organizational structure used by the Navy is probably not directly applicable to other organizations, it is the spirit that matters, the realization that there is no need to have a single fixed structure that applies to all activities. What is particularly satisfying about the Navy's structure is the flexibility coupled with a concentrated focus upon the task requirements. This is the model to emulate.

In design, the goal is that the actual development team be small, but that representatives from the larger community offer expert advice and be available when needed. Just how this is accomplished varies from situation to situation. This is the role of an informed management, and it is an arduous job.

User experience incorporates at least six areas of expertise (see chapter 9). Some people are skilled in several of these areas, but it is the rare individual who is skilled in all of them. As a result, this community requires several representatives. The several disciplines that comprise UE often come from different academic backgrounds, ranging from the hard-core science of experimental psychology, through the art or architectural school background of the visual and industrial designers, to the journalism and humanities background of the writers, to mechanical engineering and programming skills required for rapid prototyping. So, even within this single discipline, the people have different back-grounds, mean different things even when they use the same words, and come from a variety of cultures. Mesh this mix with the technical and marketing people and you can see why working on a development team can be a real challenge: exciting during periods of great creativity and productivity and frustrating during periods of noncommunication, clashing personalities, and personal and technical disagreements.

The problems of creating products for people are simply an example of real life, with its diversity, synergies, challenges, and clashes. Successful product teams, like productive communities, learn to exploit their differences to create products that deliver useful value, are a pleasure to look at and to use, and enhance people's lives.

The Organizational Structure of a Company

The traditional organizational structure of a company is that of a hierarchy. The company is divided into divisions, all reporting to the chief executive of the company, each reflecting either the product structure or its function: marketing, sales, and manufacturing. Inside each division, the company is further divided into structures that reflect, as before, either different products or subcomponents of products, or function. Eventually, at the bottom, are those who do the work.

Organizational structures have many virtues, but the major one is accountability. All employees know to whom they report, and orders are expected to flow from the top downward, with information and feedback coming from the bottom upward. This organizational structure optimizes a vertical flow of communication up and down the organization; it makes it difficult for horizontal communication to take place, for a horizontal path cuts across departments and divisions. As a result, the traditional organizational structure tends to pit one part of the company against the other; it does not facilitate harmonious interaction and cooperation. In large companies, different divisions are often located at considerable geographical separation from one another, making cooperation even more difficult.

Products, however, are usually produced horizontally across the structure. After all, to create a product requires the coordination and combination of many low-level people, from conception to shipping. This means that if the hierarchy of the company is drawn in a diagram from top to bottom, products are created and manufactured by the different groups structured horizontally across the bottom of the chart (see figure 10.2).

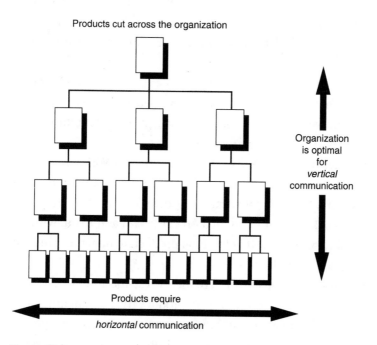

Figure 10.2

Traditional organization of a company is optimized for vertical communication. The traditional hierarchical structure of the company is not optimized for horizontal, cross-divisional interaction. Workers report to managers. Managers report to middle management, who report to the company executives. Information flows relatively smoothly up and down the organization. This organizational structure is idealized for command, for control, for accountability. It also provides clear reward structures and promotion paths. Hence, the traditional structure tends to pit one division against another. Moreover, the structure impedes horizontal communication, so it is less than optimal for the development of products.

A fundamental conflict exists between the traditional vertical organization of most companies and the functional, horizontal structure required to deliver products. Not only is the vertical organizational structure inimical to product development, but it leaves no place for functions that cut across the structure, functions such as usability, reliability, maintainability. It also makes design iteration difficult, because the organizational structure often leads to what has been called the "linear" or "waterfall" process of development. In this process, each stage passes on its results to the next, and once the pass-off has been made (once you are over the edge of the waterfall), there is no turning back.

The problem is that design is really an iterative process. Customers never know what they want until they have had a chance to use it, yet how can a company build it in the first place if they don't know what they want? Answer: Build it many times.

Iterative development means rapid prototyping. Work with the intended users, get an idea of their needs, do a quick mock-up in hours or days, and try it out. The tryouts can be done in many ways. The prototype can be quick diagrams sketched on cardboard and foam, with the customers asked to imagine it as the final product, to imagine using it in their actual place of work.

In similar ways manufacturing engineers test the initial designs to understand how difficult it would be to produce the item, maintenance engineers try to maintain them, and so on. The development process becomes a cooperative, iterative one. The initial stages of this development process often take longer and lead to more apparent frustration and complexity than the more common process, but the overall result is usually faster, less expensive, and superior.

This type of development is not a new idea. It is frequently written about, frequently practiced under many names, such as concurrent engineering, total quality control, virtual organization, and so on.[1]

This style of iterative, concurrent development isn't easy. To many people, it appears ponderous. It starts off with meetings and the collection of user data rather than with "real work." It requires people with very different backgrounds, skills, and points of view to work together smoothly and harmoniously. It messes up the traditional lines of authority of a company. At first, progress seems slow; there are few tangible, visible results of all those meetings with all those people. In the end, it is almost always faster and more efficient. Problems are addressed in the beginning, while fixes are still inexpensive. It is easy to change a design when it is still in prototype form, still done mainly with paper and foam or story boards. It is slow and expensive to change the design once it has been committed to production. Iterative, concurrent design is definitely the correct way to proceed, but it requires changing the normal pattern of doing work.

When the Reward Structure of a Company Gets in the Way

When it comes to working together, quite often two companies find it easier to form a smooth, harmonious relationship than two divisions of the same company. Why? Because of the reward structure.

In a company, individuals are rewarded and promoted on the basis of their performance. Higher-level employees might also receive part of their rewards based upon the performance of the business unit in which they work. All this sounds perfectly reasonable. In fact, it is specifically designed to get the best work out of each employee and to ensure that the employees work for the benefit of the business. If the business unit does well, the employees do well.

This reward structure has unintended consequences. The problem comes when a company has multiple business units, yet limited funds for bonuses or salary increases and limited positions available for promotion. The result is that employees are competing with one another for rewards rather than with competing companies.

Employees seek the path that is in their best interests. This is hardly a surprise, and in most businesses, that is what the reward structure is all about; it tries to arrange things so that the person's and the company's best interests are identical. Unfortunately, they aren't. Oftentimes, an employee's most feared competitor is the person in another division of the same company, for the two are competing for the same promotion, salary raise, or bonus. Most employees will act in their own best interest to do whatever it takes to improve the performance of their particular business unit, whether or not this is helpful to the competing business unit, even when this is not ideal for the company.

Suppose that during the course of designing a product, the members of the development group realize that a redesign would simplify manufacturing and maintenance, cutting the overall costs of the company and improving customer satisfaction. Do they dare do the redesign? Of course not. The redesign would not only delay the completion of their assigned tasks, but it is likely to cause them to exceed their budget. When it comes time for the performance review of the people in the group, they would suffer because they had gone over budget and been late with the product. No matter that as a result, the company saves money. The maintenance and manufacturing engineers, who might not even have been aware of the valiant efforts of the development team, would be promoted and rewarded because they had lower costs.

The only way out of this dilemma is to ensure total accountability: Rewards go to everyone in the process. The company has to be structured so that everyone is in it together. But this is not easy, not in a large company.

The reward structure has to be designed to take all critical variables into account. Thus, the charges for help lines, service, and maintenance ought to go to the development team. Perhaps service should report to developers, the better to ensure that customer complaints are tallied and understood by the developers, the better to take account of them in the next product release. So, too, with the costs of these after-sales ventures. Out of sight, out of mind, goes the folk saying, and when the costs of help desks, service, and maintenance are out of sight, they are apt to be forgotten by the development team.

It's critically important that all costs of a product be factored into the reward structure of the team, for, otherwise, those aspects will be slighted in favor of the features that do receive awards. In a similar way, it is important that all benefits be credited to the proper teams: product awards, increased sales, decreased service and maintenance, increased profit margins ought to be factored back to all who were involved.

Putting together a proper reward structure is a laborious and demanding proposition, but improper ones foster behavior that is not in the best interests of the company. The reward structure is perhaps the most important variable of all, more important than organizational structure. Set up the proper rewards and the appropriate behavior will follow.

Who Owns the Product?

"Marketing wants us to redesign the panel on the front of the product so that the features are more apparent in the store," a user-experience designer complained to me, "but our tests show that this also makes it harder to use. Now what do we do?"

This is a typical product tradeoff: in this case, ease of use versus sales appeal. Which point is correct? Both are legitimate. Both are correct. But rather than conflict, what is needed is an organization that works like a team, where everyone realizes that the goal is products that sell better, that work better, and that give pride of ownership to the users. Products that are hard to use do not provide joy to their owners. But products that don't sell in the first place don't even give ease of use a chance. How does one make this tradeoff?

Note that similar issues will arise at all stages of the product process. Engineering wants a new feature, but it will add time to the schedule and perhaps extra cost to the product. Marketing wants some new features. The user experience team wants to hide the little-used controls behind a panel to make the device look less intimidating and confusing, but marketing shows that customers purchase products because of all the features, even if they never use them once they get home. Each of these issues pits one part of the development team against the others. Each has proponents who think they own that part of the product, that they should be making the decision.

Who does own the development process? Who should make these decisions? If there is anyone in charge of the product development process, it is those involved with the business side of the company, often the product manager. The human-centered development team itself has to consist of a team of equals, all contributing their own areas of expertise. Conflicts must be resolved in an intelligent way, not by a power

The business case

Figure 10.3
Who owns the product? The foundation of the human-centered product development team is the business case for the product, and it is upon this foundation that
ownership of the product resides. Disputes among the development team almost
always result from the tensions inherent in product design; design is a series of tradeoffs where each aspect adds benefits and extracts costs. Conflicts are inevitable. Moreover, each party is correct, from their limited point of view. In the end, these tradeoffs
must be decided upon with reference to the business case for the product.

struggle. In most cases all parties are correct from their own point of
view. The resolution requires taking a higher-level look at the problem
and asking what decision is best for the business. What are the tradeoffs? How do they affect sales, customer satisfaction, the brand reputation and image, service, and maintenance? The decision is about
business, not design. It has to be decided by the senior managers, those
who hold the profit-and-loss accountability for the product.

Will a change increase functionality at a cost in schedule or price? It is
resolved by a business analysis: How much is the market willing to pay?
How important is a certain feature, both for the customer's needs and in
terms of differentiating the product from those of competitors? Will the
addition or deletion of the feature make a noticeable impact on sales? If
so, can a reasonable estimate be made of the impact? Is that impact
worth the investment?

Is there a tradeoff in usability versus perceived functions at the point
of sale? Can one estimate the increased sales that would result from an

emphasis on point-of-sales visibility? Can one estimate the impact on usability at the time of use? Will it lead to increased service calls? Will it make a significant difference in customer satisfaction that would impact word-of-mouth recommendations and future purchases by this customer?

Who owns the process? Nobody and everybody. The goal is better products for the consumer, better sales for the company—moreover, sales with fewer requirements for service and assistance. The goal is customers so satisfied and happy with the product that they become customers for life, buying more products, recommending the product, the company, and their experience to their friends and neighbors.

Who owns the product? Everyone. Who makes the decisions when there are conflicts? Management. That's what management is for: to resolve conflicts, to agree that all sides have valid points, and then to use its judgment to make business decisions. The end result is always a tradeoff. Engineering emphasizes different aspects of the product than does marketing, which in turn has different emphases from user experience. They are all valid, all important. The development process is one of continual tradeoffs: marketability, functionality, usability. That's life in the world of business.

Corporate Requirements for Human-Centered Development

What does it take to do human-centered development in a company? Total commitment. Just as quality control required the company to have such a commitment, so does human-centered development. Here is a list of the fundamental requirements:

- **Total corporate commitment**   From lowest level worker to highest level management.

- **Organizational changes**   So designers and the eventual users of the product interact.

- **A formal, human-centered product process**   The formal process puts the organizational stamp of approval on the process whereby technologists, marketing, and user experience specialists work together in a team, as equal colleagues, from the very inception of the product through the shipping and assessment of market reaction. The process should propose and be built around an iterative design and study process. And finally, it should extend beyond the final release date of the product in order to collect field data and user feedback on sales performance, repair and service requirements, usability and functionality that will drive the next release. This is where it is essential to listen to customers.

▪ **An engineering discipline of human-centered development** So that when user experience personnel are given the opportunity to work at all stages of the process, they are able to do so effectively, demonstrating their potential. This is especially difficult because the several disciplines that are involved have diverse backgrounds, which makes communication and a shared vision difficult. Nonetheless, a shared vision is essential.

Without the proper organizational structure, without the proper development process, even organizations with committed, dedicated individuals can fail.

What Is the Proper Organizational Home for User Experience?

One standard question about the appropriate organization of a user experience development group arises frequently: Should there be one central group, with members farmed out to the various projects of the company, or should the group be distributed, people hired to work wherever they are needed? Answer: It depends upon the company and its culture.

The development teams have to be a close-knit, working group. All the key development talent have to be together, working in concert. This is the point behind concurrent development. Do they have to belong to the same organization? No.

Having the development talent dispersed throughout the organization so that each individual works within and is assigned to the product group is my preferred way to get the work done. It's not the only possibility.

Having a central group has its value as well. Here, the group can have sufficient critical mass that it has all the skills required for UE development. Recall that I listed six critical skills for UE, a set unlikely to be found in a single individual. If UE is dispersed throughout the product groups, any individual group might not have all the necessary skill sets. In addition, not all skills are required at all phases of the project, so with dispersed membership, there are times when workers have nothing to do and times when they are overloaded. In a central group, there can be sufficient distribution over jobs to use all members effectively. And a central group allows for sharing of ideas and knowledge, so that the whole group continually grows in ability.

The central group has the difficulty of being removed from the action, being distant from the actual development activities. If there is a central group, then it is best to have it structured so that its members are assigned to particular projects, ideally moving to join those project teams.

There are other considerations as well. The social science and artistic talents of designers are not apt to be well understood by engineering or marketing organizations. When it comes to evaluations and promotions, the UE members can be at a disadvantage. Everyone can agree that they produce worthwhile results, but their skills are not apt to be rated as highly as that of the skilled engineering specialist. For this purpose it is often better to be judged by peers who truly understand the contributions, the amount of effort required, and the kind of knowledge and talent involved.

I favor matrixed or virtual organizations. Let the UE team be hired and work for individual projects, but let there be a virtual central organization, with regular staff meetings and development seminars. Ensure that the leader of the virtual team is involved in project reviews as well as in personnel assessment. The virtual team can also serve as a central clearinghouse of talent, so that if a UE talent is needed for a project, perhaps that person could be borrowed from another project.

Often, the correct organizational structure depends on the maturity of the company. When a company has just begun to incorporate UE, it probably needs a strong central group that reports high up in the hierarchy of the corporation, thereby giving the group visibility, authority, and clout. The UE personnel are then assigned to virtual or matrixed project teams. As the organization matures and begins to develop its understanding and appreciation for these skills, the need for a central team diminishes. In the end, it is probably not needed at all.

Many industrial design groups have opted for a strong central presence. Industrial and graphic design helps set the corporate identity, and the strong industrial design manager has always thought it important to have high visibility in the corporation, in many cases reporting directly to the CEO of the company. The reasoning is sound: This projects a strong message to everyone else that this is an area that is being taken seriously by the company. It's nice if you can get it, but it isn't realistic to expect UE to report at this level. Moreover, reporting to the corporate level of an organization can also be the kiss of death. It may isolate the group from the product teams where the work is being done. It tends to lead toward a police mentality—"we are the design police." Effective work is cooperative work. A complete disassociation from the groups with whom eventual cooperation is required is not a good thing.

The problems of effective management are formidable. Any solution seems to have as many weaknesses as strengths. The real problem is our biological heritage; we work well in small groups, groups of fewer than ten, probably around five. Add to this the biological/cultural drives for status and recognition and there are the fundamental bases for conflicts. Small companies can often work smoothly and harmoniously. But when a company has thousands of employees—and some companies have hundreds of thousands, while governments and armies can have millions—then there is no correct answer. Whatever organizational structure is used will be intricately convoluted and never right.

The most important thing to remember is that it is results that matter. No organizational structure is perfect; every one has its problems. In the end, what matters are results.

Human-Centered Development Is Not Enough

I'm obviously a strong advocate of user experience in product development, a strong supporter of human-centered development. But, let me emphasize, this is not enough.

"You keep saying ease of use is important," I am often admonished, "yet Apple had superior ease of use and it failed to become the market leader. How can you justify the emphasis on ease of use when you look at Apple's current position in the marketplace?" Good question. The story of Apple Computer is instructive.

The Macintosh initially did succeed. It had all three legs of the tripod in place: good technology, good marketing, and an excellent user experience, from industrial design through innovative ease of use. But, then, why did Apple as a company get into such difficulty? The answer is that although ease of use and high quality industrial design are important in the consumer market, it isn't enough. Human-centered development alone cannot save a product.

Note that two earlier products, The Xerox Star and the Apple Lisa, had great design and ease of use, but they both failed. They came before their time; the technology wasn't yet ready. As a result, they were too expensive, too slow, too limited in capability. They were easy to use, but there wasn't much they could do.

The Apple Macintosh overcame these problems. Not only was it an elegant, human-centered development, but it came equipped with a set of useful programming applications, a printer that produced a pretty close reproduction of what was visible on the screen, and a price that, although high, was within the range of millions of customers. The Macintosh succeeded for almost ten years. That's a long time in this business.

In the long run, Apple failed because it chose a flawed marketing strategy. Oh, yes, the tactical execution was superb, so Apple enjoyed an effective campaign, clever advertisements, and a quick capturing of brand recognition. But the strategy achieved short-term gains at the expense of long-term viability.

Apple positioned itself as the maverick, the computer "for the rest of us." That is, Apple wanted nothing to do with traditional business, with the world of official forms and procedures, of the routine working day with its rules and regulations. Apple was for the creative thinkers of society: artists, writers, students, youth. Bad idea. Because Apple shunned the world of business while IBM courted it, the IBM PC and its spreadsheet, Lotus 1–2–3, soon dominated that marketplace. The name "IBM" made the small, personal computer legitimate in the eyes of business in a way that Apple could never do.

Note that for any comparison of the products, Macintosh was far superior. The IBM PC was limited in power, complex, and difficult to learn. Its operating system, DOS, was rudimentary, and quirky. The Apple Macintosh was elegant, powerful and easy to learn. It had a modern operating system. It had a graphical user interface, with windows, keyboard, and mouse, and it could display and print graphics and a variety of fonts and styles. DOS had just the keyboard and commands that had to be memorized or, more often than not, looked up in a book. Printing graphics was a chore, as was displaying them on the screen. The DOS system had lots of manuals, and they had to be used; with the Macintosh, you never had to use the manual.

So what? DOS and the IBM PC were good enough to serve the needs of the business community. Apple restricted itself to the home, school, and the graphic arts industry. For a while, these were large enough to sustain the company. But by shunning business, Apple had taken itself out of the market over the long run.

The marketplace positioning of Apple versus IBM was one of the factors in Apple's fall from grace. The Apple II was the first successful personal computer, so it initially had the benefits that come from being first. But IBM's courtship of industry led to its dominance in the business world. Not only did Apple not care, it bragged about the fact that it was not used in business.

Remember the argument about substitutable and nonsubstitutable goods? The market for nonsubstitutable goods leads to a winner-take-all business situation. Operating systems are nonsubstitutable goods. At first, the difference in infrastructures didn't matter, because the IBM PC dominated in the business market whereas the Apple II dominated within the home and educational markets. However, in the decades that followed, these different markets began to merge. People wanted the same computers at home as they used at work so they could bring their work home. Many schools felt it was their responsibility to use whatever the dominant system was for industry, whether or not this was appropriate for education. Because it is difficult for a company, school or household to cope with incompatible, conflicting operating systems, this tended to push the market toward one system, not on the basis of product superiority, but rather on the basis of convenience. Hence the domination of Microsoft's DOS over the Apple II and later, the Macintosh operating system. The domination had its roots in those early days, and it has grown ever since. Today, decades later, the domination is almost complete, despite the dramatic changes in computer equipment since that time, despite that, in those early days, the Apple Macintosh operating system was greatly superior to that of DOS.

When Apple introduced the Macintosh computer, it emphasized the virtues of user experience. The Macintosh was well developed from every point of view: superb technology, good industrial design, an excellent marketing campaign, and the best user experience in the business. It truly was easy to use—the average user never had to read the manuals. The Macintosh developed a loyal following. It did become the machine of choice for "the rest of us," for the nonbusiness world, just as the advertising proclaimed. For a long time, Apple was able to grow rapidly and profitably by exploiting its unrivaled core competency of user experience. Apple charged a high price for its machines, but its customers were willing to make sacrifices to buy them; nothing else offered such usability and such emphasis on design, on graphical displays. Macintosh was especially popular in the school systems, among university students and faculty, and in the worlds of graphic arts, entertainment, and desktop publishing. Emphasis on design paid off.

Business wants standards before elegance, and for historical reasons they had standardized on the IBM PC and, therefore, Microsoft DOS. Microsoft, meanwhile, understood the advantages of the Macintosh user experience, and therefore, after numerous efforts, brought out a successful graphical user interface system of its own: Windows. By the fourth go-around, Microsoft had a successful product, Windows 95. Now, the advantage of the Macintosh was much diminished; add to this the onslaught of Microsoft's extensive marketing campaign and the desire of computer users to have a single standard infrastructure, and soon the positive feedback cycle took hold. More companies developed software products for Windows than for Macintosh. As a result, even users who preferred their Macintosh felt compelled to switch to Windows in order to get the full range of products. And the more people that switched, the more other software companies started making Windows products and stopped making Macintosh ones. Eventually the result was the dominance of a market by a single standard.

Apple showed that superior user experience can make a difference, but that this alone isn't sufficient. Apple had technological superiority as well, but two legs of the tripod will not keep it standing: It needs all three legs. Apple's marketing leg emphasized the minority status of its customers. In fact, its marketing slogan, "The computer for the rest of us," glorified the fact that it was not meant to be the solution for everyone. It clearly implied that Apple intended to occupy a privileged minority position. A healthy minority to be sure, but a minority nonetheless. This is a bad idea when it comes to operating systems. When you have a nonsubstitutable good you need to be the dominant player. This requires careful attention to the market, careful and continued leadership to ensure that yours is the most popular system. Apple failed to do this.

In the world of high technology, any technical advantages are shortlived; others will soon catch up. The race is to the swift, but even the swift can lose if they don't always keep running. Remember Aesop's fable: This is how the tortoise beat the hare.

Nothing Worthwhile Is Easy

Remember Thomas Edison? The technologies on which he founded his numerous companies were usually first and best. He understood the importance of systems analysis and product structure. He did everything right except for one thing: He failed to understand his customers. Many of Edison's companies failed.

In infrastructure products, market share is what matters. The market buys things based on availability, functionality, price, and marketing images. The technology need only be "good enough."

Today, in the world of high technology, we are victims of our own success. We have let technology lead the way, pushing ever harder to newer, faster, and more powerful systems, with nary a moment to rest, contemplate, and reflect upon why, how, and for whom all this energy has been expended. In the process, although we have made many wonderful technological leaps, we have left humanity behind. Much of humanity is estranged from the technology, wary of it, fearful of it, and frightened of the future. These same emotions are increasingly common even among those of us who are technologically astute, who nominally are both friends and creators. Technology for the sake of technology is not an appropriate way to proceed.

There is a better way. It is possible to build systems that relate to people, that are task-centered, human-centered. But it requires high-technology businesses to change the way they do things, to move to simpler technologies that are a better match with people's activities. It requires a change to emphasize the human needs, to emphasize development for people. Such a change will not come effortlessly. It requires a new process for product development, one that involves the social side of development as much as the engineering and marketing sides. It requires bringing a new discipline—user experience—to the development table. And it requires that this new discipline live up to the challenges before it.

The current infrastructure for personal computers has outlived its usefulness. Although it was well designed for the problems and technology of the 1980s, it no longer works when faced with the problems and technologies of the twenty-first century. Moreover, the technology of the personal computer gets more problematic every year.

The only way out is through a break with tradition to a technology that becomes invisible, a disruptive technology that focuses on simplicity, pride of ownership, joy of use: the result of a human-centered development philosophy. The path to human-centered development will require changing some long-honored habitual ways of doing business. It requires restructuring the product process and reorganizing the company, causing temporary upheaval for everyone. The transformation is demanding because it involves people, organizations, and culture. But the outcome is worthy. Along this path lies a new attitude of increased acceptance of technology, a technology that is invisible and thoroughly integrated into tools for the tasks and activities people wish to perform. Nothing worthwhile is easy.

11
Disruptive Technologies

Years ago I took a scuba diving course at my university. This was an advanced course, primarily for professionals, being taught at the Scripps Institution for Oceanography in La Jolla, California. One day, the instructor taught us about ocean currents. He lectured about how they were generated and illustrated what they looked like with rough sketches on the blackboard. We were told about various riptides, including the dreaded undertow and why it need not be feared, and we were told what to do if we found ourselves in one. Then we went outside the classroom to stand on the cliff overlooking the beach where we could spot the riptides, so we would know what they looked like firsthand. There was a big rip right on the north side of the pier. Most of us were bored with this part of the course. We were all experienced swimmers and familiar with rips. The surfers even sought them out, for the fastest way to get from the beach to beyond the breaking waves was to find a riptide and let it pull you out to sea.

A few days later we had an ocean swimming test. This was January, and even in Southern California the water was cold. We were supposed to enter the water just south of the pier, swim out through the breaking waves, around the pier, and back in to the beach. I swam to the end of the pier, around to the right, and headed back to shore. By then I was cold and tired. I looked up at the pier as I swam and noticed that I wasn't making much progress, so I increased my efforts. "I really am tired," I thought to myself, "look how slowly I'm swimming." Nobody else was around me—was I going to be the last one in? I swam even harder. The harder I swam, the more tired I got, tired and cold. I began to worry.

I finally stopped swimming and looked around. The rest of the class was all back on land. And there, on the shore, was the instructor looking at me, laughing. He pointed to his right. "You're in a rip," he shouted, "swim to your left."

Oh. No wonder I wasn't making any progress. No wonder that while I stopped swimming I was moving backward, out to sea. After all those lessons I had failed to recognize the riptide from inside. I only understood it sketched on a blackboard, or looking down on it from above, from the top of the cliff. I quickly began to swim parallel to the beach for a short distance, then turned and swam to land. Simple, once you knew what was happening. How many people have succumbed because they fought hard against the riptide until they drowned, exhausted by the struggle, chilled by the cold water? Turn at right angles and the path is smooth. A few feet and you are clear.

Disruptive Technologies

Most technological industries pass through many generations. Most are incremental, offering better technologies for doing the same work within the old paradigm. Some are disruptive, changing the entire course of the industry. Disruptive, revolutionary changes are the ones that change people's lives, and these are the changes most difficult for companies to cope with. Change is never easy from within an industry. After all, any industry has come to believe in itself, for that is how it has managed to succeed. Any new approaches will start off as small, simple, and weak. Such is the case with all new technological developments, with what have come to be called *disruptive technologies*.[1]

The phonograph moved from cylinders to discs, from acoustic machines to electronic ones with vacuum-tube amplifiers and electric motors. It standardized on 78 rpm platters. Then it changed to 33 1/3 rpm and 45 rpm, with an initial, almost deadly fight between these last two "standards" until each found its own niche in the market. With time the phonograph industry changed so dramatically that today we don't even call it by that name; today it is the recording industry, and the technology is tape and various forms of compact disc: CD, mini-CD, DVD. All of these changes were incremental, for they didn't change the basic nature of the business.

The radio was disruptive and revolutionary: It almost killed the phonograph industry. Before radio, the only way people could listen in their home to musicians and other performers was with the phonograph and as a result, the phonograph could be found in nearly every home. But with radio, people could hear concerts, news, and entertainment for hours on end—free. The phonograph industry went into a massive decline.

How did the phonograph industry react when the radio was first introduced? Did it take note of the threat and attempt to counteract it? No. It should have entered the radio business, realizing that its real function was entertainment, with the technology being secondary. Not only did it not fight the threat, it didn't even notice it. Thomas Edison said that as far as he could tell, the radio had "no commercial future."

Such responses to revolutionary, disruptive technologies are typical. It's possible to form a large collection of such statements. Here are some:[2]

- Edison turned down the radio: "No commercial future."

- Western Union turned down the telephone: "It will never be more than a toy. . . . This 'telephone' has too many shortcomings to be seriously considered as a means of communication. The device is inherently of no value to us." (Western Union internal memo, 1876.)

- In the early 1920s, David Sarnoff urged his associates to invest in radio. They responded that "the wireless music box has no imaginable commercial value. Who would pay for a message sent to nobody in particular?" Sarnoff went on to head RCA, which then eventually bought out the major phonograph company, Victor.

- Thomas J. Watson, Sr., founder and head of IBM, turned down the computer (but Watson, Jr., persisted).

- The use of computers in business was thought to be a fad. In 1957, an editor of business books for the publisher Prentice Hall said "I have traveled the length and breadth of this country and talked with the best people, and I can assure you that data processing is a fad that won't last out the year."

- What is the future of computers? "There is no reason anyone would want a computer in their home," said Ken Olson, president, chairman and founder of Digital Equipment Corp., in 1977.

To be fair to Ken Olson, about thirty years ago I spent an evening with some very prominent computer scientists trying to figure out why people would ever want computers in their homes. All of us, me included, failed to find a convincing reason. We, of course, wanted them, but we were technologists. We couldn't think of why the average person would use them. Among the many things we failed to think about were games. As for the internet, sure, we used it for sharing computer programs, scientific data, writing papers, and sending email, but what did that have to do with the average person? (This was long before the advent of graphical browsers; we used such things as telnet, command languages, and FTP—today all neatly hidden behind the friendly pictures and links of the graphical browser.)

- Kodak turned down Land's Polaroid camera (and later paid Polaroid multiple millions for copying their patents).

- Kodak turned down the Xerox copier.

- Apple Computer turned down the Mosaic internet browser, after helping pay for its development at the University of Illinois Supercomputer Center. It decided there was no commercial value.

- Steve Jobs and Steve Wozniak took their home-built computer to Hewlett-Packard to try to convince them to make it into a product. HP turned them down, so, instead, they started their own company: Apple Computer.

- "Heavier-than-air flying machines are impossible," said Lord Kelvin, president of the Royal Society, in 1895. This, mind you, is the famous Lord Kelvin after whom the Kelvin temperature scale is named and who, in 1866, supervised the laying of a transatlantic cable.

Clayton Christensen has examined how established companies fail to take new disruptive technologies seriously. An example from his book is instructive.[3] In the early days of the steam shovel, the goal was to move as much earth as possible, to dig big, deep holes for things such as mining and construction excavation. The industry made the transition from steam engines to gasoline and diesel engines and then to electric engines. Each transition was a major change for the companies, but each was incremental in nature. The basic design of the shovel and the basic nature of the work did not have to change. These are sustaining changes, not disruptive ones.

When hydraulically controlled machines were introduced into the excavation industry, they were seen as toys. They did not have the power or reliability required for the massive tasks of excavating huge mineshafts. They did simplify the control problem; hydraulics did not require the extensive cable networks of the cable-actuated systems, so they were potentially more reliable and easier to maintain. Still, their performance was so inferior that the thirty cable-activated excavator companies active in the 1950s chose to ignore hydraulics.

Hydraulically controlled machines were disruptive to the established business. New companies recognized that there was a new marketplace: small, flexible machines that could dig a trench from the backyard of a home to the street for sewer or water lines, or that could maneuver inside of a building to dig holes. They developed an entirely new digger—the backhoe—for a market that seemed entirely unrelated to that of the large excavators—digging small holes and trenches for small contractors. At first, this market was inconsequential, so the amount of money involved was not enough to interest the large companies. But the market developed. It grew bigger. Hydraulically operated machines got better. They started to move into the domain of the larger machines. By the time the major companies recognized the threat, it was too late. Of the thirty companies that existed in the 1950s, only three remain today. The industry is dominated by companies that did not then exist.

A number of relevant factors dissuade existing companies from taking new technologies seriously:

- New technologies usually are initially inferior to the existing ones.

- Large companies require large business markets. A ten-billion-dollar-a-year company isn't interested in investing in small markets. After all, if it wants to grow by 10 percent in a year (and most high-technology companies aim for a larger figure than that), it has to grow by a billion dollars. No new business concept starts off anywhere near that size. New technologies, even if considered viable, are just not important enough to be of interest to established companies; they are usually relevant only to a small market. The common way of putting it is "that's just a toy." That's what the mainframe and mini-computer manufacturers said about the first personal computers, such as the Apple II. They were correct at the time.

- Any logical analysis of the return on investment shows that spending a few million dollars on improving the existing products will bring a greater return than the same funds spent on trying to design and develop new products for an unknown market. The size of the early market for new technologies is small, composed of the early adopters and niche arenas where the virtues of the new technology outweigh the disadvantages. The majority of consumers are late adopters, notoriously slow about accepting new technologies.

- Most divisions of a company are operated on a profit-and-loss basis, usually measured quarterly, sometimes yearly. The manager of the division is rewarded by how much of a profit is made. If some resources are diverted to start a new enterprise, even one that might someday be successful, it can only take away from the immediate profitability, thereby reducing the reward, the salary, the bonus, and the promotion possibilities for the current manager.

- New products often cut across divisions, but it is difficult to get divisions of a company to coordinate their efforts. This is especially true if one is starting an operation that might harm another. Why should a division let another in the same company bring out a product that it thinks would harm its sales? Although total sales of the two divisions might be larger than sales of either one alone, each probably loses some sales to the other, and most managers are rewarded on the profit and loss statement for their division, not for how well their individual sacrifice might have aided the company. The reward, bonus, and promotion policies of most companies penalize altruistic behavior, even when the altruism is beneficial to the company as a whole. It is often easier to get two companies to work together than two divisions within the same company. The managers from the different companies are not competing for the same promotions, raises, or bonus pools. If the joint enterprise excels, both companies win.

- A gravity well is exerted by the existing product stream. Given that the new technology is apt to be inferior to the established one, especially in the early days of its development, any new product that looks anything like the existing one will be unfavorably compared with it. Even if the new product is intended for a new domain, if it looks like the old one it will be judged by the same criteria, and invariably it will be found lacking. This is the gravity well trap: The old product sucks the new one within its gravity field and then destroys it.

Information Appliances as a Disruptive Technology

Information appliances are a disruptive technology. As such, their introduction is apt to be painful, difficult, and, at first, unsuccessful. The first appliances are apt to be underpowered and overpriced, incapable of producing the results required by the consumer. Worse, the very same functions will be available from existing technologies at lower cost and higher performance.

New disruptive technologies always have this property, yet eventually they not only succeed, they dominate. The new technology is never quite the same as the existing one, and in the differences lie the benefits. The best strategy is to deploy the new technology in those specialty areas where the virtues far outweigh the cost. After they have succeeded in these small areas, they can pick off other small areas—niches—one by one, then as the underlying technology matures, they can slowly start taking on mainstream applications.

This is how Christensen describes the events for the industries of small disk drives and hydraulic digging machines.[4] The new, disruptive products got started by capturing one niche opportunity after another. In this way they could start making a small profit early, while simultaneously gaining valuable market experience, customer support, and brand recognition. In these cases, the virtues of the disruptive devices lay in their smaller sizes, allowing them to be used in numerous situations where the earlier technologies of large disk drives and steam shovels could not be. Their value was so high in these special situations that they readily overcame their limited performance.

The strategy is to cover the niche markets thoroughly, while developing the technology to the point where its costs and performance migrate to a satisfactory level for other markets. Eventually, the technology will be sufficient for the average consumer. Meanwhile, the company that builds through specialty markets has gained considerable experience, has developed a brand reputation, and has avoided losing money. The strategy should first target the early adopters, those who need the virtues of the technology and are willing to pay more and suffer some inconvenience to get it. It is inadvisable to deploy an early technology on the consumer market, for this is made up of late adopters, who will not purchase until they are assured of convenience and economy.

Disruptive technologies are always new ones, starting off at the early adopter side of the technology life-cycle (figure 2.4, page 35). The technology is insufficient for most customers, the market small. These new technologies are never ready for the mass market. They are too expensive, their abilities too limited; in comparison with existing technologies, they are toys, and expensive ones at that. This is why it is best to focus upon the unique properties of the new, disruptive technologies and market them to those who need that uniqueness. Market first to the niches, then expand.

The rule that it would be wise to start with specialized markets before moving on to the consumer is not common sense to most companies; they prefer to jump immediately to the mass market. Some companies have succeeded by going directly for the consumer market, but only at great cost; they had to invest a large amount of money and wait many years to see their gamble pay off. This is what RCA did with color television. Most companies don't have enough capital or patience to invest for such a long period. The approach via specialized markets conserves capital while advancing the technology and the product.

It is difficult for a company to invest in a disruptive technology when it already has successful products using the existing technologies. In fact, it is difficult for any large company to take disruptive technologies seriously. Large companies need huge successes in order to grow, often billion-dollar opportunities. On this scale, niche markets seem insignificant. Any expenditure of funds aimed at starting the new, small, doubtful industry seems better spent, and guaranteed of greater reward, on the existing product lines. Even if a company invests in the new technology, as soon as it encounters financial difficulty in its main market it is apt to borrow funds from the new enterprise to save the existing ones. Finally, even if a new disruptive technology gets established and shows signs of success, the managers of the divisions producing the existing products may feel threatened and kill off the new devices in order to protect their own business sectors.

The only way to get new technologies going within a large company is to protect them from the entrenched interests of market size, market competition, and financial needs. This can be done only if it is put into a new division, with no monetary or managerial ties to existing ones. This is difficult for large companies, which is one reason so many disruptive technologies come from small, fledgling companies for whom sales into a niche market represents huge success and who have no existing industry to protect or that can drain away funds.

Bower and Christensen put it this way:

Managers must beware of ignoring new technologies that don't initially meet the needs of their mainstream customers. None of the established leaders in the disk-drive industry learned from the experiences of those that fell before them. Seagate paid the price for allowing start-ups to lead the way into emerging markets. Small, hungry organizations are good at agilely changing product and market strategies. Every company that has tried to manage mainstream and disruptive businesses within a single organization has failed. In order that it may live, a corporation must be willing to see business units die.[5]

Information appliances are a disruptive industry. Each appliance is relatively expensive, yet inferior compared to the broad range of capabilities offered by existing devices. In the case of information appliances, the major competitor is the personal computer.

Even today, in their youthful, primitive state, information appliances have their attractions. They are simpler and easier to use than the computer. Their physical shapes, form, and interaction styles are tuned to fit the task. The required electronics and computer hardware and software can be embedded within the devices where they are invisible.

Information appliances offer ease of use, convenience, and simplicity. They offer to simplify life. Although expensive and limited in power today, with time they will improve in performance and decrease in cost. They will become more effective. And when there is a variety available that can communicate with one another, their power will grow rapidly. Today information appliances are disruptive. In time they will become commonplace and taken for granted. Information appliances are on the way.

Why It's Hard to See the World from Inside a Company

Now we see why it is so difficult for computer companies to change, so difficult for them to move away from the computer toward other approaches. Mind you, the computer industry understands the problems and the challenges. It understands the alternatives as well, and many of its leaders believe that information appliances are inevitable. But the industry is stuck in the riptide of technology. It struggles harder and harder to compete, but it can't figure out how to escape; it is too closely involved. And just as I suffered from cold and fatigue, it suffers from the pressures of competition and the dreaded quarterly earnings report. Nobody has time to think, nobody has time to plan. New products are due every six months. If you slow down, your competition will leap ahead of you. The computer industry thinks that the way to escape is to swim even harder, to bring out more and more products that push the technology envelope, that are cheaper, faster, more powerful.

In the scuba class there was an instructor to guide us, a knowledgeable diver who deliberately led his class into a riptide so that we would all experience it from within while we were being watched, while it was safe to learn from the experience. Now when I go swimming and find myself in a rip, I laugh and swim parallel to the shore for a bit. I know what to do. If only the computer industry had such a wise instructor.

Alas, the computer industry is instructed by technology addicts, people themselves caught going against the rip. "Work harder," they call out. "Get more computer power, more speed, more memory." No, when you are caught in a never-ending fight for survival against a powerful tide, the solution is to relax and move at right angles to the current. Don't try to overpower the problem, learn to bypass it. The problem is that while you are caught in the situation, the remedy seems counterintuitive. Worse, in those initial stages of moving at right angles, you will also slip backward. No technology company wants to retreat; no stockholder would allow a company to do that for a few quarters. Everyone would rather drown.

History is filled with examples of old trades continuing in their set ways, failing to see the changes happening around them. Even when they noticed the disruptive technologies, even when they realized that the traditional way of doing business was threatened, the established trades commonly responded by staying on the same path. They did not see any advantages to change. The new methods moved into unexplored territory, and every analysis showed it to be dark, forbidding, and not nearly as profitable as the current business.

Carriage makers persisted long after the horseless carriage was catching on with the population. Some adapted by making bodies for the new automobiles, but most did not. They kept making better and better carriages. And they argued that these newfangled machines were dangerous. Horses were dependable and safe; the new horseless carriages were neither. A horse could find its way safely home even if the driver was inattentive or lost. With a car, an inattentive driver is a dangerous driver. Their argument was correct, but irrelevant. You don't see very many carriage makers around anymore.

It is not unusual that one established business may fail to see the threat from some other, often inferior new enterprise. Major examples can be found by looking at the history of transportation.

- In the past, most shipping within a country was through riverways and canals. The boat shipping industry minimized the importance of railroads, for early trains were expensive, noisy, and smoky, with limited carrying capacity. The laying of rails was a tremendously expensive operation. Railroads did not appear to be competitive with boat shipping.

- In similar fashion, the railroad industry minimized the importance of airplanes, for airplanes were very expensive, with even more limited capacity than trains. They were also dangerous. Why would passengers risk discomfort and even their lives on an airplane when they could travel in luxury aboard a train, complete with dining cars and bedrooms?

- A similar story was told about the relevance of the airplane to ocean travel. Luxury passenger ships plied the waters. Airplanes could barely make it across the Atlantic and had even more difficulty over the Pacific. Airplanes might be fine for the brave few who had to get where they were going quickly, but the rest would take the ships or, on land, railroads.

- Those in the radio industry minimized the importance of television, for radio was firmly entrenched and television sets expensive, unreliable, and difficult to use. The movie industry scoffed at TV, and early films invariably made fun of it by showing sets with tiny screens and a noisy, unstable picture. That is, of course, when they deigned to show them at all. How could small, fuzzy, black-and-white pictures compete with the glamour of large-screen images, in color, with full sound, viewed in a glorious, palatial theater?

- The typewriter industry ignored the computer industry and the advent of word processors in general purpose personal computers.

With the benefit of hindsight it is easy to scoff at the carriage makers, or the early telegraph company officials who thought the telephone was a toy, or the camera company that said a Xerox copier was impractical, but at the time these all seemed like reasonable arguments. Most of the proposed new ideas that established companies rejected should have been rejected. Today we only hear about the few that turned out to be successes, in most cases only after a large infusion of money, time, and resources. We don't hear about all those equally good-sounding ideas that never succeeded.

When Customers Are Wrong

I was flying back from a computer industry trade show when some of my company's customers on board the airplane recognized me. "What a disappointing show," they complained.

"Why?" I asked.

"Because there wasn't any neat, new technology," they replied.

Sigh: That's the problem. Our customers demand exactly the wrong thing from us. They won't let us change. Problem is, these are the wrong customers. And they are wrong about what is important.

Our best customers think that computers are about new technology. In my opinion, computers should be about the development of good tools that help us get some work done, simply, efficiently, and with enjoyment. To my mind, the best computer is one that is hardly noticed; we should notice our tools only when they give trouble. For far too many of our most vocal customers, the pleasure comes from the computer itself, and when there are problems, they take pride in their ability to overcome them.

Why are our customers wrong? Simple: Our current customers are the technology addicts, the early adopters. These are the people for whom technology is its own reward, or perhaps those whose need for the technology is so strong that they overlook all other issues. When a company tries to make the transition from technology-driven products into the world of mass-marketed consumer products, its current customers will be from the world of technologists. These are precisely the wrong people to ask how best to attract the new breed of customer, the vast majority of people who fear technology, who are conservative, who want products only when they are convinced that they will get value for their money, value without pain.

What is wrong with the computer industry? It's caught in a technology trap. It grew up in an era when the technology was never quite sufficient for the demands placed upon it. Engineers ruled the day, and the customers clamored for more and more technology, more and more features. But today, the industry is fifty years old. It has reached maturity. The technology is far more than sufficient for the needs of most people. Still, the industry cannot change its ways. It feels that the key to success is bringing out new and fancy technology. Unfortunately, customers have been led to think the same.

At all the major trade shows the goal is to introduce neat, cool technology. The newspaper columnists expect it, the computer magazine writers expect it, and even the average consumer has come to expect it. If a company dared to bring out a simplified, easier-to-use system, it would be panned in the trade press. "Why, look how underpowered it is," the columnist would sneer, "it lacks so many critical features that we have all come to take for granted." Companies are stuck in the feature-comparison list. The mindset of the computer industry is mired in the past, in the era of technology-driven products.

If things are so bad, why do customers buy today's computers? For several reasons. In the workplace, they have no choice. Their employers buy them; they have indeed become essential to today's work environment. Why do they buy them for themselves and their families? One, they do want the benefits of the information age, and even though they dislike and even fear the technology they have no choice. Two, they want to take work home, so they need the same computing environment at home as they have at the office. Three, they want them for their children, for educational purposes. And four, they buy them out of guilt and envy, to keep up with their neighbors. But my visits to the homes of these customers have convinced me they are not happy; they often do not like what they have bought. They suffer quietly, usually blaming themselves for their perceived lack of technical skills. Moreover, these customers are not likely to attend the industry trade shows, so they are not the ones who talk to our marketing staff, engineers, or executives.

With its complacency and narcissism, the computer industry reminds me of the carriage makers. After all, the computer industry has grown up catering to the technologically sophisticated. Everyday users have been made to feel inferior, cowered into submission. They don't clamor for a change because they feel that the problems they face are the result of their own inadequacies.

Is fancy new technology wrong? Am I saying we should not listen to our customers? How can I say our customers are wrong? Isn't *not* listening to his customers the mistake that Thomas Edison made?

Yes, we should not always listen to our customers. Yes, I think our customers can be wrong in what they say. And no, this is not the same mistake that Edison made. Our customers are loyalists; they will follow us to our death beds, which is exactly the problem. The bulk of our customers are technology enthusiasts, a small percentage of the world's population. We should be designing products for that vast, large crowd of people who don't use computers or who do only to the extent that they are forced to. These people are not the ones clamoring for new technology. These people are conservative, they are skeptical. They want technology that is useful, that provides value. These are our future customers. These are the people we should listen to.

Don't Talk Only with Your Customers—Talk with Your Noncustomers

It is very natural to want to talk to one's customers. And who better to talk to than your most satisfied customers? Ask them for advice, keep them happy, keep them buying more of your products. It is always cheaper to sell a new product to an established, satisfied customer than to try to convert a new one. Maintaining a successful, warm, supportive relationship with customers is essential for success. But this is not enough. It is essential to understand your noncustomers.

If you have a product that you want to sell to the world, don't talk only to your customers, especially your most satisfied ones. Talk to those who are having problems and to those who don't buy your product at all.

Make a product for your loyal followers and you are stuck in a rut. Make a product that appeals to those who do not buy today and you are on to something. These people only want to use new technology when it truly benefits them, when the benefits far exceed the costs and when they will have to exert minimum effort to use it.

This is such an important issue, let me highlight it:

*It is always more important to talk to those who are not buying your product than those who are. It is always more important to talk to those who buy a product **and** complain than those who buy and are satisfied. There are always far more people in the world who do not buy a product than who do. Even if a product is the market leader with 100 percent market share, there are still more people outside the market than within it. The future sales potential lies with those who today are not customers, not with those who are satisfied ones.*

There is a huge chasm between people who first buy a product just because it's a new technology and the vast majority of folks who wait until it helps them in their lives. Technology companies sell to that first group; successful companies learn how to sell to that second group. Big difference. Someone ought to write a book[6] explaining the differences. Someone did: Geoffrey Moore. In fact, he wrote two books, both of which should be required reading: *Crossing the Chasm* and *Inside the Tornado*. Someone ought to write a book explaining why companies are so resistant to change, why asking the existing customers what they want is a recipe for failure. Someone did: Clayton Christensen, *The Innovator's Dilemma: When New Technologies Cause Great Firms to Fail*. Now someone ought to write a book explaining why despite the best will in the world, despite the fact that the executives of companies have read these books and understood the lessons, they still fail. Well, part of that lesson is in this book.

12

A World of Information Appliances

The PC is maturing from a universally adaptable, "one-size-fits-all" system into a wide range of targeted appliances designed to solve specific user applications.
— Gordon Moore, cofounder and chairman emeritus, Intel Corporation.[1]

Whether we will have information appliances is not in doubt; they already exist and their number is increasing. The only questions are *when* and *how*, not *if*. This book presents a scenario for *how;* the *when* depends upon the congruence of the multiple unknowns that propel business and industry.

The current business model of the computer industry is not particularly attractive. Most computer manufacturers are engaged in a constant struggle to make a profit. Because the technology has matured, almost anyone can manufacture a computer today. In fact, each of us can put our own computer together. All that is necessary is to visit an electronics store, whether in person, by catalog, or over the internet, and pick a suitable cabinet and power supply, cpu card, memory, hard drive, modem, and one or two other components and just plug them all together. The only tool that is required is a screwdriver. Buy a software package and you are in business. Indeed, many of the largest computer sellers do little more themselves; they scout out the lowest-cost manufacturer of each component from around the world, find some low-cost location in which to assemble the parts, and voila! a computer. All that distinguishes some brands from others is the name that is printed on the cabinet.

In this business, prices are extremely competitive, relentlessly being driven lower and lower. Moreover, there is little any manufacturer can do to distinguish its wares from the competition. The software is rigidly controlled by Microsoft, and even if a particular brand manages to add some innovative feature this year, Microsoft is apt to incorporate it into the Windows operating system next year, ending that means of differentiation. In a similar way Intel controls the hardware, setting the standards that all manufacturers are forced to follow. Both hardware and software are nonsubstitutable goods, and each is dominated by a single company; deviant producers cannot survive for long.

But even though the world of personal computers is a frustratingly difficult business proposition, and even though the world of information appliances has begun and new products beckon, the thought of change can be frightening. Information appliances bring their own sets of challenges. Even the bold and adventurous hesitate to take the plunge. Why? The reasons are numerous. Information appliances are as yet an unproved business. Their success requires cooperative agreements about communication standards, agreements that do not yet exist. Historically, standards take considerable time to develop. Moreover, because appliances are consumer items, they will have to sell for relatively small amounts of money, which translates into little profit from each sale.

Finally, the technology itself is not quite ready; the most critical technologies for information appliances are flat-screen displays, batteries, and wireless communication, all problem areas in today's world of information technology. All three areas are making remarkable progress, all are expected to be at acceptable levels of price and performance "real soon now," but at the moment they are too expensive for consumer products.

No wonder that everyone is jittery. No wonder that even the most advanced companies see virtue in waiting. If you are a small, new company, there is nothing to lose in entering the information appliance market. Your costs are low, with no historical base of customers and products that require continued support. Even a relatively small profit is satisfying. If you are a large company, your overhead costs are high. There is a large existing base of customers and products that must be supported. Moreover, the short-term financial story always argues against new enterprises. That is, the same money that is proposed to be spent on a new fledgling venture brings a higher short-term return if invested in the existing business.

Large established companies have another reason to hold back: They don't have to be first to win. A small company has to be first to get its name before the public, to position itself in the new business and to establish brand recognition. The large companies can hold back, waiting and watching. Let the small companies take the risk, let them establish the field. Then, the large companies can pick and choose, avoiding the areas that didn't seem to work, moving afterward into those product areas that do seem to be successful. Buy out the successful, but still struggling smaller companies. Buy them or compete with them. Even if a large company starts into a new area years after it has been established, its name and brand reputation allow it instant credibility. It's a hard world out there; let the small players take the risks and establish the field, then walk in and take over. Three cheers for capitalism.

The preceding scenario depicts the strategy that many large, successful companies have followed for years. But those who attempt it should be aware that the risk is high. Success requires that all those new entrants be small and struggling, that when they start to be successful, it will be possible to move into the field and dominate. History shows that it doesn't always work that way.

Christensen's analyses of disruptive technologies demonstrate that time after time, big companies ignore new technologies for too long a period.[2] He documents a depressing list of companies and industries that tried to hold back and as a result were destroyed. IBM underestimated the power of small personal computers and suffered grievously. Manufacturers of hard disk drives who waited out the emergence of newer, smaller drive technologies no longer exist. Steam engine digging machines who watched the hydraulic digging machines emerge no longer exist. To wait out the battle sounds intelligent, but the risk is high.

The Business Model of Information Appliances

The business model of the information appliance is very different from that of the personal computer. This is a new, disruptive industry, and everything is changed: the design principles, the marketing, the role it plays in business, family, and education. And the manner by which companies make their money.

Appliances are consumer products, whereas computers are technology products; therein lies the fundamental difference in the market. Computers emphasize technology, appliances emphasize convenience, ease of use; they downplay or even hide the technology. Computers are targeted at technology enthusiasts, even though a larger segment of buyers is buying them. Computer companies stand in strong contrast to consumer electronics and consumer appliance companies.

The major difference in these two markets reveals itself clearly in a comparison of their business models, as shown in figure 12.1. In the high-tech world, profits come from the technology itself, from the sale of hardware and software. The continuing revenue stream is generated by the "subscription" model of marketing, which includes a planned obsolescence of both hardware and software.

The business model of the information appliance industry is much more like that of consumer products, especially household appliances, hardware, and consumer electronics. In the consumer electronics market, companies sell relatively inexpensive devices that last for years with no maintenance. Fierce competition in this market results in low profit margins. Growth is reasonable, but not at the rate to which high-tech firms are accustomed. Sales volumes can be huge, however.

With low profit margins, how do companies make money in consumer appliances? By providing content and services. It is no accident that consumer electronic firms such as Sony and Philips participate in all levels of the value chain. They make devices, and in many cases, the underlying components. They make consumables such as tapes, floppy diskettes, CDs, and DVDs. They own recording studios and have long-term contracts with artists. Sony owns a company that makes the digital

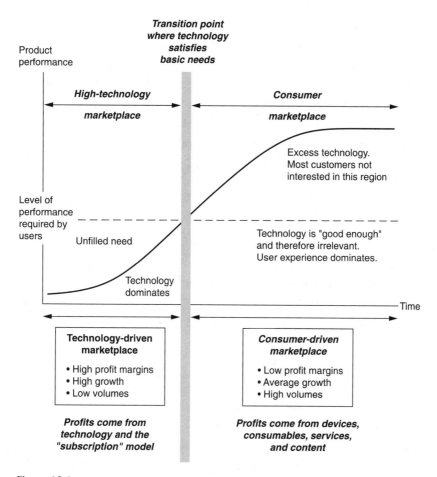

Figure 12.1

The business story accompanying the transition from a technology-centered market to a consumer-centered one. When technology reaches the point that it satisfies user needs, consumers no longer seek the best technology; they seek the most convenient one, the one with the most satisfactory user experience, the lowest cost, and the highest reliability. In some cases, they seek prestige. Brand name and reputation become major selling factors. Profit margins drop, but sales volumes rise; the entire business structure changes. As a result, the company itself must change if it is to survive the transition.

maps used in automobile routing devices and many mapping and direction-giving applications. And Sony owns a motion picture studio. Disney goes straight for services and content, ignoring devices and consumables. Disney stores sell many Disney products, but they are all manufactured by other people, with Disney taking a royalty. Go to a Disney theme park, and you will probably stay at a Disney hotel and eat in Disney restaurants. Disney will take photographs of you and your family and put them on mugs and T-shirts, which they will sell to you. The only part of the trip they do not make money on is the air transportation, although they recently acquired a line of holiday cruise ships.

In the world of information appliances, the devices are the enablers of the consumer experience, but they are only a part of the picture, and a small one at that. The prudent company will diversify from an initial emphasis on devices into providing a full complement of content and services for their customers. The goal should be to provide the total user experience.

Devices

Devices may very well be the area of least profit in the information appliance business, but that does not mean they should be neglected. There is a subtlety to the business case that many in the computer industry overlook: In the appliance industry, it is quite common for people to buy several of each device, not just the one-per-family model that dominates in the computer industry.

When devices are inexpensive, easy to use, and specialized, then it makes sense to buy them as needed for convenience. Families have several television sets, and many radios and tape players. Sure, only one is really required, but having several avoids conflicts when different members of the family wish to use the same device at the same time. It's most convenient to locate the devices where they will be needed, rather than to move them around. Thus, tape players are built into automobiles and are a permanent part of audio equipment. A portable, waterproof one might be reserved for exercising, while a smaller one is used while on errands or around the house.

How many information appliances will a family want? Who knows? How many cameras? One for each person? How many printers? Why not have printers wherever they are needed? One in the kitchen for shopping lists. One by the writing appliance. One built into the newspaper appliance that prints out the daily news and reports of interest. One providing information about shows, travel, and interesting products via the set-top box (increasingly becoming an internal part of the television set itself). A photographic-quality printer permanently loaded with glossy, photographic-quality paper where the family photographs are kept. If anyone wants a copy, it can be produced immediately, on the spot.

Printers will be everywhere, for they will no longer be thought of as general purpose printers. Instead, they will just be considered expeditious ways of getting information and images onto paper, wherever and whenever it is needed. One printer is part of the photography studio, and it is labeled "photograph out." Another is for shopping lists, and it should be labeled "shopping list." There's one for checks. Printers will become like clocks, electric motors, and embedded computer chips. They'll be wherever they are needed; nobody will question why there are more than one.

Before long people will begin to think of the appliance in connection with their activities. Music. Photography. Addresses. Shopping list. Personal finances. Health. When we think of them by activity, we are apt to purchase whatever is most suited for the task it involves. In this way, we never think "I already have an information appliance. Why should I buy another one?" Instead, we buy what is appropriate for the activity.

Consumables, Content, and Services

Information appliances should be thought of as systems, not isolated devices. The goal is to provide solutions for the consumer, not just electronic gadgets. The physical device is only one piece of the entire story. The successful business will provide all the pieces. Those pieces include consumables, content, and services.

Conventional photography provides a useful analogy. The business of photography includes much more than cameras. Photography requires a variety of accessories, such as lenses, tripods, carrying bags, cleaning material. It requires film, batteries, print paper, developing supplies, and darkroom equipment. It requires commercial services that will process the film for those not interested in doing it themselves and print the pictures or deliver them in electronic form, on discs or on the internet. It provides reprints, cropping, and enlargements. Even though anyone can take a photograph, professionals can take better ones, and so there will forever be a service business of professional photographers to photograph individuals, families, and special events such as weddings. Courses on photography are needed, covering the artistic aspect of selecting the subjects, composing the shot, setting up the appropriate lighting, and producing the most effective print. There is more business and money in these subsidiary activities than in the sale of the camera itself. So it should be with information appliances.

Digital photography requires much the same set of services and goods, substituting electronic media for film and computer enhancement and printing for darkrooms. Some information appliances will serve as home photographic studios, and the owners of these studios will probably wish to purchase memory appliances, viewing appliances, and photographic paper. They may wish to transmit some of their photos to friends and relatives, thus requiring communication appliances and suitable viewers or printers. And the need for lenses, tripods, lights, and instructional courses, books, and tutorial videos and computer-guided learning courses on how best to use these and how best to process and finish the photographs will proliferate.

Manufacturers of computer printers make more money off the supplies than the devices: toner for laser printers, ink and cartridges for inkjet printers, and specialized paper for quality presentations, for cards, celebrations, certificates, photographs. More business is generated helping people create greeting cards, calendars, announcements, and news-letters. Consumables and services, together.

Medical appliances will need communication services, perhaps special-purpose consumables for collecting blood and other body fluids and for recording temperature. Expert systems that provide advice.

Those who purchase learning and entertainment appliances will need to purchase content for the devices. There will be an ever-increasing supply of instructional material suitable for all ages and purposes: for traditional school, from preschool through graduate school. Course material for business. And learning material for the retired, for the interested, for the curious: material on the world, on the arts, languages, hobbies, sports, music. The need is enormous. The business of providing entertainment content is already well established; there is no reason this will ever diminish.

Many of the companies in the high-tech world may be uncomfortable with this list of consumables, services, and content; this is not the sort of business they are used to. Today's world of technology can be content with selling just the device or just the software.

Mature industries work differently than do growing, emerging ones. As the earlier chapters demonstrate, mature industries require a different approach to marketing and product development than do developing ones. The same is true for the nature of the products that are to be sold. The current computer business forces artificial obsolescence upon its customers, requiring continual upgrading of hardware and software. Under the new scheme, appliances seldom become obsolete. Instead, people will want multiple devices, consumables, services, and content. This is a different business model than today's high-tech industry is used to, but it is one very familiar to the consumer appliance, electronics, and entertainment industries.

Privacy Concerns

The new technologies for communication and computation pose serious privacy concerns. When cameras are so small that they can be hidden in every device imaginable, when radio transmitters are so small that they can be embedded in cameras, in the walls, in clothing so as to be undetectable, then the chances of unwarranted surveillance increase. Personal data will more and more often be stored electronically, accessible to many people from many locations. Large databases of personal and private information are already accumulating. A great deal of information is stored about every citizen, but much of it is incorrect, for the ease of collection of information is not matched by ease of validation.

These issues are not a result of information appliances. They arise from the rapid developments in technology, perhaps starting with the evolution of governments and record keeping multiple centuries ago, but made more efficient by modern database technologies. The rise of large numbers of appliances will only intensify the issue. The rise of large databases of knowledge about individual citizens, their health, their purchasing patterns, and their activities raise numerous concerns. It doesn't help that the methods of collection and storage are imperfect, so that the records on any individual are apt to contain erroneous information, out-of-date records, and records that actually pertain to a different person (perhaps bearing the same or similar name).

When we start transmitting personal information from one location to another, it is essential to ensure privacy and to prevent fraud. The technology already exists for doing this: encryption. The term *encryption* refers to a means for encoding information such as text, messages, and pictures in such a way that other people cannot view it without decoding. Decryption then requires either access to the secret key or else an enormous amount of computing power to try all possible combinations or exploit clever tricks to decipher the code without the key. Encryption methods come in various strengths of difficulty in unscrambling the code in the absence of the key.

Most national governments are concerned about the use of information and communication technologies to aid criminals, terrorists, and foreign espionage agents. As a result they want to prohibit the use of strong encryption. Strong encryption is an encoding that is virtually impossible for an unauthorized person to decipher. Governments are often opposed to this because they want their own investigative agencies, which usually have access to the world's most powerful computers, to be able to read all information traffic. Citizens and corporations are concerned that weak encryption can be decoded by an ever-increasing number of parties who group together large numbers of the most powerful personal computers and that governments—their own and foreign ones—who have access to more powerful machines will routinely decode the messages and use the information for their private advantage. The topic is highly controversial. The roadblocks are political. These are legitimate concerns and they lead to political tension between those who want to safeguard their private information from others and the governments that are concerned about the use of these same technologies by organized crime, terrorists, and other miscreants.

Key recovery and key escrow schemes are provisions for people who use encryption to place a copy of the decoding key in some trusted place—an escrow agency—where in principle the government can only get access to it by a court order. Key recovery is quite important. Remember, with strong encryption, no key means no data; it may be impossible to break the code. You will lose access to your own records if you forget the key. Similarly a family may lose access to its important papers if the keeper of the records dies. A company loses access to its data if a key employee leaves (or dies) without telling others the secret key. It is essential to have some trusted place where the secrets can be kept, with faith that they will not be released for any unauthorized use. But who would you trust?

Many citizens do not trust governments to use this power with discretion; every government in the world has a history of breaching trust, even when such violations are prohibited by law, and even when they are enforced (but enforced only for those violations that are discovered). Governments and escrow agencies, of course, are composed of people, and individual people are sometimes curious, misdirected, and evil (or paid or controlled by those who are). Yet another reason not to trust the sanctity of the escrow process.

These problems will eventually be resolved, but probably with different solutions in different parts of the world, and not always in a manner satisfactory to the various parties. At the very least, the encryption will be sufficient to discourage casual eavesdroppers from access to private information. Ideally, nobody could get access, except those for whom the information is intended or, in the case of demonstrated criminal culpability, by means of a court order.

The Tradeoff between Privacy and Ease of Use

The need for privacy, alas, creates a tradeoff between the need for security and ease of use. In the ideal world, it would be possible to go to an information appliance, turn it on and instantly use it for its intended purpose, with no delay required for the electronics to warm up, no delay for the underlying computer systems to turn on and establish the context. All information appliances would work like our calculators: When you needed them, you would simply push the "on" button and start calculating. Because of the privacy issues, this simplicity is denied us whenever confidential or otherwise restricted information is involved.

In general, the more secure a device, the more hassle legitimate users will face. It will be necessary to identify yourself, to prove that you are the person you claim to be and, in some cases, demonstrate that you have both the authority and a need to get access to the information. Sometimes this will require the cooperation of another person or organization, such as a bank. Publishers will want to control access to their news or financial reports, or even movies. The identification process may be tedious.

Today, the most widely used method of verification is passwords, but these are faulty for several reasons. Passwords work best when they are long, complex, and randomly generated from both letters and digits, uppercase and lowercase, certainly with no words, names, or dates. In other words, good passwords are those that are difficult to remember. On top of that, the best security is obtained when different devices and services use different passwords that are changed frequently so that if one password is discovered, it won't allow access to everything. All these requirements are most unfriendly to people. Human memory works best with meaningful material, and when overloaded with a large number of passwords that change frequently and that contain nonsensical sequences, our memory systems balk. The result is that either we violate the rules or, worse, we write down the passwords, which spells disaster should the written list fall into the wrong hands.

The security issues are severe. In my opinion, the only practical solution is identification through a physical device, some electronic version of a key, coupled with some biometric identification, such as fingerprint, retinal scan, or recognition of voice, face, or hand shape. A simple password might also be required, but with the other methods in place, the password could be short and easy to remember. No one of these methods is fully secure; each has known problems and weaknesses. But combine two or three imperfect methods and the result is a very high degree of security. This system also overcomes the enormous memory load of the current schemes that cause people to choose inappropriate passwords or to write them down.

Privacy issues are of critical importance, but they are also extremely complex. They pit convenience against security, business interest against national security, trust in individuals against trust in governments. This is a topic that has elicited excellent studies and reports,[3] even if the basic issues have not yet been resolved. Political disagreements are never easy to overcome.

The Vision: A World of Information Appliances

Now comes the fun. The stage has been set, the players are in their places, the overture is complete. Time to do information appliances. The vision is clear. Move to the third generation of the personal computer or, if you will, a generation of personal technologies, the generation where the technology disappears into the tool, serving valuable functions, but keeping out of the way. The generation where the computer disappears into tools specific to tasks. The generation of the invisible computer.

The first steps have already occurred. We already use a variety of information appliances, usually without even being aware of the fact—which is the way it ought to be. The list of existing information appliances is surprisingly long. Electronic reference books, address books, calendars and diaries. Dual- and multiple-language dictionaries and encyclopedias. Physician's guides, trip guides. The navigation systems for automobiles that provide specific driving instructions and sometimes restaurant, hotel, and entertainment information relevant to the trip plan and the current location. Digital cameras. The standalone printer that prints anything beamed to it by a standardized infrared protocol (today used only for digital cameras, but wait, the range of devices will soon expand). Electronic test equipment, such as oscilloscopes, voltmeters, and circuit checkers. The wide variety of calculators, some simple, some specialized for business, for real estate, for statistics, or for algebra and calculus, some that contain communication protocols, some that don't. The stock quote machine, carried in the pocket, always up to date, personalizable to reveal just those statistics and quotes of interest to the owner. The cellular telephone. The fax. The pager. The variety of specialized game machines for the home. The ever-increasing number of internet appliances for browsing, for email, and for a variety of services and catalog purchases.

Most of these appliances have taken only the first step. They perform sophisticated information processing in ways appropriate to the task and the environment without requiring guidance from their users. They fit the task. They have been designed with the specific needs of the consumer in mind: They provide value, ease of use, and simplicity. But they are isolated from one another. They seldom communicate, except perhaps through proprietary protocols so that the devices of one manufacturer can interact only with other devices of the same brand. As a result, these information appliances have only partially fulfilled their potential.

I envision a thriving appliance industry offering a large choice to the consumer. Different manufacturers will have different philosophies of what their customers need, thereby providing consumers with a wide array of choices; whatever their preferences in devices, in selection of which tasks and activities should go together, will be available. Couple this with a standardized, international protocol for sharing information so that any manufacturer's device can share information with the devices of any other manufacturer. The result will be whole systems of powerful, interconnected appliances, offering possibilities not even contemplated today. We already see this working in the music industry with its array of instruments intended for a large range of musical tastes, abilities, and pocketbooks. We see it working in the consumer electronics industry with its huge variety of kitchen, shop, entertainment and business appliances. The result is a healthy market for all concerned, whether consumer, retailer, or manufacturer.

Although industry may question the change, consumers do not; for the consumer, there is nothing but benefits. From the consumer's point of view, the change is highly desirable: lower cost, increased functionality, new services, and useful, informative, and enjoyable content.

Less fuss and bother. Simpler, more convenient devices. Great flexibility and versatility. New modes of interaction, of learning, of conducting business and recreation. Increased reliability. More pleasure. It is a magnificent win.

The successful family of information appliances will be built around the people who use them and the tasks to be performed. Products in the world of information technology have suffered far too long under the existing technology-centered designs. It is time for a change, time for a human-centered design philosophy. People are not machines, they have very different requirements.

Today, it is the individual who must conform to the needs of technology. It is time to make technology conform to the needs of people.

Appendix
Examples of Information Appliances

The Information Appliance Revolution in Photography

"I always take a picture of the inside of my refrigerator before I go shopping," a woman told me. "When I get to the store and I can't remember whether or not we need milk, I simply look at the camera display to see what was in the refrigerator."

Imagine a camera the size of a gumdrop, so inexpensive it can be given away. Cameras could be built into everything. Afraid of forgetting where you parked your car in the parking lot? Take a photograph, and when you want to return, view the picture on the electronic display of your photo appliance, the better to find your way back.

See an item at the store you think your family might be interested in? Take a picture. When you return home, show it to your family on the electronic photo viewer, or beam it to the home television set so everyone can see it at once, or send it to the printer appliance and get an instant photographic print. When cameras are everywhere and displays or prints instantly available, the uses of photographs expand enormously.

Meet a group of new people at a business conference and instantly photograph each other. I have already used a digital camera to make a tiny thumbnail sized print of the people I was talking with, conveniently printed on paper with adhesive on the back. I stuck the photograph into my research notebook so that I now have a permanent, visual reminder of the person whose ideas I recorded.

Once it is possible to send a photograph from one device to another, the usage possibilities increase. Send to a storage device and the print is saved; send to a fax and you can choose between transmitting the photograph to a friend or using the fax machine as an inexpensive, low-quality printer. Send to a television set and the image is displayed for group watching. Send to a friend's camera and the friend now has a copy of the picture. Ah! Now we are getting interesting.

Find the photo kiosk. Send your pictures to the kiosk for instant prints, or put them up on an internet web site so you can tell your friends the address and password so they can see what you are doing. Professional photographers can sell their pictures in the kiosk, sending them to your camera or making a print. When you return home from a trip, your camera will contain a collection of images, some which you took, some which other people may have taken, some you might have purchased, and some which might not even be camera images, but faxes or newspaper and magazine articles that were scanned, photographed, or extracted from the internet. And even before your return, family members could be sharing the experience. Suddenly, our entire conception of "camera" is changed. A camera is an image-gathering device, gathering some through the lens, some through the communication channel. All can be viewed on the camera's display, all can be sent to other devices for storage, manipulation, display, or printing.

The photography story shows the real power of information appliances: New ways of working pop up that never existed before. A camera that ends up with pictures you didn't take. The ability to use any printing device as a way of getting copies of your photos. The ability to move images from one device to another, each performing with the device whatever primary function it was designed for: storing, viewing, website placement, printing, transmitting or faxing, or studio manipulation in the home darkroom of the future. New tools, new activities. All this with an absolute minimum of complexity.

The Home Medical Advisor

The age of medical sensors that are sufficiently inexpensive, rugged, and reliable for the home is just emerging. [1] The possibilities are large: home urinalysis, blood tests such as blood sugar or white-cell count, blood pressure and pulse, body temperature, and weight. Asthma patients could do home pulmonary assessment. EKG readings of heart activity are possible. And, of course, the home breath analyzer. A physician may ask that critical sensor readings be automatically transmitted to the primary health care center. That way when patients called or visited, their physicians would already have their measurements and recent medical history.

Simple home advisory systems seem practical using the technology called *expert systems*. These would be more powerful, automated versions of some of the home medical books that now exist, more precise and useful because as input, they would have the outputs of the home medical appliances. The advisor would know your body temperature, weight, pulse, and other basic medical parameters. It could ask a carefully sequenced set of questions to guide you toward a likely diagnosis and recommended actions. Are there liability problems? Yes, but the advisor can be designed to be very conservative, much as are the existing books. They would give useful explanations and descriptions, suggest when it is important to be concerned and when you can relax, but they always would be designed to err in the direction of safety, recommending that you consult your physician when there was any doubt. They would also make such consultation more productive by providing an information record that will help both the patient and the physician know the facts, instead of relying upon the patient's faulty memory.

The Weather and Traffic Display

Want to know the weather forecast or traffic conditions for your daily commute? Just look up on the wall at the weather and traffic display. It's somewhat like a clock, meant to be hung on the wall, perhaps in the kitchen. The clock is an appliance that continually shows the correct time. If you aren't interested in the time, you don't look at the clock. If you want the time, there it is, effortlessly available. So, too, with the traffic display.

You don't want traffic or weather? You would prefer the latest sports scores, or stock market results? No problem: That's what information appliances are for. If there is enough demand, someone will make just what you are looking for. Want a device that allows you to select your source of information? That makes for a slightly more complex device, but, once again, if there is sufficient demand, someone will make it. Proponents of "push" technology, which provides services that "push" information relevant to their consumers onto their computers, please take note. The wall-hanging information display is a perfect vehicle for your services, and far simpler for the user than today's computer implementations.

The Home Shopping List

It's easy to think of ways of improving upon the average home shopping list. Paper and pencil work quite well, except that they never seem to be available when they are needed. How many times have you needed the list at the store while it was still in its assigned location in the kitchen? Wouldn't it be nice if you could pull out your pocket information display and request the list? One moment it's at home, out of reach; the next moment there's a nice copy on the portable, hand-held information display appliance.

How would this work, especially if the list were written with paper and pencil? Ah, the wonders of modern technology. As long as the paper was written on the proper pad of paper or sensor board, or, alternatively, as long as a motion- and location-sensitive pen was used, the information would simultaneously be captured electronically as well as physically, the one form for reading at home, the other for remote access.

The Gardening Appliance

The same philosophy that works for medical advice will work for the garden, except here it isn't so necessary to err on the side of conservatism. The information appliance can contain color photographs, videos of planting, pruning, and grafting techniques; sensors to measure ground moisture and acidity to control the watering schedule and recommend fertilizer. It can do a soil analysis, perhaps analyze the leaves for health; aim the gardening camera at those bugs you found on the plant and have it identify them and suggest remedies.

Intelligent Reference Guides

Home medical advisors and gardening advisors are examples of smart reference guides. Imagine an automobile information appliance advisor that can help diagnose the car's ailments and show what to do, complete with photographs and videos.

There is already a small but thriving business of providing portable reference dictionaries, language translators, currency converters, and travel information. Add a global positioning satellite receiver (GPS) so the information appliance knows where it is, and the information could be tailored for the location.

Walk into a store and the floor plan and daily sales flash on the screen of your display appliance. Hike in the mountains and your location, elevation, and map appear on the screen. Need first aid on the trail? Advice is available on the display.

Automobile guidance systems already exist, displaying a map of the locale to the driver, along with directions for driving to any desired location. The directions are displayed on a simple screen with arrows pointing in the direction of the desired travel, with the more complex map display disabled in the interests of safety except when the car is stationary. Most units also have voice output, so they can instruct the driver by speaking: "Approaching left turn. Turn left now." I have already found these units very valuable in rental cars when I am traveling in unfamiliar locations.

Because the units use CD-ROM technology to store the maps, it is possible to select what information is available. Instead of maps and directions, it is possible to get enhanced maps that show the facilities along the route: restaurants, hotels, scenic attractions. Some contain advertisements that pop up when the automobile is within range of the attraction. In Japan I have seen units that displayed photographs of the food and menus of the restaurants along the route and pictures and descriptions of ski trails.

Looking for a house? Your real estate agent sends photographs and home information of potential locations to your home-buying advisor appliance. As you make the rounds of homes, you can take written and voice notes, as well as photographs, using the built-in camera. Later, as you review the prospects in your home, perhaps sending the information about each home to your home television set so the entire family can review it, the advisor can also tell about schools and shops and its mortgage calculator lets you figure out if you can afford it.

The Home Financial Center

Imagine a simple information appliance that specializes in home finances: bill paying, family financial reviews, and at the end of each year, income taxes. The financial appliance is networked to the bank and perhaps a stockbroker and financial advisor. Send it information from the checkbook appliance, the one you carry in your pocket. Use it with the smart-card credit card appliance. The home financial center pays bills electronically where possible, otherwise it automatically prints checks and addresses envelopes.

What is the advantage of a specialized family home finance appliance when all of this could already be done on a home computer? Because this is easier, dedicated to the task, and tucked away in a private workplace so it can be used or ignored at will. It always remembers the last operations it did. It is always ready to do the next ones, immediately, with no warm-up, no search for the proper application and files. It lets family members do financial matters where they are most comfortable, and in private. The financial center appliance follows the design maxim: "Put the tool where the work is done: don't be forced to work where the tool is."

The Internet Appliance

Can appliances take advantage of the internet? Will there be internet appliances? Of course. In fact, I expect the use of the internet to be so pervasive, so natural, and so commonplace that the very notion of calling something "an internet appliance" will be completely unnecessary.

With the advent of the internet, everyone is rushing into the act, inventing "internet appliances" that allow for browsing on almost every medium and device imaginable, from portable telephones, to handheld units, to "screen telephones" (regular home telephones that have small display screens on them), television sets, and, of course, computers.

Are these viable devices? Are these really appliances? Yes and no. The term *internet appliance* isn't very useful, for it simply names the technology that is to be used rather than say what tasks are to be performed. The functions have already been covered: entertainment, education, music, social communication, and so on. Will these use the internet? Maybe. Will their functionality and value be thereby improved? Maybe.

The internet is a rich source of data, of information, and of knowledge. It affords social interaction and communication. Where these are appropriate to the activity, they should be included; otherwise they should be omitted. Moreover, the internet requires a large infrastructure that at times may get in the way of the use of the appliance. From the appliance to the internet one must have a telephone line or cable connection, a radio link, or some means of making the connection. In some locations this may be difficult or impossible. In some cases, the connection rate may be slow or expensive. In general, internet appliances will find their way into the world of devices just like any other. Connection to the internet has great potential, and it will be provided naturally in the development of appliances whose functions require or are enhanced by the connection. The internet is a powerful infrastructure. Where appropriate, information appliances should exploit its power.

Embedded in the Walls and Furniture

Appliances do not have to be things that are visible; they can be embedded within many of the structures of everyday life—the walls of our homes, offices, and schools; in our automobiles; in airplanes seats; in furniture. As the world of embedded computers expands, many of our activities will receive automatic support from the infrastructure, often without our even being aware of the devices.

All we have to do is couple the power of communication networks with the new array of wireless devices, and then, no matter where we are, the information we need is available. And the information we generate can be shared by all.

Does an information appliance have to be small? Does it have to be portable? Can it be on the desk? Can it be large? The answer to the size question is all of the above. The point of information appliances is to fulfill people's needs in a natural manner, to provide benefits and pleasure without the encumbrance of technological complexity. Most information appliances will be small, many will be portable. But size and portability are secondary, derived from their function and the needs they are designed to support. Some will be small, some large. Some will be portable, some stationary.

Write on a whiteboard in our office or classroom and the information can readily be transmitted to others. The teacher's notes can be sent to each student. Material written in the office can be sent to coworkers, or to the class, or home, for further work. Identification chips will allow people to identify themselves to otherwise locked doors or protected information devices. Already we see chips in automobiles that tell the tollgate that this car has already paid its toll, or that pay for gasoline in a filling station. Many industrial workers wear badges that automatically open doors when they are waved near the badge sensor. Groceries could be automatically checked out of a supermarket when the shopper walks through a sensing field, with transponders on each item automatically registering themselves.

The supermarket checkout stand can be considered one big appliance; it reads the barcodes on the groceries, automatically weighs and computes the price of fruits and vegetables, accepts electronic money, whether credit card or electronic cash, and prints itemized receipts. The store uses the information to determine what clusters of foods people like to purchase together, the better to keep accurate inventory, so it can order new stocks when necessary. The information can be used in many ways, some beneficial to the store, some beneficial to the shopper—and some invading the shopper's privacy. The latter needs to be guarded against. The point right now, however, is primarily to point out that appliances need not be restricted to small devices carried on the person.

The Ultimate Appliances: Embedded in Our Clothes, Implanted in Our Bodies

Although size is not a defining parameter, I fully expect to see small, portable appliances. Already I can carry calculators, cellular telephones, cameras, electronic address books, and reminder lists in my shirt pocket. I am sure the size will decrease even more. Some will indeed be wearable, clipped onto our bodies or clothes like eyeglasses, watches, and jewelry. Some will be built into our clothes. And some might even be permanently implanted within our bodies, always available, always with us.

The latest craze is wearable devices that are literally woven into the fabric of clothes, so small and lightweight that you don't know you are wearing them. Put on a pair of shoes, and voila, you have donned an electric power generating plant and radio transmitter (after all, each footstep can generate sufficient electric energy to power numerous low-power devices). Put on a shirt and you have put on communication channels, body sensors, and even electronic jewelry that changes color to match your other clothes, your environment, maybe even your mood.

Consider the value of eyeglass appliances. Many of us already wear eyeglasses during our entire waking hours. Why not supplant them with more power? Add a small electronic display to the glasses, perhaps displaying the image on the bottom part of the lens (adjusted optically so that the images appear at a comfortable viewing distance), and we could have all sorts of valuable information with us at all times. Put a small camera on the eyeglasses so that when you were talking to someone, the camera could quickly photograph the face and compare it with a database of all the people you had previously met, then unobtrusively display the person's name and other information.

Let the camera record all your experiences; you need never forget anything. Lose a favorite sweater?[2] Why, just review the photographs until you find it again, and of course the most recent photo to show the sweater also reveals its location.

The idea of body implants bothers most people. Today, they are limited to medical devices, such as metal pins and plates to strengthen bones, hip and knee sockets, artificial heart valves, or electronic pacemakers to control the heartbeat. Artificial lenses are implanted in the eyes after the removal of cataracts. Some people have the lenses of their eyes altered by scalpel or laser beam. Why shouldn't hearing aids be implanted inside the body, so they are always available?

Now go beyond health aids. Perhaps an accountant would like an implanted calculator so that computations are effortlessly available, perhaps voice activated, with the answers coming back via synthetic speech. Telephones and other communication devices could also be surgically implanted; my favorite location is in that tiny fold of skin just beneath the ear, a location well placed to provide a home for both microphone and earphone via bone conduction. In all these devices power could be provided by simple electromagnetic coupling from outside the body. Do these ideas sound strange and repulsive? Although the idea of implanted appliances may be difficult to accept, note the rise of medical implants: heart pacemakers, kidney pumps, auditory prostheses that stimulate the auditory nerve, and artificial limbs and sockets. Can credit cards, telephones, or global positioning navigator appliances be far behind?

Notes

Chapter One

1. **Duryea was the first.** Daimler and Benz were first in the world, with their two companies starting around 1885, merging in 1926 and now sold under the name of Mercedes-Benz. For them, being first helped. The Duryea brothers' company started in 1895 and sold thirteen cars before it failed. Then the Stevens-Duryea company made high-priced limousines until its demise in the 1920s: being first provided no real advantage.

2. **The history of the phonograph is illustrative.** The fascinating history of Edison's several phonograph companies and of the feuds between Edison, Berliner, and almost everyone else can be found in W. L. Welch and L. B. S. Burt, *From Tinfoil to Stereo: The Acoustic Years of the Recording Industry, 1877–1929* (Gainesville: University Press of Florida, 1994).

3. **Edison's phonograph had a number of superior features.** E. Thompson, "Machines, Music, and the Quest for Fidelity: Marketing the Edison Phonograph in America, 1877–1925," *The Musical Quarterly* 79 (1995): 131–171. I am thankful to Emily Thompson of the University of Pennsylvania for her assistance in helping me track down the story of Edison and the phonograph.

4. **An audience could not distinguish the sounds produced by his phonograph from those of a live singer.** See Thompson (1995), note 3.

5. **If you had your choice of attending two concerts.** Victor advertisement, *National Geographic,* November–December 1917. (Quoted in Thompson [1995], note 3.)

Chapter Two

1. **The very talents of a company that made it successful in the early stages of a technology are exactly wrong for the latter phases.** The discussion of the life cycle of a technology owes much to two major sources. First, and primary, is the "crossing the chasm" argument of Geoffrey Moore. His is an important book, and although it is

continually referred to within Silicon Valley, I fear that few have actually understood it. Too bad. G. A. Moore, *Crossing the Chasm: Marketing and Selling High-Tech Goods to Mainstream Customers* (New York: HarperBusiness, 1991).

Second is the discussion of product life cycle provided by Clayton Christensen, especially in chapter 8 of his book: C. M. Christensen, *The Innovator's Dilemma: When New Technologies Cause Great Firms to Fail* (Boston: Harvard Business School Press, 1997). See note 8 of his chapter 8 (p. 182) for a good source of articles on product life cycle.

2. **For many years, those who study the way innovative ideas and products enter society.** The classification scheme for adopters of innovative technology has a long history. The classic text in this field is Everett Rogers's *Diffusion of Innovations,* now in its fourth edition. The story of the classification of adopters into categories of "innovators," "early adopters," "early majority," "late majority," and "laggards" is told in his Chapter Seven, "Innovativeness and adopter categories," pp. 252–280. This is the source of the categories that Geoffrey Moore used in his works. See E. M. Rogers, *Diffusion of Innovations,* 4th edition (New York: The Free Press, 1995).

Rogers and his colleagues showed that innovation spread slowly, with early adopters being different kinds of people than late adopters. Moore showed that a high-technology company had to change its behavior and its marketing as the customer base changes. My message is that in addition to the lessons from Rogers and Moore, the product has to be different. It isn't enough to change the marketing—the entire product must change.

3. **Geoffrey Moore called it a "tornado."** G. A. Moore, *Inside the Tornado: Marketing Strategies from Silicon Valley's Cutting Edge* (New York: HarperBusiness, 1995).

4. **Many of the developers of systems in the marketplace today would do well to study the Star.** See D. C. Smith, R. Kimball, W. Verplank, and E. Harslem, "Designing the Star User Interface," *Byte* 7, no. 4 (April 1982): 242–282. For a retrospective look back at the Star and the lessons learned, see J. Johnson, T. L. Roberts, W. Verplank, D. C. Smith, C. H. Irby, M. Beard, and K. Mackey, "The Xerox Star: A Retrospective," *IEEE Computer* 22, no. 9 (September 1989), 11–29. Reprinted in *Readings in Human-Computer Interaction: Toward the Year 2000,* R. M. Baecker, J. Grudin, W. A. S. Buxton, and S. Greenberg, eds. (San Francisco: Morgan Kaufmann, 1995), pp. 53–70.

5. **The Xerox Star suffered a number of faults. It was ahead of its time.** These opinions come from several sources. First is my own experience in watching the birth and death of the Star, as well as studies my students and I made of a group of early users. Second is conversations with a number of the developers, many of whom are my close friends, including especially David Liddle, who headed the Star team. The conclusions, however, are my own, and are not necessarily shared by the Star team.

The retrospective analysis by a group from the original Star team is consistent with my analysis. Their article, especially the last section entitled "Lessons from experience" expands upon these points: Johnson, Roberts, Verplank, Smith, Irby, Beard, and Mackey, "The Xerox Star," in Baecker, Grudin, Buxton, Greenberg, eds., *Readings in Human-Computer Interaction*, pp. 53–70.

6. **One critical aspect of marketing is the positioning of the product in the marketplace.** See A. Ries and J. Trout, *The 22 Immutable Laws of Marketing* (New York: HarperCollins, 1993); A. Ries and J. Trout, *Positioning: The Battle for Your Mind* (New York: McGraw-Hill, 1986, First ed., revised).

Among the 22 "laws" these are of most relevance to my discussion:

Law 1: It's better to be first than it is to be better." (p. 2)
Law 3: "It's better to be first in the mind than to be first in the marketplace." (p. 14)
Law 4: "Marketing is not a battle of products, it's a battle of perceptions." (p. 18)

"Most marketing mistakes stem from the assumption that you're fighting a product battle rooted in reality. All the laws of this book are derived from the exact opposite point of view" (p. 20).

7. **Transform products into "objects of desire."** A. Forty, *Objects of Desire* (New York: Pantheon Books, 1986).

Chapter Three

1. **Raskin had coined the term in 1978.** Personal (email) correspondence with Jef Raskin, December 20, 1997. The term first appeared in an internal Apple document. Also cited in "Special Report on Information Appliances," *Business Week* 22 (November 1993): 110. Raskin's company, Information Appliance, still exists, and the name is trademarked. (When I showed Raskin this section, he apologized for his behavior fifteen years ago, explaining that he had just been lectured by his lawyer about his "continued negligence with respect to getting people to sign nondisclosures before discussing things," and my visit triggered an overreaction.

2. **. . . the encryption key that you alone would hold.** This leads to a complex discussion about privacy and the tradeoff between the rights of individuals and of governments, or the rights of companies and their employees. In general, governments wish to restrict the power of encryption to thwart crime and fraud. They want to make it so that under certain circumstances, usually requiring permission of a legal authority, they could decode the information without permission. In addition, it would be foolhardy to store all your important papers under a password that only you yourself knew; suppose you became incapacitated or died—there has to be some way that others can get access to your information when necessary, perhaps as authorized by you in a will or other document. Similarly, companies will want to ensure that they can access company data stored by employees when employees are no longer around, whether they are ill, dead, or no longer working for the company. On the other hand many do not want governments to hold power over their privacy. There is ample

precedent for a lack of faith in governmental integrity. This is a very important and critical argument. I return to this topic in chapter 12.

Chapter Four

1. **Creeping featurism is what I called this problem in 1988.** D. A. Norman, *The Psychology of Everyday Things* (New York: Basic Books, 1988), p. 172. (Also published in paperback as D. A. Norman, *The Design of Everyday Things* [New York: Doubleday, 1990]).
   The numerical values for the number of commands in the 1992 and 1997 versions of Microsoft Word come from W. W. Gibbs, "Taking Computers to Task," *Scientific American* 277, no. 1 (July 1997): 88.

2. **Nathan's First law: "Software is a gas. . . . "** Statements made in 1997 at the ACM's 50th Anniversary party, at their annual convention in San Jose, California. These are actually paraphrases, not actual quotations, for although I was in attendance, I was not taking notes. But these are precisely the sentiments that Nathan expressed: for corroboration, see Wayt Gibbs's provocative article, "Taking Computers to Task," 82–89 (see note 1).

3. **Together with a hardy band of souls.** The ABC group consisted of Thomas Erickson, Charlie Hill, Austin Henderson, Dan Russell, Harry Saddler, and Mitch Stein, all of whom have left Apple.

4. **What happened? See the endnote.** Activity-based computing never did make it to product. The idea failed for many reasons. It was a disruptive technology offered to an industry that wasn't interested. It suffered from all the common ailments of disruptive technologies (discussed in chapter 11). In part, the idea failed because it connected itself to a superior, new technology (object-oriented component parts) that itself never reached any market acceptance. In part, it was too difficult to convince the critical senior executive staff that the approach would make a difference in the marketplace. Apple was already suffering from its use of a nonstandard operating system, the nonsubstitutable, infrastructure problem, and it wasn't clear why offering a nonstandard set of applications would help in this battle, even if the new approach was a superior way of doing things.
   Apple had developed a component-based software architecture that it called "OpenDoc" (as in Open standards for Documents), which provided the perfect vehicle upon which to implement activity-based computing. It was easy to convince the members of Apple's OpenDoc team and together we made the rounds of the other companies that were part of the OpenDoc consortium. But OpenDoc had its own political problems, both within Apple and outside, so this effort never got off the ground. OpenDoc itself failed to receive widespread usage, and it was finally abandoned. Established companies, even innovative ones (which Apple prided itself on being), have great difficulty in moving outside the established paradigm.

5. **In the scientific research field of activity theory.** See B. Nardi, ed., *Context and Consciousness: Activity Theory and Human-Computer Interaction* (Cambridge, MA: MIT Press, 1996). My interest first started in the early 1980s: see Y. Miyata and D. A. Norman, "Psychological Issues in Support of Multiple Activities," in *User Centered System Design,* ed. D. A. Norman and S. W. Draper (Hillsdale, NJ: Lawrence Erlbaum Associates, 1986).

6. **There have been numerous attempts.** Austin Henderson and Stuart Card of the Xerox Palo Alto Research Center developed an early version of Activity Spaces, "Rooms," which a division of Xerox released as a product. D. A. Henderson, Jr., and S. K. Card, "Rooms: The Use of Multiple Virtual Workspaces to Reduce Space Contention in a Window-Based Graphical User Interface," *TOGS* 5, no. 3 (1986): 211–243. "Lotus Notes," a business communication and organizing tool by the Lotus Corporation includes related notions, although within a restricted (confining) framework. To be completely successful requires a somewhat different model of software than the current application-based framework. It requires component-based software as well as the appropriate task-centered design philosophy (hence our use of Open Doc: see note 4).

Chapter Five

1. **The mythical man-month.** F. P. Brooks, Jr., *The Mythical Man-Month: Essays on Software Engineering,* anniversary edition (Reading, MA: Addison-Wesley, 1995). (Reissuance, with additions, of the original 1975 publication, including "No silver bullet.")

2. **There is no silver bullet.** I am tempted to cite as an authoritative reference on my behalf a critical article in *Scientific American* that makes many of these same points, both for speech and for three-dimensional space. The only problem is that this article buttresses its case by citing me as one of its authorities, and there is a limit to how much circular cross-citation one ought to do. But, obviously, I recommend the article: W. W. Gibbs, "Taking Computers to Task," *Scientific American* 277, no. 1 (July 1997): 82–89. (From the table of contents: "Will new 3-D interfaces, speech recognition and other highly touted computer technologies do anything to make workers more productive? A no-nonsense look at the value of new computer features, from the over-hyped to the overlooked.")

3. **A telephone messaging system called Wildfire.** Wildfire Communications, Inc., 20 Maguire Road, Lexington, MA 02173. For a demo, in the United States, call 1-800-WILDFIRE.

4. **Well, there are agents and there are agents.** A good review of the state of the art is in the book edited by Jeffrey Bradshaw. Proponents, opponents, skeptics, and

agnostics all get to make their case. J. Bradshaw, ed., *Software Agents* (Menlo Park, CA, and Cambridge, MA: AAAI Press/The MIT Press, 1997). My own contribution to this book is entitled "How Might People Interact with Agents?"

Chapter Six

1. **In the world's marketplaces, technical quality is only one of many variables.** These analyses owe much to the work of the economists W. Brian Arthur and Paul A. David: See Arthur (1988, 1994) Arthur and Lane (1993), David (1985, 1997).

2. **I have been a happy man . . . when I no longer had an email address.** Quote from the section "Frequently asked questions" on Prof. Donald Knuth's personal web page. Also see Steve Talbot's electronic journal, *NETFUTURE* 45 (April 9, 1997).
   Donald Knuth: http://www-cs-faculty.Stanford.edu/~knuth/
   NETFUTURE: http://www.ora.com/people/staff/stevet/netfuture/
Knuth is a heavy user of the internet, complete with a home page and his photograph. In other words, he doesn't mind technology, but he wants to be in control of his time. He writes books and technical articles, for which he needs undisturbed time, something with which most authors will sympathize. If you want to send him email, send it to his secretary, who screens items sent him. Regular postal mail gets the same treatment: He reads postal mail only once a month, faxes perhaps once every three months.

Chapter Seven

1. **It requires a biblical name to fool you.** T. A. Erickson and M. E. Mattson, "From Words to Meaning: A Semantic Illusion," *Journal of Verbal Learning and Verbal Behavior* 20 (1981): 540–552. The paper that started the quest for understanding why people have trouble discovering the problem with the question, "How many animals of each kind did Moses take on the ark?"
   Reder and Kusbit followed-up on the work and present numerous other examples of sentences that show this effect. L. M. Reder and G. W. Kusbit, "Locus of the Moses Illusion: Imperfect Encoding, Retrieval, or Match?" *Journal of Memory and Language* 30 (1991): 385–406.

2. **Humans versus computers.** This section modified from D. A. Norman, "Why It's Good That Computers Don't Work Like the Brain." In *Beyond Calculation: The Next Fifty Years of Computing,* ed. P. J. Denning and R. M. Metcalfe (New York: Copernicus: Springer-Verlag, 1997).

3. **The one best way.** R. Kanigel, *The One Best Way: Frederick Winslow Taylor and the Enigma of Efficiency* (New York: Viking, 1997).

4. **The question is, at what price?** For an excellent, in-depth analysis of the price paid in the name of efficiency, see J. Rifkin, *The End of Work: The Decline of the Global Labor Force and the Dawn of the Post-Market Era* (New York: G. P. Putnam's Sons, 1995).

5. **His book, *The Principles of Scientific Management*.** F. W. Taylor, *The Principles of Scientific Management* (New York: Harper & Brothers, 1911). (See note 6.)

6. **Taylor stated that it was necessary to reduce all work to the routine.** Taylor's work is described well in three books. First, there is Taylor's major work, cited in note 5. Second, there is the masterful and critical biography of Taylor, one that illustrates the paradox between what Taylor professed and how he himself lived and acted: Kanigel, *The One Best Way*. Finally, there is Rabinbach's masterful treatment of the impact of changing views of human behavior, the rise of the scientific method (even when it wasn't very scientific), and the impact of Taylor not only on modern work, but on political ideologies as well, especially Marxism and Fascism: A. Rabinbach, *The Human Motor: Energy, Fatigue, and the Origins of Modernity* (New York: Basic Books, 1990). Also see "Taylorismus + Fordismus = Amerikanismus," chapter 6 of T. P. Hughes, *American Genesis: A Century of Invention and Technological Enthusiasm, 1870–1970* (New York: Viking, 1989).

7. **A repair crew disconnects a pump from service in a nuclear power plant.** This is an oversimplified account of some of the many factors of the Three-Mile Island nuclear power accident. See J. G. Kemeny et al., *Report of the President's Commission on the Accident at Three Mile Island* (New York: Pergamon, 1979); E. Rubenstein, "The Accident That Shouldn't Have Happened," *IEEE Spectrum* 16, no. 11 (November 1979): 33–42.

8. **A hospital x-ray technician enters a dosage for an x-ray machine, then corrects the setting.** See Appendix A, Medical devices: The Therac-25 story, in N. G. Leveson, *Safeware: System Safety and Computers* (Reading, MA: Addison-Wesley, 1995). This book also includes nice appendices on The Therac-25 story (x-ray overdosage), the Bhopal chemical disaster, the Apollo 13 incident, DC-10s, and the NASA Challenger. And the various nuclear power industry problems, including Three Mile Island and Chernobyl.

9. **There are better ways of developing software.** See Leveson, *Safeware* (note 8). For a scary discussion of the failures of system design, see P. Neumann, *Computer-Related Risks* (Reading, MA: Addison-Wesley, 1995).

10. **If the Navy would follow formal procedures and a strict hierarchy of rank, the result would very likely be an increase in the accident rate.** See Hutchins' analysis of crew training and error management in ship navigation: E. Hutchins, *Cognition in the Wild* (Cambridge, MA: MIT Press, 1995). See also T. R. La Porte, and P. M. Consolini, "Working in Practice but Not in Theory: Theoretical Challenges of

High-Reliability Organizations," *Journal of Public Administration Research and Theory,* 1991, 19–47.

These issues are well treated by Robert Pool in both his book and the excerpt in the journal *Technology Review:* R. Pool, *Beyond Engineering: How Society Shapes Technology* (New York: Oxford University Press, 1997). R. Pool, "When Failure Is Not an Option," *Technology Review* 100, no. 5 (1997): 38–45. (Also see http://web.mit.edu/techreview/).

11. **Attributes of humans and machines presented from today's machine-centered point of view.** This chart and the following chart of the human-centered view come from D. A. Norman, *Things That Make Us Smart* (Reading, MA: Addison-Wesley, 1993).

Chapter Eight

1. **It was also the era of increased complexity of life and of a regimented work style.** The classic book on this topic, one I highly recommend, is S. Giedion, *Mechanization Takes Command: A Contribution to Anonymous History* (Oxford: Oxford University Press, 1948). Republished in 1969 by W. W. Norton & Co. (New York).

2. **Henry Ford's assembly line philosophy ("Fordism") and Frederick Taylor's principles of scientific management ("Taylorism") specified work practices throughout the world.** T. P. Hughes, *American Genesis: A Century of Invention and Technological Enthusiasm, 1870–1970* (New York: Viking, 1989), chapter 6: Taylorismus + Fordismus = Amerikanismus, pp. 249–294.

3. **At the start of the industrial revolution.** O. L. Bettmann, *The Good Old Days— They Were Terrible!* (New York: Random House, 1994).

4. **If the discovery of electricity changed the face of the earth** . . . A. D. Bragdon, *Ingenious Inventions of Domestic Utility* (New York: Harper & Row, 1989), p. 148.

5. **The plough, almost 500 years ago.** T. I. Williams, *The History of Invention: From Stone Axes to Silicon Chips* (London: Macdonald & Co.; New York: Facts on File Publications, 1987), p. 202.

6. **"Give the Phonograph a thorough trial of two weeks."** From *The Phonograph and How to Use It. Being a short history of its invention and development containing also directions helpful hints and plain talk as to its care and use, etc.* (p. 175). Originally published in 1900 by the National Phonograph Company. Facsimile edition published 1971 by Allen Koenigsberg, New York.

7. **"To acquire all the dexterity in its use."** *The Phonograph and How to Use It,* p. 109. (See note 6.)

8. **Robert Pool argues that complexity follows almost inevitably from the need to improve.** R. Pool, *Beyond Engineering: How Society Shapes Technology* (New York: Oxford University Press, 1997). See chapter 4, "Complexity."

9. **"The five fundamentals of radio reception."** Radio Corporation of America, *Radio Enters the Home: How to Enjoy Popular Radio Broadcasting. With complete instructions and description of apparatus. For those who desire to be entertained with concerts, lectures, dance music—as well as for the radio amateur* (New York: Radio Corporation of America, 1922).

10. **I once argued that modern technology is complex to the user because its operations are invisible.** In D. A. Norman, *The Psychology of Everyday Things* (New York: Basic Books, 1988). Also published in paperback as D. A. Norman, *The Design of Everyday Things* (New York: Doubleday, 1990).

11. **I called this state "knowledge in the world."** In chapter 3 of *The Psychology of Everyday Things*, "Knowledge in the Head and in the World." (See note 10.)

Chapter Nine

1. **One method that I particularly like is called *contextual design*.** See H. Beyer and K. Holtzblatt, *Contextual Design: Defining Customer-Centered Systems* (San Francisco: Morgan Kaufmann, 1998). (http://www.incontextenterprises.com).

2. **There are numerous books on the subject.** R. M. Baecker, J. Grudin, W. A. S. Buxton, and S. Greenberg, ed. *Readings in Human-Computer Interaction: Toward the Year 2000* (San Francisco: Morgan Kaufmann, 1995); H. Beyer and K. Holtzblatt, *Contextual Design: Defining Customer-Centered Systems* (San Francisco: Morgan Kaufmann, 1998); M. Helander, ed., *Handbook of Human-Computer Interaction* (New York: North-Holland, 1998), and the more recent edition, M. G. Helander, T. K. Kandauer, and P. V. Prabhu, eds., *Handbook of Human-Computer Interaction,* 2d ed. (Amsterdam: North-Holland, 1997); W. M. Newman and M. G. Lamming, *Interactive System Design* (Wokingham, UK: Addison-Wesley, 1995); D. A. Norman, *The Design of Everyday Things;* D. A. Norman and S. W. Draper, eds., *User Centered System Design* (Hillsdale, NJ: Lawrence Erlbaum Associates, 1986); B. Shneiderman, *Designing the User Interface: Strategies for Effective Human-Computer Interaction* (Reading, MA: Addison-Wesley, 1998). (See http://www.aw.com/DTUI for updates, reviews, and discussion.) This is the standard text on interface design: thorough, with excellent suggestions for control, search, and interaction that have never been incorporated into products, even though they should have been. Why not? For many of the reasons described in this book. Excellent though they may be, the designers of contemporary systems could never see how to get proprietary advantage; H. Thimbleby, *User Interface Design* (Reading, MA: Addison-Wesley/ACM Press, 1990). Also see the Association for Computing Machinery's Special Interest Group (a SIG) on Computer-Human Interaction, SIGCHI, and its

tutorial sessions and similar societies in other countries (http://www.acm.org/sigchi/).

3. **The results will be approximate rather than exact.** The tools of experimental psychology are often quite inappropriate for user testing. The user tester is looking for large phenomena not small ones; the results are required quickly; and great accuracy is not required. Large effects can be discovered with much simpler designs than the small phenomena usually being tested by the scientist, and the need for quick, approximate results allows for much more rapid, less carefully controlled experiments. In user testing, one only needs results that are "good enough." It is not necessary to have the very best design.

An excellent discussion of rapid testing methods is provided by Jakob Nielsen: J. Nielsen, *Usability Engineering* (Boston: AP Professional, 1993).

4. **Contextual inquiry by the proponents of contextual design.** Nielsen reviews rapid testing methods in his two books: J. Nielsen, *Usability Engineering,* and J. Nielsen and R. L. Mack, eds., *Usability Inspection Methods* (New York: John Wiley & Sons, 1994).

Contextual inquiry, a form of rapid ethnography, is discussed in detail in chapters 2, 3, and 4 of Beyer and Holtzblatt, *Contextual Design.*

5. **Mindless automation can be more dangerous than no automation, a topic I have explored elsewhere.** I covered the topic of aviation automation in D. A. Norman, *The Design of Everyday Things;* "The 'problem' of automation: Inappropriate feedback and interaction, not 'over-automation,'" in D. E. Broadbent, A. Baddeley, and J. T. Reason, eds., *Human Factors in Hazardous Situations* (Oxford: Oxford University Press, 1990), pp. 585–593; and also in my chapter "Coffee Cups in the Cockpit" in D. A. Norman, *Turn Signals Are the Facial Expressions of Automobiles* (Reading, MA: Addison-Wesley, 1992), pp. 154–174.

This was the theme of my book, *Things That Make Us Smart* (Reading, MA: Addison-Wesley, 1993).

Let me hasten to add, however, that there is a large and important discipline of aviation psychology (human factors in aviation), which has addressed these problems in great detail, with great effectiveness, both for military and commercial aviation. My papers and insights all derive from my interactions with this community of scientists, aided by NASA's aviation safety program.

Chapter Ten

1. **Concurrent engineering, total quality control, virtual organization, and so on.** The best review of concurrent engineering and a large number of related techniques is in W. H. Davidow and M. S. Malone, *The Virtual Corporation: Structuring and Revitalizing the Corporation for the 21st Century* (New York: HarperBusiness, 1992). Concurrent engineering is treated on pp. 91–93, but the entire chapter (chapter 5: "The

Future by Design," pp. 87–106) is relevant, and while you are at it, look through the entire book. I learned about concurrent engineering from R. I. Winner, J. P. Pennell, H. E. Bertrand, and M. M. G. Slusarczuk, *The Role of Concurrent Engineering in Weapons System Acquisition* (IDA Report R-338), (Alexandria, VA: Institute for Defense Analysis, December 1988); also see *CSERIAC Gateway* 1, no. 3 (Summer 1990), available from CSERIAC Program office, AAMRL/HE/CSERIAC, Wright-Patterson AFB, OH 45433–6573, (513) 255–4842, CSERIAC@falcon.aamrl.wpafb.af.m; and also look at Tom Peters: T. Peters, *Liberation Management: Necessary Disorganization for the Nanosecond Nineties* (New York: Knopf, 1992). Also see D. G. Reinertsen, *Managing the Design Factory* (New York: Free Press, 1997).

Chapter Eleven

1. **What have come to be called *disruptive technologies*.** See C. M. Christensen, *The Innovator's Dilemma: When New Technologies Cause Great Firms to Fail* (Boston: Harvard Business School Press, 1997). Some of the arguments in this chapter are from Christensen, for example, the story about the steam and hydraulic excavators. Most are my own, from my own experiences. We see the issues in very similar ways, but my analysis comes from experience whereas his comes from a more scholarly, thorough analysis of business cases from a variety of industries.

2. **It's possible to form a large collection of such statements. Here are some.** This list comes from many sources. I have collected them over the years and, alas, have not always been diligent about recording the sources. I thank David G. Curry for many of these.

3. **An example from his book is instructive.** Christensen, *The Innovator's Dilemma*. See note 1.

4. **This is how Christensen describes the events for the industries of small disk drives and hydraulic digging machines.** Christensen, *The Innovator's Dilemma*. See note 1.

5. **A corporation must be willing to see business units die.** J. L. Bower and C. M. Christensen, "Disruptive Technologies: Catching the Wave," *Harvard Business Review* 15 (January–February 1995): 43–53.

6. **Someone ought to write a book.** G. A. Moore, *Crossing the Chasm: Marketing and Selling High-Tech Goods to Mainstream Customers* (New York: HarperBusiness, 1991); G. A. Moore, *Inside the Tornado: Marketing Strategies from Silicon Valley's Cutting Edge* (New York: HarperBusiness, 1995); Christensen, *The innovator's dilemma* (see note 1).

Chapter Twelve

1. **"The PC is maturing from . . . "** Quotation from the Intel web page (January 1998): "Gordon Moore on Moore's law." http://developer.intel.com/solutions/archive/issue2/feature.htm

2. **Big companies ignore new technologies for too long a period.** This, of course, was the theme of chapter 11. See C. M. Christensen, *The Innovator's Dilemma: When New Technologies Cause Great Firms to Fail* (Boston: Harvard Business School Press, 1997).

3. **This is a topic that has elicited excellent studies and reports.** For a thorough but very readable discussion that reveals the entire complexity of the problem, I recommend the report by the Computer Science and Telecommunications Board (CSTB) of the National Academy of Sciences: K. W. Dam and H. Lin, eds., *Cryptography's Role in Securing the Information Society* (Washington, DC: National Academy Press, 1996). This influential report is widely used in government on all sides of the issue. The CSTB is composed of scientists and professionals from the communication and telecommunication industry who provide expert advice to the government. (I'm a current member of the board, but was not when this report was written.)

Appendix

1. **The age of medical sensors . . .** The age of cheap sensors was first pointed out to me by Paul Saffo of the Institute for The Future (Menlo Park, CA) in private conversation. See P. Saffo, "Sensors: The Next Wave of Innovation," *Communications of the ACM* 40, no. 2 (1997): 93–97.

2. **Lose a favorite sweater?** This example is inspired by the story of Steve Mann who has worn eyeglasses like these for some time and who actually did discover a lost sweater by exactly this procedure. S. Mann, "Wearable Computing: A First Step toward Personal Imaging," *IEEE Computer Magazine* 30, no. 2 (February 1997): 25–32.

References

Arthur, W. B. (1988) "Competing Technologies: An Overview." In *Technical Change and Economic Theory.* Edited by G. Dosi, C. Freeman, R. Nelson, G. Silverberg, and L. Soete. London and New York: Pinter, pp. 590–607.

Arthur, W. B. (1994) *Increasing Returns and Path Dependence in the Economy.* Ann Arbor: University of Michigan Press.

Arthur, W. B., and Lane, D. A. (1993). "Information Contagion." *Structural Change and Economic Dynamics* 4: 81–104.

Baecker, R. M., Grudin, J., Buxton, W. A. S., and Greenberg, S., eds. (1995). *Readings in Human-Computer Interaction: Toward the Year 2000.* San Francisco: Morgan Kaufmann.

Bettmann, O. L. (1974). *The Good Old Days—They Were Terrible!* New York: Random House.

Beyer, H., and Holtzblatt, K. (1998). *Contextual Design: Defining Customer-Centered Systems.* San Francisco: Morgan Kaufmann. (http://www.incontextenterprises.com).

Bower, J. L., and Christensen, C. M. (1995). "Disruptive Technologies: Catching the Wave." *Harvard Business Review* 15 (January–February): 43–53.

Bradshaw, J., ed. (1997). *Software Agents.* Menlo Park, CA, and Cambridge, MA: AAAI Press/The MIT Press.

Bragdon, A. D. (1989). *Ingenious Inventions of Domestic Utility.* New York: Harper & Row.

Brooks, F. P., Jr. (1995). *The Mythical Man-Month: Essays on Software Engineering,* anniversary edition. Reading, MA: Addison-Wesley. (Reissue, with additions, of the original 1975 publication, including "No Silver Bullet—Essence and Accident.")

Christensen, C. M. (1997). *The Innovator's Dilemma: When New Technologies Cause Great Firms to Fail.* Boston: Harvard Business School Press.

Dam, K. W., and Lin, H., eds. (1996). *Cryptography's Role in Securing the Information Society.* Washington, DC: National Academy Press.

David, P. A. (1985). "Clio and the Economics of QWERTY." *American Economic Review* 75:332–337.

David, P. A. *Path Dependence and the Quest for Historical Economics: One More Chorus of the Ballad of QWERTY.* (Discussion papers in economic and social history.) University of Oxford, November 20, 1997.

Davidow, W. H., and Malone, M. S. (1992). *The Virtual Corporation: Structuring and Revitalizing the Corporation for the 21st Century.* New York: HarperBusiness.

Erickson, T. A., and Mattson, M. E. (1981). "From Words to Meaning: A Semantic Illusion." *Journal of Verbal Learning and Verbal Behavior* 20:540–552.

Forty, A. (1986). *Objects of Desire.* New York: Pantheon Books.

Gibbs, W. W. (1997). "Taking Computers to Task." *Scientific American 277,* no. 1 (July): 82–89.

Giedion, S. (1948). *Mechanization Takes Command: A Contribution to Anonymous History.* Oxford: Oxford University Press. Republished in 1969 by W. W. Norton & Co. (New York).

Helander, M., ed. (1988). *Handbook of Human-Computer Interaction.* New York: North-Holland.

Helander, M. G., Kandauer, T. K., and Prabhu, P. V., eds. (1997). *Handbook of Human-Computer Interaction,* 2d ed. Amsterdam: North-Holland.

Henderson, D. A., Jr., and Card, S. K. (1986). "Rooms: The Use of Multiple Virtual Workspaces to Reduce Space Contention in a Window-Based Graphical User Interface." ACM *Transactions on Graphics* 5, no. 3: 211–243.

Hughes, T. P. (1989). *American Genesis: A Century of Invention and Technological Enthusiasm, 1870–1970.* New York: Viking.

Hutchins, E. (1995). *Cognition in the Wild.* Cambridge, MA: MIT Press.

Johnson, J., Roberts, T. L., Verplank, W., Smith, D. C., Irby, C. H., Beard, M., and Mackey, K. (1989). "The Xerox Star: A Retrospective." *IEEE Computer* 22, no. 9 (September): 11–29. Reprinted in *Readings in Human-Computer Interaction: Toward the Year 2000.* Edited by R. M. Baecker, J. Grudin, W. A. S. Buxton, and S. Greenberg (San Francisco: Morgan Kaufmann, 1995), pp. 53–70.

Kanigel, R. (1997). *The One Best Way: Frederick Winslow Taylor and the Enigma of Efficiency.* New York: Viking.

Kemeny, J. G., et al. (1979). *Report of the President's Commission on the Accident at Three Mile Island.* New York: Pergamon.

La Porte, T. R., and Consolini, P. M. (1991). "Working in Practice but Not in Theory: Theoretical Challenges of High-Reliability Organizations." *Journal of Public Administration Research and Theory,* 19–47.

Leveson, N. G. (1995). *Safeware: System Safety and Computers.* Reading, MA: Addison-Wesley.

Mann, S. (1997). "Wearable Computing: A First Step toward Personal Imaging." *IEEE Computer Magazine* 30, no. 2 (February): 25–32.

Miyata, Y., and Norman, D. A. (1986). "Psychological Issues in Support of Multiple Activities." In *User Centered System Design.* Edited by D. A. Norman and S. W. Draper. Hillsdale, NJ: Lawrence Erlbaum Associates.

Moore, G. A. (1991). *Crossing the Chasm: Marketing and Selling High-Tech Goods to Mainstream Customers.* New York: HarperBusiness.

Moore, G. A. (1995). *Inside the Tornado: Marketing Strategies from Silicon Valley's Cutting Edge.* New York: HarperBusiness.

Nardi, B., ed. (1996). *Context and Consciousness: Activity Theory and Human-Computer Interaction.* Cambridge, MA: MIT Press.

National Phonograph Co. (1900). *The Phonograph and How to Use It. Being a short history of its invention and development containing also directions helpful hints and plain talk as to its care and use, etc.* West Orange, NJ: National Phonograph Co. (A facsimile edition was published in 1971 by Allen Koenigsberg, New York.)

Neumann, P. (1995). *Computer-Related Risks.* Reading, MA: Addison-Wesley.

Newman, W. M., and Lamming, M. G. (1995). *Interactive System Design.* Wokingham, UK: Addison-Wesley.

Nielsen, J. (1993). *Usability Engineering.* Boston: Academic Press Professional.

Nielsen, J., and Mack, R. L., eds. (1994). *Usability Inspection Methods.* New York: John Wiley & Sons.

Norman, D. A. (1988). *The Psychology of Everyday Things.* New York: Basic Books. Also published in paperback as D. A. Norman, *The Design of Everyday Things* (New York: Doubleday, 1990).

Norman, D. A. (1990). *The Design of Everyday Things.* New York: Doubleday. Originally published as D. A. Norman, *The Psychology of Everyday Things* (New York: Basic Books, 1988).

Norman, D. A. (1990). "The 'Problem' of Automation: Inappropriate Feedback and Interaction, not 'Over-automation.'" In *Human Factors in Hazardous Situations.* Edited by D. E. Broadbent, A. Baddeley, and J. T. Reason. Oxford: Oxford University Press, pp. 585–593.

Norman, D. A. (1992). *Turn Signals Are the Facial Expressions of Automobiles*. Reading, MA: Addison-Wesley.

Norman, D. A. (1993). *Things That Make Us Smart*. Reading, MA: Addison-Wesley.

Norman, D. A. (1997). "How Might People Interact with Agents." In *Software Agents*. Edited by J. Bradshaw. Menlo Park, CA, and Cambridge, MA: AAAI Press/The MIT Press.

Norman, D. A. (1997). "Why It's Good That Computers Don't Work Like the Brain." In *Beyond Calculation: The Next Fifty Years of Computing*. Edited by P. J. Denning and R. M. Metcalfe. New York: Copernicus: Springer-Verlag.

Norman, D. A., and Draper, S. W., eds. (1986). *User Centered System Design*. Hillsdale, NJ: Lawrence Erlbaum Associates.

Norman, D. A., and Fisher, D. (1984). "Why Alphabetic Keyboards Are Not Easy to Use: Keyboard Layout Doesn't Much Matter." *Human Factors* 24:509–519.

Peters, T. (1992). *Liberation Management: Necessary Disorganization for the Nanosecond Nineties*. New York: Knopf.

Pool, R. (1997). *Beyond Engineering: How Society Shapes Technology*. New York: Oxford University Press.

Pool, R. (1997). "When Failure Is Not an Option." *Technology Review* 100, no. 5:38–45. (http://web.mit.edu/techreview/).

Rabinbach, A. (1990). *The Human Motor: Energy, Fatigue, and the Origins of Modernity*. New York: Basic Books.

Radio Corporation of America. (1922). *Radio Enters the Home: How to Enjoy Popular Radio Broadcasting. With complete instructions and description of apparatus. For those who desire to be entertained with concerts, lectures, dance music—as well as for the radio amateur*. New York: Radio Corporation of America. (Reprinted by the Vestal Press Ltd., Vestal, NY 13850.)

Reder, L. M., and Kusbit, G. W. (1991). "Locus of the Moses Illusion: Imperfect Encoding, Retrieval, or Match?" *Journal of Memory and Language* 30:385–406.

Reinertsen, D. G. (1997). *Managing the Design Factory*. New York: Free Press.

Ries, A., and Trout, J. (1986). *Positioning: The Battle for Your Mind*. First ed., revised. New York: McGraw-Hill.

Ries, A., and Trout, J. (1993). *The 22 Immutable Laws of Marketing*. New York: HarperCollins.

Rifkin, J. (1995). *The End of Work: The Decline of the Global Labor Force and the Dawn of the Post-Market Era*. New York: G. P. Putnam's Sons.

Rogers, E. M. (1995). *Diffusion of Innovations*. Fourth edition. New York: The Free Press.

Rubenstein, E. (1979). "The Accident That Shouldn't Have Happened." *IEEE Spectrum* 16, no. 11 (November): 33–42.

Saffo, P. (1997). "Sensors: The Next Wave of Innovation." *Communications of the ACM* 40, no. 2:93–97.

Sexton, G. A. (1988). Cockpit-crew systems design and automation. In *Human Factors in Aviation*. Edited by E. L. Wiener and D. C. Nagel. San Diego: Academic Press.

Shneiderman, B. (1998). *Designing the User Interface: Strategies for Effective Human-Computer Interaction*. Reading, MA: Addison-Wesley. (http://www.aw.com/DTUI.)

Smith, D. C., Kimball, R., Verplank, W., and Harslem, E. (1982). "Designing the Star User Interface." *Byte* 7, no. 4 (April):242–282.

Taylor, F. W. (1911). *The Principles of Scientific Management*. New York: Harper & Brothers.

Thimbleby, H. (1990). *User Interface Design*. Reading, MA: Addison-Wesley (ACM Press).

Thompson, E. (1995). "Machines, Music, and the Quest for Fidelity: Marketing the Edison Phonograph in America, 1877–1925." *The Musical Quarterly* 79:131–171.

Welch, W. L. and Burt, L. B. S. (1994). *From Tinfoil to Stereo: The Acoustic Years of the Recording Industry, 1877–1929*. Gainesville: University Press of Florida.

Williams, T. I. (1987). *The History of Invention: From Stone Axes to Silicon Chips*. New York: Facts on File Publications. Also published by London: Macdonald & Co.

Winner, R. I., Pennell, J. P., Bertrand, H. E., and Slusarczuk, M. M. G. (1988). *The Role of Concurrent Engineering in Weapons System Acquisition (IDA Report R-338)*. Alexandria, VA: Institute for Defense Analysis, December 1988.

Index

User experience (cont.)
  marketing and, 199–201
  organizational home for, proper, 222–228
  special discipline for, 195–199
  with technology and marketing, 199–201
User-testers, 190, 282n.3

Verplank, W., 274–275nn.4–5
Versatility (design principle), 67, 261
VHS video cassette recorder, 8, 117, 119
Victor Talking Machine Company, 1, 8, 10–13, 273n.5
Victrola, 10, 12
Virtual organization, 216–217, 282–283n.1
Virtual reality, 100–104
Visicalc, 24, 42
Visual recognition, 100–101
Voice mail, 18
Voice recognition, 100

Watches, 29–30, 166
Waterfall product development, 216
Watson, T. J., Sr., 233
Watt, J., 171
Wax cylinder phonograph, 273n.3
Wearable Computing (Mann), 284n.3
Weather display, 265–266
Welch, W. L., 273n.2
Western Union, 233
Wildfire messaging system, 100, 277n.3
Williams, T. I., 280n.5
Windows (Microsoft) operating system, 8, 41, 73, 117–119, 122, 227
Winner, R. I., 283n.1
Wireless telephone, 166
Wizards (help systems), 105–107
Word (Microsoft), 80, 177–178, 276n.1
Word processor, 177–178
Wozniak, S., 234
Wristwatch, 29–30

X-ray dosage, 151, 155, 279n.8
Xerox
  copier, 234
  Rooms, 277n.6
  Star, 41–44, 73, 225, 274–275nn.4–5
"The Xerox Star," 274–275nn.4–5